Responsible Business

Responsible Business

Making strategic decisions to benefit people, the planet and profits

Annemieke Roobeek
Jacques de Swart
Myrthe van der Plas

KoganPage

First published in English in Great Britain and the United States in 2018 by Kogan Page Limited

2nd Floor, 45 Gee Street	c/o Martin P Hill Consulting	4737/23 Ansari Road
London	122 W 27th Street	Daryaganj
EC1V 3RS	New York, NY 10001	New Delhi 110002
United Kingdom	USA	India

ISBN   978 0 7494 8060 8
E-ISBN   978 0 7494 8061 5

British Library Cataloguing-in-Publication Data

A CIP record for this book is available from the British Library.

Typeset by Integra Software Services Pvt. Ltd., Pondicherry
Print production managed by Jellyfish
Printed and bound in Great Britain by Ashford Colour Press Ltd.

CONTENTS

ACKNOWLEDGEMENTS

Research is continuously developing and new theories are always rising to form the basis of new research. Much happens in isolation and an interdisciplinary approach is rare rather than common. However, being affiliated to Nyenrode Business Universiteit and to advisory companies we are used to collaborative research; interdisciplinarity is essential to answer questions that are relevant to society, the environment and organizations. We tested the resulting concept via action research, an interactive and iterative research process.

For the development of our strategic decision-making approach, multiple disciplines have been brought together to facilitate scientific cross-pollination, and therefore we would like to thank everyone who has contributed to the creation of this book.

For the cases: Feike Sijbesma, Fokko Wientjes, Paulette van Ommen, Jos de Visser, Martin Borsje and Patrick Van Bael from DSM; Bert Stuij from the Energy Delta Institute and Ronald de Vries from Rabobank for the opportunity to discuss our approach in the energy sector with students from the mini-MBA on Energy Transition and Innovation; Roy Wolbrink from KLIKO/Rimetaal; Michiel Buchel and Jouke Konijn from NEMO; Anouk ten Arve, Dominique Vijverberg, Karlijn Hillen and Klaas Visser from the IZZ Foundation; Jacco Swart, Jurrie Groenendijk, Theo Hermsen, Ron Francis, Marc Boele and Edu Jansing from KNVB; Frank van Eekeren from Universiteit Utrecht; Joep Goessens and Bart van Ingen from N.E.C. Nijmegen; Pieter van Boheemen and Wouter Bruins from Amplino for their support and insights; Erik van der Meulen from Kirkman Company for his 'shared value' expertise in the NEMO and Rimetaal cases; Jacques Reijniers for sharing his knowledge on purchasing management in the Rimetaal case; and Marco Florijn from the municipality of Eindhoven for the Refugees case.

From MeetingMoreMinds: Ivar Kolvoort, Monique de Ritter, Floris de Vries and Stephanie van Balsfoort for their insights and critical review.

From PwC: Wineke Haagsma, Robert van der Laan and Sandra Hazenberg, who continuously gave us their support and belief in our approach; Jeroen Hoexum, Mila Harmelink, Krista Jaarsma and Simon Lok from the Data Analytics group for their part in improving the methodology and the Responsible Business Simulator; Jurian Goei, Pieter Veuger and Steven Schotanus for facilitating us to further develop the methodology; Charlotte Bech, Coen Hennipman and Daan Stroosnier from the Data Analytics group for their help in improving the simulation model via the operationalization of one or more of the cases described; and subject matter experts Dorine Helmer and Hans Schoolderman for their contribution to the DSM case; Jonas Rietbergen and Maaike Platenburg for the Amplino case, Lina Lukoseviciute for the KNVB case, and Michiel Beijersbergen, Wendelina Botjes and Wim Wensink for the Refugees case.

Last but not least, Peggy van Schaik for supporting us with some of the translations and for her patience during the writing process; Christophe Frere and Patrick van Gent from AIMMS for brainstorming with us on the practical implementation of the Responsible Business Simulator as a software platform; Elke Vergoossen and Elke Parsa from Boom publishers for their support throughout the process; and of course Lucy Carter and Nancy Wallace from Kogan Page for their valuable input and the pleasant collaboration.

ABOUT THE AUTHORS

Annemieke Roobeek has been a Professor of Strategy and Transformation Management at Nyenrode Business Universiteit since 1997, the fourth professorship of her career. Previously she was Professor of Technology and Economics (Nyenrode), Wibaut Professor of Metropolitan Affairs (University of Amsterdam) and Professor of Management of Complexity (University of Amsterdam). She is Founder/CEO of MeetingMoreMinds, advisory for intercompany networking and ecosystem design.

Jacques de Swart is Professor of Applied Mathematics at Nyenrode Business University and partner within PwC, where he is responsible for the Data Analytics group. He has over 25 years of modelling experience.

Myrthe van der Plas holds master's degrees in both Econometrics and Communication and is a GARP certified Financial Risk Manager. She works as Manager within the Data Analytics group of PwC and has been involved in most of the practical applications of strategic decision making. She also teaches courses on Strategic Decision Making at several universities.

PREFACE

In this age of transformation, disruptive technologies and systems change, there is momentum for an innovative, combined quantitative and qualitative approach to strategic decision making. There is a need to move beyond the traditional spreadsheets for financially based decision making, and beyond intuition and personal conviction for including non-financial aspects. The combined forces of data science and interactive strategy in the Responsible Business Simulator unleash the collective intelligence of the boardroom, professionals, stakeholders and the wealth of public knowledge. This combined approach provides a solid base for decisions and investments shaping the future of companies.

The tipping point draws nearer for new paradigms such as the circular economy. The historic Paris Agreement on climate change, adopted by 192 countries in December 2015, is a clear signal to stimulate renewable energy, cleaner technologies and massive investments in infrastructure. Rethinking of supply chains, use and re-use of materials, modes of transport and ways of working will have tremendous impact on reaching a better balance between People, Planet and Profit. Add to this the implementation of a range of disruptive technologies, ranging from the Internet of Things to 3D printing, advanced robotics, genomics and personalized health care, and the conclusion is that the world is changing at a rapid speed and companies have to respond by making strategic decisions.

Although the tipping point is being approached through a multitude of developments, this does not mean that it is easy to implement sustainable business practices. The frontrunners, still a relatively small group of companies but quickly growing in size, are leading the way but often pay a high price for their conviction that – in the long run – they are doing the right thing for all concerned, including themselves. Many businesses and organizations are struggling with the strategic choice of structurally implementing sustainable and inclusive business practices. It is exactly in this phase, when we are moving towards the tipping point and when a turnaround in management thinking is taking place to favour more sustainable operations, that it is essential to be able to make rational decisions on the basis of facts and figures both for financial and non-financial reasons. This is where the Responsible Business Simulator comes into play.

Based on weighted key outputs, which have been designated as keys for success by management and employees in an interactive process, the Responsible Business Simulator can provide concrete forecasts about the impact of sustainable investments on medium-term operational results. Those forecasts are presented in simulations that can be fine-tuned to different conditions, hence the fact that the model is referred to as a 'simulator'.

The Responsible Business Simulator is innovative in more than one sense. It is an advanced mathematical calculation model that neutralizes bias and objectifies the strategic decision-making process, because it uses weighted key outputs. In addition, it attaches value – in the form of scenarios – to historical data on a company and to the opinions of external experts. Using these scenarios, which blend historical facts with impartial external expertise, the model is able to estimate the probability that a particular option for a strategy based on sustainability and social inclusivity will have a positive or less positive impact on the company. It simulates the reactions of decision makers and employees, presenting various probabilities in a comprehensible way. The combination of a strategic dialogue about the key outputs for success and the weighted scenarios is calculated statistically and presented visually. The results allow the board, management and employees to take a decision on the basis of hard facts on financial and non-financial items.

Finally, the model allows decision makers to tweak the results so that they can determine their own timeline, along which all aspects of the triple bottom line and the three Ps of People, Planet and Profit can be incorporated and calculated.

In the real world, however, strategic decisions are not always rational. Other considerations always creep in. We are of the opinion that the added value of a rational model, such as the Responsible Business Simulator, lies precisely in the fact that it can clarify highly diffuse strategic considerations. This can lead to greater insight on the part of the decision makers, to better prospects for investors and shareholders, and to more transparency and accountability vis-à-vis the stakeholders – both internal within the company, and external in society as a whole.

The vision of the book

The combination of interactive strategic decision making and advanced data analytics gives companies, organizations and governmental agencies new insights for balanced investment decisions in the era of sustainability and an inclusive society. The strategic dialogue in an action research setting unleashes the informal and formal knowledge underlying the long-term mission of the organization and its potential to realize its goals. Data science techniques allow the comparison of large amounts of data for visualizing different scenarios. The combined effort of qualitative and quantitative approaches is powerful for decision makers who have to meet financial and non-financial objectives in a society at the brink of a new paradigm.

The combination of these forces is what distinguishes this book from existing approaches. As authors with strategy and data analytics backgrounds we have a track record of proven results both in academia and in the advisory practice for international companies and the public sector. Our purpose in writing was to provide a book that is a practical description of the strategic decision-making tool that we have developed and its application in highly diverse settings in companies and organizations. The book is also the gateway to an advanced software tool that allows you as the reader to play around with the data for strategic decision making.

We hope this book will inspire students at universities and business schools, as well as being a practical guide for advisories, consultants, investors and policy makers in developing a feasible sustainability strategy for companies and the public sector. The book will appeal to a broad range of readers, from those who are interested in finance and economics and modelling, to those who are involved in strategy and broader sustainability and inclusivity issues. The fact that the insights and software tools can be used immediately lowers the threshold for professionals, from advisories to the financial industry, as well as for students in the classroom to study the cases. For strategists the advantage of using data science will be an eye-opener, as it is for data-driven IT-based consultancies and investors to learn from the strategic dialogue and the added value of iterative, interactive decision making in highly diverse teams. For all target groups the challenge is to understand the underlying complexity of factors that give evidence of the choices to be made within the internal and external contexts of the company or organization.

Strategy is no longer the exclusive domain of the boardroom, although major decisions are taken here. The need for interaction with internal and external experts, as well as stakeholders and opinion leaders has become crucial. The strategy concepts in this book are underlain by theories around multi-stakeholder management, strategic dialogue and unleashing knowledge potential by empowerment, as well as theoretical concepts underlying action research and grounded theory.

How the book is organized

The book starts with chapters that describe the transformative forces and paradigm changes that are under way. In Chapter 1 we start with the rise of the notion of sustainability and how we are moving from awareness to systems change in a circular economy and an inclusive society. We offer examples of frontrunners in business who are giving flavour to this profound change in the economy. Chapter 2 explains the use of the Responsible Business Simulator in seven steps. The reader gets a step-by-step introduction to the different phases of the decision-making process. This chapter is the basis for understanding the approach taken. In the subsequent chapters we describe concepts that try to achieve a better balance between the interests of companies, shareholders and stakeholders. We dig deeper into the concept of shared value in Chapter 3, and in Chapter 4 we argue that there is no alternative to sustainability. In this chapter we offer arguments for the potential of innovations stemming from sustainability and give many examples of disruptive changes under way.

In Chapter 5 the importance of stakeholder management and interactivity in strategic decision-making processes is elucidated. We pose that collaboration is necessary for new insights and actionable results. To give the reader a better idea of the combined forces of the strategic dialogue based on action research and the application of data science for neutralizing information and knowledge into facts and figures, we describe the methodologies used in Chapter 6, which concludes this part of the book.

The application of the strategic dialogue and the use of the Responsible Business Simulator form the core and are illustrated in the cases in chapters 8 until 14. To understand the working of the methodology and the Responsible Business Simulator in practice we undertook a range of case studies. We applied the combined methodology in various companies, from a global science-based company to a health organization, and from a social enterprise and a science museum to a metalworking company and a national football association. We chose these highly diverse companies and organizations on purpose to investigate the usefulness of the Responsible Business Simulator and our combined quantitative and qualitative approach.

Each of the cases starts with a short introduction, some facts about the company or organization, and the strategic issue at stake. The cases show how the strategic dialogue triggers the conversation and the search for solutions. The data process is illustrated by the visualizations of each of the steps in the decision-making process. The first three cases are more oriented towards the P of Planet. DSM, the globally operating company active in health, nutrition and materials, is a frontrunner in balancing People, Planet and Profit. In the case of DSM the strategic issue is how to anticipate climate change by addressing the environmental and carbon footprint and finding options to reduce greenhouse gas emissions. The second case discusses the decision of how to repair the roof of the Science Museum NEMO's landmark building in Amsterdam. Should they go for a simple repair and maintenance solution or is it possible to create a sustainable roof that gives space to an outdoor exhibition with even more attractions for the public? In the third case we shift the focus to a highly specialized metalworking company, Rimetaal, that does its utmost to score high in all three Ps, but has difficulties in selling its sustainable waste collection systems to local municipalities. In this case we describe the surprising outcome and how the company changed its business model based on the Responsible Business Simulator.

In the subsequent cases we focus more on the P of People. In the case of IZZ, the strategic issue is creating a better working environment in health care and decreasing costs for health and stress-related absenteeism. We created the inputs for the simulation model together with the IZZ professionals. They were so eager to understand the model that they learned its workings and now support decision-making processes at many health institutions. Another example of the application of the combined methodology and the use of the Responsible Business Simulator is the case of the Royal Dutch Football Association (KNVB). Football is seen as the glue for a stronger and tighter society. Football is promoted, because it contributes to better physical as well as mental health. We also know that football (matches) can be associated with aggression and violence, so here the question was how to increase the attractive parts of football and turn down the negative trends. The case illustrates how the societal contribution of sports can be quantified. Another example of the use of the Responsible Business Simulator is the European refugee crisis and how this new approach can help to get the facts onto the table while at the same time doing justice to the emotions expressed by stakeholders. The application of strategic decision making towards a circular economy and an inclusive society in this context has the purpose of supporting policy makers in their decision making regarding their response to the refugee crisis on a fact-based dialogue. The final case study looks at how to attract investment to a social enterprise that develops portable malaria diagnostics. Amplino, the diagnostics company, claims it can bring the most advanced diagnostic method with a portable device to remote areas, offering lower costs with fewer medical staff. In this case all the Ps of People, Planet and Profit come together. It is a nice illustration of clarifying the options by assessing the risk appetite for the investors. With the Responsible Business Simulator, potential investors could make a better decision based on a better foundation.

In our closing chapter we invite you to explore with us the world of inter-disciplinary research, collaboration and interactive strategy combined with highly advanced data science for better strategic decision making in the age of transformation and systems change.

> Readers can access the Responsible Business Simulator
> at www.koganpage.com/ResponsibleBusiness.

Working towards responsibility in business and society

From awareness to systems change

With the extreme weather events taking place all around the globe in recent years, few deny climate change any longer. The images of massive floods in Paris and London, shrinking icefields on the poles, and the years of drought in sub-Saharan countries in Africa show us the impact of climate change. The problem of climate change goes beyond the type of energy we are using. The shift from fossil fuel to renewable energies and clean technologies will certainly help to reduce the amount of greenhouse gas emissions, but it won't be enough. It will substitute part of the energy demand, but the demand for energy, materials, water, food, cars and computers will continue to increase as long as the logic of the economic system remains the same.

Awareness of a need for systemic change started among scientists, farmers and grassroots activists in the 1960s, when heavily polluted rivers in industrial countries were endangering food production and health. This seems long behind us nowadays, with strict regulation in place in Western countries, but it does not mean the problem is solved. With the internationalization of production to developing and emerging countries, the problem has become global. Living in a global world, many products are produced in countries in Asia, South America and parts of Africa; the mobile phone purchased in London will have been produced in China with intricate supply chains of rare materials, energy streams and prescribed designs that come from remote places of the world. As a consequence, the challenge to safeguard the planet as well as the health of its people with transparent governance has become even more urgent than before. At the same time the many efforts taken by global, regional and national initiatives to bring the world into a better ecological balance show the complexity of the issues at stake. With the United Nations Global Development Goals 2030, a new and ambitious agenda has been set for the decades ahead. In combination with the successful Paris Climate

Change Conference COP21 in December 2015, we are entering a new era. We have entered the age of systems change, circular economy and social inclusion, where companies, politicians, citizens, farmers, NGOs and the academic community have to rethink the logics of the economic system. Sustainable growth is perhaps one of the greatest challenges humankind is facing. Systemic change requires profound insight into the logic of the current economic system. The move towards a circular economy and social inclusion requires more than redesigning products and recycling. It is also about finding better work – life balances, taking into account externalities in pricing of products and services, reducing inequality, and making the world a better place for all.

The rise of the notion of sustainability

The notion of 'sustainability' has been defined in the literature in an almost infinite variety of ways (Elkington, 1997); a timeline of events is presented in Figure 1.1. When the Club of Rome, an interdisciplinary think tank, published its report titled 'The Limits to Growth' in 1972, it was the first time that the possible long-term consequences of economic actions on the climate had been presented on a global scale (Meadows et al, 1972). The report caused a great deal of concern and fuelled much debate.

The present-day activities of the Club of Rome focus less on the end of growth and more on sustainability in a broad sense. At around the same time as the Club of Rome's report, the term 'sustainable development' was receiving substantial attention following the United Nations Conference on the Human Environment (1972), which resulted – 15 years later – in

Figure 1.1   Sustainability awareness and action timeline 1972–2015

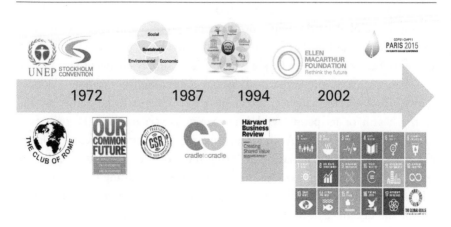

the Brundtland Report of 1987. That report was later published in book form, under the title *Our Common Future*, by the World Commission on Environment and Development (WECD, 1987). The Commission defined sustainable development as follows: 'The development that meets the needs of the present without compromising the ability of future generations to meet their own needs' (WECD, 1987, p. 8). The Brundtland definition has been applied consistently during the many UN conferences held on this subject, such as the UN Earth Summit in Rio de Janeiro in 1992, the Kyoto Protocol of 1997, and the Climate Conferences in Copenhagen in 2009, Dublin in 2011 and Paris in 2015. According to Rogers and Hudson (2011), the following four core elements can be distinguished from this definition:

1 recognition of sustainability as a global problem, with global responsibilities;

2 recognition of the limits of growth, or at least of the necessity to structure growth so as to take advantage of the options that are least destructive for the natural environment;

3 recognition of social equality as an important consideration, especially in offering opportunities for economic and social progress for less-developed countries;

4 giving long-term planning over future generations a new priority, and recognizing the fact that market economies tend to lean on short-term interests and are often at risk of losing sight of long-term goals.

As can be seen from this explanation of the UN definition of sustainability, it is a highly complex subject and one that can be approached from a variety of directions.

With the awareness of the importance and impact of sustainability, with the Triple Bottom Line with People, Planet and Profit as its pillars, the rise of corporate social responsibility (CSR) initiatives in companies, advisories and NGOs started during the 1990s (Elkington, 1997). In the early 2000s the Cradle to Cradle design concept became popular among companies that wanted to redesign their products and supply chains to prevent waste. All material inputs and outputs of this design concept are seen as nutrients which can be reused or recycled (McDonough and Braungart, 2002). With this Cradle to Cradle concept a big leap forward was made towards what was coined a decade later by the Ellen MacArthur Foundation as a circular economy in 2012. The Ellen MacArthur Foundation is advocating for an accelerated transition to a circular model with numerous business and economic opportunities. As such, the three pillars of the TBL become integrated (Ellen MacArthur

Foundation, 2012). This integration of the People, Planet and Profit pillars continues with the concept of Shared Value Creation, developed by Porter and Kramer and adopted by many companies (Porter and Kramer, 2011). The central premise of shared value is that there is a mutual dependence between the competitiveness of a company and the health of the communities around it. Recognition of these connections between the 3Ps can lead to opportunities spurring both societal and economic progress. In a short period of time this concept has gained inroads in businesses worldwide. At a societal level, the United Nations Development Programme (UNDP) has worked on Sustainable Development Goals (SDGs). As successors of the Millennium Development Goals, these 17 SDGs cover social, ecological and economic objectives, and include both developing and developed countries to help achieve these goals. According to the UN, businesses and companies worldwide have been and will be at the forefront of creating this change. This UNDP intergovernmental platform has made positive inroads in boardrooms and governments' agendas.

We are approaching the 'tipping point' of sustainable business operations. More and more enterprises and organizations, including governments, have used recent annual reports and strategic policy papers to point out that sustainability has become a crucial factor in the way in which they design and produce their products and services (Nidumolo, Prahalad and Rangaswami, 2009). The increasing customer demand for sustainability, the high cost of energy, the finite nature of raw materials, and the negative impact that present-day production methods have on the environment are all prompting more inventive and sustainable alternatives.

Sustainability reflected in the use of standards

For many years international indices such as the Dow Jones Sustainability Index (DJSI, started in 1999) were paid only scant attention. Today, however, a large part of a company's reputation and credibility relies on the fact that they have a good ranking in this and similar indices. Via the media, companies proudly boast of their standing in the annual DJSI sustainability 'contest', and are increasingly eager to be acknowledged in the DJSI as the worldwide frontrunner in their sector. Production processes are examined and screened for sustainability elements. Aside from the fact that it provides better social and environmental conditions, companies are learning that investing in sustainability can also lead to cost savings in the longer term. Sustainability has become a mark of competitiveness.

The list of worldwide sector frontrunners mentioned in the DJSI Industry Group Leader Reports from 2010 to 2017 include AirFrance-KLM Group, Abbott Laboratories, Sodexo, Fujitsu, Swiss Re, KLM, DSM, AkzoNobel, Philips, Unilever, ING, Siemens, LG Electronics, and Woolworths (Dow Jones Sustainability Indices, 2017). Enterprises such as Ahold Delhaize NV are now deliberately investing more in sustainability than in previous years in order to achieve a higher ranking in the index. After all, if a competitor achieves a higher score this might give investors a reason to transfer their funds to that competitor. The 2017 DJSI revealed new entrants by companies among others ABN AMRO, Samsung Electronics, Hugo Boss, Carrefour SA, ASML Holding NV, and Infosys Ltd. The importance of sustainability therefore goes much deeper – for many enterprises – than simply applying ecologically responsible production processes. It has become a strategic choice in keeping ahead of the competition.

The triple bottom line or TBL standard uses a somewhat wider definition of sustainability. The TBL aims to measure the financial, social and environmental performance of a company over time, rather than merely the traditional measure of corporate profit. TBL is based on three pillars: People, Planet and Profit (PPP). These pillars were formulated by John Elkington in his book *Cannibals with Forks: The triple bottom line of 21st-century business* (Elkington, 1997). Even then they were not entirely new: the interpretation of People, Planet and Profit had already been broached in the United Nation's Brundtland report of 1987 (WECD, 1987).

What makes the triple bottom line – whether expressed as TBL or as PPP – such an interesting framework is the fact that in 2007 it became the UN standard for the full cost accounting of the public sector. It is used to calculate eco-footprint and goes beyond the scope of the DJSI in the sense that economic operating results are not considered solely in terms of sustainability, but are appraised in conjunction with social aspects.

It ought to be noted that a difficulty posed by the TBL is the fact that it is extremely difficult to capture environmental and social standards in one value. In order to 'weigh' the three Ps against each other, one must account for Profit in the same terms as People and Planet. The Responsible Business Simulator, which will be introduced in Chapter 2, provides a solution to this problem.

Corporate Social Responsibility, or CSR, is used as an umbrella term derived from the TBL to describe entrepreneurial behaviour. In the case of the TBL, it is explicitly clear that companies must not only account for their performance to shareholders but also to other stakeholders (Wheeler, Colbert and Freeman, 2003). The concept of profit has to be 'weighted' against the two other pillars. A stakeholder is anyone who is or becomes directly or indirectly involved in or affected by the activities of a company or organization. The TBL puts a great deal of emphasis on the reciprocity between a company, the community within which it operates, the natural resources it uses and the people who work for it (Rogers and Hudson, 2011). A company that operates according to the principles of the TBL or People, Planet and Profit will not use toxic substances, cause environmental pollution, trade in arms or weapons, or use child labour.

Increasing awareness of the important role of stakeholders has gradually led to positive results. For example, companies such as Nike and Tesco were forced to reconsider some of their corporate malpractices in countries where social and environmental standards were not regulated. Within the United States, there was an increase of 12 per cent (between 2012 and 2014) in companies engaging with investors on sustainability issues. Moreover, 35 per cent of companies engaged in substantive stakeholder dialogues in 2014, as opposed to 28 per cent in 2012 (Ceres/Sustainalytics, 2014). A good example of a company that increased awareness among its stakeholders of its environmental impact is PUMA, the sportswear company based in Germany. PUMA was the first to develop an environmental profit and loss account in 2010, which revealed that the company's environmental impact was almost 72 per cent of its profit. It turned out that PUMA's supply chain was responsible for 94 per cent of this environmental impact. This information helped PUMA to focus innovation on their supply chain and on designing products with less environmental impact (Puma, 2011).

In the financial industry standards are up and coming. In particular, the trend is set by the leading pension funds that have massive amounts to invest. The so-called ESG considerations include Environmental, Social and Governance aspects that can or should be taken into account in assessing investments in countries, companies or projects. Aspects of the Environmental considerations are, for example, sustainable resources, clean technology, climate change and low carbon. Social considerations include controversial weapons, repressive regimes, adult entertainment, landmines, gambling, tobacco, diversity and alcohol. Considerations under Government are, for example, board independence, majority ownership, financial planning, financial reporting and executive pay. PGGM, a world player in pensions, states in its 2014 Annual Report that ESG factors were analysed in 100 per cent of the new investments in external funds that year. This particular pension company has specific areas of focus: climate change and reduction of pollution and emissions, water scarcity, healthcare, food security, a stable financial system that serves the real economy, good corporate governance, and safeguarding human rights (PGGM, 2015).

The UN Global Impact Assessment on the transformation of business (2015) speaks of 'a modern corporate sustainability movement'. The assessment concludes that the UN Global Compact, as the world's largest corporate sustainability initiative, together with new impulses from the business community on sustainability as described above, have had a significant impact on the development of sustainability over the past 15 years. Business has become more strategic, systematic, integrated, transparent and collaborative regarding sustainability.

In last decade, space has been created for alternative ways of running a business, based on concepts of social enterprises, B-Corps and shared value creation, described by Porter and Kramer (2011), which will be addressed extensively in Chapter 3 (Austin and Reficco, 2009; Eggers and Macmillan, 2013; Mair, Battalina and Cardenas, 2012; Short, Moss and Lumpkin, 2009). The enterprise or organization is not an isolated entity, and its purpose should not only be to create value for shareholders. It must continually assess the impact of its actions on the various parties directly and indirectly involved: the stakeholders. Shell used to call this a 'license to operate', and businesses these days are increasingly finding that they need some sort of social certificate of good conduct to be able to continue their activities. Nowadays companies who want to do good, want to do better. The focus is not only on a licence to operate, but also on social and environmental impact, transparency and good governance.

This new attitude increases the complexity of strategic and investment decisions. When you add external factors, such as limited resources, energy transition, future demographics, hyper-transparency, growing wealth gap and exponential increase in technology into the mix, it is no wonder that management sometimes finds itself caught in a maelstrom (UN Global Compact, 2015). It will be clear that there are now many more factors and actors to be taken into account than there were in the past. But what value should you attach to them in relation to the strategic goals you are trying to achieve? How can you translate those values into concrete and manageable actions? How can you visualize the various options? And which decision best suits your enterprise or organization? The strategic decision-making process and the Responsible Business Simulator help to reduce that complexity to manageable proportions for decision makers and advisers in the world of business. Making use of the results of data and dialogue is a powerful way of getting a better oversight in decision making.

Circular economy approach

Our current economy can largely be described as a linear one. From resource extraction to production process to consumerism, it is a one-way ticket. This *take–make–dispose* approach results in a highly inefficient and, more importantly, unsustainable use of our resources. Not only does this lead to an increasing scarcity of resources, it also brings along waste and pollution, which causes enormous costs in the public domain. Here we elaborate on the phenomenon of a circular economy, the inevitable perspective for an economy with limited resources. A circular economy, as defined by the Ellen MacArthur Foundation (2012), is an economy that is restorative and regenerative by intention and design, and which aims to keep products, components and materials at their highest utility and value at all times. So a circular economy is very careful with resources, trying its best to 'circulate' them throughout the economy indefinitely without wasting any of them.

There are six trends visible that move the economy towards a circular one. Although this list is not exhaustive, we see these as the main drivers for such a circular future:

1 *Increasing demand for resources and energy.* With an increasing global population, coupled with a sharply increasing middle class, the demand for resources and energy surges.

2 *Innovative technologies.* Using new technologies (eg Internet of Things, Big Data, etc) enables producers to increase the value in their production chain, to analyse the material life cycle and employ new design and production methods.

3 *Urbanization.* The increase in urbanization makes it easier and more cost-effective to track, gather, reclaim and share parts or whole products and materials.

4 *Governmental pressure.* Governments and legislators are becoming more aware of sustainability issues and are creating legislation to contribute to these issues (eg Paris COP21).

5 *More conscious consumers.* Consumers are becoming more critical of their own consumption behaviour, being more conscious of their impact. There is societal momentum directed towards sustainability.

6 *Consumers get used to access over ownership.* People are getting used to having access to the performance of a product instead of simply owning one (eg car sharing via Uber or house sharing via Airbnb); this leads to an increased efficiency in the use of products.

Within a circular economy one can distinguish two 'sub-circles', based on the compostability of waste: a biological circle and a technological one (Figure 1.2). A linear economy essentially leads to treating both types of 'waste' the same, meaning they are being dumped in landfills and incinerated, resulting in large amounts of toxins being released into the environment. The first step towards a circular economy is making the essential distinction between biological and technical materials. The difference lies in the return of biological nutrients to the food chain, which is not possible with technical materials. The focus within the technical realm consequently lies on the reuse, remanufacturing or recycling of these waste materials. Keeping soil at its highest possible value is a crucial part of sustaining this biological circle. Through this new circle process, the quality of all materials is optimized, which results in the pressure being taken off the manufacturing end of the model, as well as the waste disposal end. As both far ends of the model are being 'pushed down', the first steps towards a circular economy are taken. Last, but definitely not least, the energy necessary to fuel this cycle should be renewable by nature, to decrease resource dependence and increase system resilience (Ellen MacArthur Foundation, 2015).

Although the public in general highly values recycling, from a circular perspective it is the last resort when aiming to 'close the loop'. Recycling often reduces the quality of materials, 'downcycling', which limits their usability. While regaining raw material from used products in this way we lose valuable information related to these used products, such as product idea, design and technical specifications. The different sub-circles, as shown in Figure 1.2, are focused on maximizing the use of products, distinguishing them on the basis of their inherent characteristics.

Products that need the least change in order for them to be reused are represented in the innermost circle. Typically, these products require maintenance and should be prevented from entering the outer cycles of remanufacturing and recycling, in order to optimize potential savings on the shares of material, labour, energy, capital, and the associated externalities (such as greenhouse gas emissions, water and toxicity). The next circle, as one moves towards the outside, focuses on reuse and redistribution. If, due to the specific characteristics of the product this is not possible, remanufacturing, refurbishing and, last, recycling are the options, in that order. Needless to say, the more products that stay within the inner circle, the less negative impact on the environment and the more positive impact on profit through potential saving (such as material, labour, etc). Consequently, the leakage to landfill and incineration is minimized (Ellen MacArthur Foundation, 2015).

Critics propagating the unsustainable character of a linear economy usually focus on how deeply consumerism is embedded in our western society. Instead of including every aspect of the *take–make–dispose* approach, these critics limit their solution thinking to one side of the coin. Consumerism might

Figure 1.2 Circular economy (Ellen MacArthur Foundation, 2012)

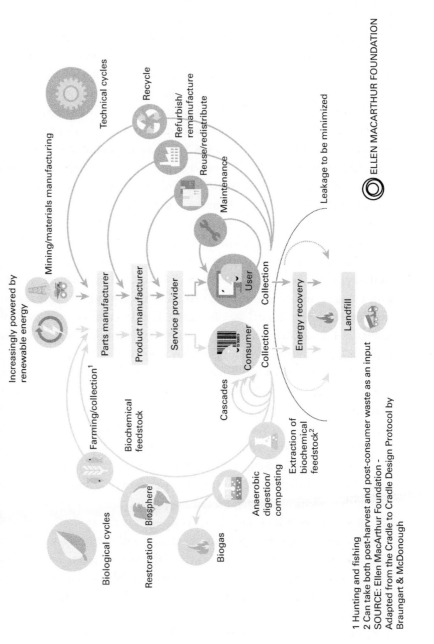

CIRCULAR ECONOMY - *an industrial system that is restorative by design*

Increasingly powered by renewable energy

Mining/materials manufacturing

Technical cycles

Recycle

Refurbish/ remanufacture

Reuse/redistribute

Maintenance

Parts manufacturer

Product manufacturer

Service provider

User

Collection

Consumer

Collection

Cascades

Biochemical feedstock

Farming/collection[1]

Biological cycles

Restoration

Biosphere

Biogas

Anaerobic digestion/ composting

Extraction of biochemical feedstock[2]

Energy recovery

Landfill

Leakage to be minimized

ELLEN MACARTHUR FOUNDATION

1 Hunting and fishing
2 Can take both post-harvest and post-consumer waste as an input
SOURCE: Ellen MacArthur Foundation -
Adapted from the Cradle to Cradle Design Protocol by
Braungart & McDonough

be the engine that keeps the manufacturers manufacturing, the producers producing and waste disposal at full throttle; nevertheless, changing consumerism as an attitude in the population has proven to be nearly impossible. By taking the economy as a whole within the loop of circular economy, other solutions come to mind. Stahel (1982) developed a new economic model that helps to facilitate the changes of a circular economy. As this author re-evaluates how we look at ownership, he introduces 'performance-based contracting'. In this model, ownership as we know it today makes way for a fee that the user pays for the performance of a product. Consumers do not pay for ownership of the product, but instead pay for the performance the product delivers. The producers keep ownership, which means, ideally, that the product is returned to the producer after the consumer has enjoyed its performance. Convincing consumers to recycle their products is taken out of the equation by returning the control over the product to the producers once the performance has been fulfilled. A recent voice in the public debate is Kate Raworth, author of Doughnut Economics. She writes that the traditional way of economics is broken and that radical reframing of economics for a new generation is necessary given the challenges at stake (Raworth, 2017).

Circular economy in business practices

In September 2014, the European Commission adopted a zero-waste programme, establishing a legal framework for an EU-wide circular economy. Not only did the commission predict that this new framework will boost recycling and prevent the waste of valuable materials, it will also create new jobs, economic growth, new business models, and reduce greenhouse gas emissions. By 2030, EU citizens can expect their municipal waste to be recycled by at least 7 per cent and all packaging materials by at least 80 per cent. On top of that, it is estimated that the circular economy can save European businesses €600 billion (European Commission, 2014).

The French car maker Renault, partner of the Ellen MacArthur Foundation, is an excellent example of a large business that has implemented circular economy principles. Renault remanufactures different mechanical subassemblies, manages raw material streams and has implemented an access-over-ownership model, so that customers need not buy a car anymore. Renault even has a whole factory mostly dedicated to the production of remanufactured car parts (Ellen MacArthur Foundation, 2013).

Another example of a company transitioning to circularity is Philips, which became a strategic partner of the Ellen MacArthur Foundation in 2013. Their business model innovation is aimed at implementing performance-based contracting in multiple sectors. Firstly, Philips started allowing customers buy 'illumination services' instead of lightbulbs. Consumers pay a service fee for the light, after which Philips reuses and recycles the equipment. In the meantime, Philips keeps maintaining and upgrading the systems in order to extend their durability. Other products are subjected to material recovery; old systems are refurbished using old components instead of creating new materials from scratch. Underlying these methods is a shift by Philips towards renewable energy for lighting. New LED technology, for example, reduces the need to build more power plants (Philips, 2014). A similar revenue model was implemented with regard to MRI machines for use in hospitals. Selling MRI services instead of machines, Philips is able to take control of the remanufacturing, refurbishment and reuse of the equipment (Philips, 2016).

These product design approaches have strong ties with the Cradle to Cradle philosophy developed by designer William McDonough and chemist Michael Braungart. This philosophy reshapes the way we think about product design. It encourages rich and smart design that is not detrimental to the environment or human health. In addition, Cradle to Cradle seeks to replace eco-efficiency (simply reducing 'negative eco-footprints') with eco-effective supply (creating 'positive eco-footprints'). Essential to achieving this goal are, for example, the principles of material health and material reutilization: only materials that provide nutrients for safe, continuous cycling of the flow of biological and technological nutrients should be used. The driving forces underlying these two principles are the notions of Renewable Energy, Water Stewardship and Social Fairness. As one can see, the Cradle to Cradle philosophy is an excellent design-led approach to the principles of circularity (McDonough and Braungart, 2002).

The Cradle to Cradle philosophy is successfully implemented by BMA Ergonomics, which, for more than 20 years, has been specializing in making office chairs. Their office chairs are 99 per cent recyclable and each new chair is made of at least 50 per cent recycled materials. On top of this, BMA offers their clients a buyback guarantee, which gives BMA the certainty that the chairs will be processed in a way that keeps the materials at their highest values. Small parts suitable for reuse are immediately returned to the production process, unusable components are returned to the supplier for processing, and any defective or worn parts can be replaced to give BMA chairs a second life (BMA Ergonomics, 2015).

In transitioning to a circular economy, we will be viewing a disruptive overhaul of many economic systems, affecting every sector imaginable. We expect change in the following five sectors to be most influential, and disruptive, in the near future:

1 Logistics: waste flows from one company will form the resources for another. Logistics companies will have to connect companies from different material chains in increasingly complex networks. Trucks will probably never drive completely empty.

2 Retail and marketing: circular products and services will need accompanying revenue models. To regain resources and efficiently process them producers will probably remain owners of their products or use buyback schemes.

3 Finance: a change from ownership to usage has many finance-related consequences for producers and consumers alike. Risk needs to be addressed and financial instruments, like mortgages, need to be overhauled. Banks can also become important players in connecting different chains.

4 Product design: products will have to be designed for circularity; they should be reusable and modular, meaning they are easy to take apart. These parts then need to be easy to replace or repair, and the product as a whole needs to be easily refurbished.

5 Material design: materials should be made from resources that are already reused without loss in value and can be reused again. Moreover, circular materials and parts should either consist of only one material or be easily separable into single materials.

These disruptions are already taking place and a few global frontrunners are showing that using business logic to further circular goals is not only possible, but effective. The following examples are all multinationals ranked highly on the DJSI, and they show the frontier of implementing circular principles into business models (Dutch Sustainable Growth Coalition, 2015).

AkzoNobel operates globally in the paints, coatings and speciality chemicals sectors while pursuing sustainability goals. They have a sustainability strategy built upon three key elements: sustainable business, resource efficiency and capable, engaged people. One of the goals AkzoNobel set for itself was to minimize obsolete paint throughout the complete value chain. A business case was built around this issue. AkzoNobel started to invest in their relationship with GDB, a company specializing in processing both obsolete and waste paint. Rather than paying for the disposal of paint, AkzoNobel can now make money from selling this paint as a raw material to GDB, saving the company €4.5 million euros in 2013 (AkzoNobel, 2016; Dutch Sustainable Growth Coalition, 2015). GDB, in turn, sells the lower-quality and cheaper paint in developing countries. Moreover, AkzoNobel is investing in a project to collect waste paint from professional users and consumers. Some of this paint can be used as a new raw material and the rest will be remanufactured for community use. This project is being trialled in the UK, where 10 per cent of paint goes to waste, and if successful it will be rolled out in other European countries (Dutch Sustainable Growth Coalition, 2015).

Having a long history as a global brewer with a large portfolio of brands, Heineken has also set sustainability as a core business priority; as part of its corporate strategy it has formulated a number of commitments under the name 'Brewing a Better World' (Heineken, 2016). Specifically, Heineken's circular approach consists of four key activities (Dutch Sustainable Growth Coalition, 2015): recycling kegs, bottles and other packaging materials; reducing water and energy use across the entire organization; renewable energy initiatives to install wind turbines and solar panels at breweries; and lastly, reusing brewers' grains as cattle feed, as well as reusing glass bottles. Heineken's branded beer bottle is the most striking example of how circular principles can be executed on a large scale. These bottles are cleaned and refilled up to 30 times and in the Netherlands alone, just a small piece of Heineken's global market, they refill over 100 million bottles annually. The savings hereby realized in packaging operations are substantial (Dutch Sustainable Growth Coalition, 2015).

KLM is a leading air transportation company and part of the Air France–KLM Group. KLM is at the forefront of sustainable transport, and in 2015 they were placed first on the DJSI in the airlines sector for the 11th time (KLM, 2016). As a transport provider, KLM is largely dependent on its suppliers for sustainable and more circular products. However, by continuously renewing its sustainable procurement policy and its suppliers' code of conduct KLM has shown itself to be a catalyst for circularity in the whole value chain (Dutch Sustainable Growth Coalition, 2015). The problem of waste was also seen by KLM as an opportunity. From having only two waste flows for years, they now have 14, with paper, plastic, wood and glass being the main ones. All these waste flows are subject to reuse, upcycling, recycling and recovery. As early as the design phase, KLM is collaborating with its suppliers to ensure the highest value of parts and products after their life cycle. Besides waste management, KLM is a leader in biofuels. In 2010 they founded the biofuel supplier SkyNRG and in 2012 they launched the KLM Corporate BioFuel Programme. This programme enables corporate customers to choose to pay a surcharge that covers the price difference between kerosene and biofuel. Together with their corporate partners this programme lets people fly on biofuels, reducing their carbon footprint (Dutch Sustainable Growth Coalition, 2015; KLM, 2016).

The Responsible Business Simulator and the circular economy

Benefits of making strategic decisisons based on data and dialogue:

1 Unleashes the combined power of explorative and strategic dialogue with the art of advanced modelling.

2 Operationalizes circular economy-related issues.

3 Facilitates boardroom discussion with facts, figures and visuals that are created on the spot.

4 Captures every element brought up in strategic dialogues.

5 Integrates the financial and non-financial objectives of strategic decisions and clarifies potential trade-offs.

6 Stimulates out-of-the-box thinking.

7 Creates robust, sustainable decisions.

8 Provides many visual displays to explain complex interdependencies.

9 Creates shared value for multiple stakeholders.

10 Creates transparency in business dynamics.

11 Documents all assumptions, steps and sources underlying a strategic decision.

12 Allows users to incorporate new insight into existing models without programming.

13 Extends the two-dimensional world of spreadsheets into a highly multi-dimensional world.

14 Provides access to all types of data sources.

15 Discloses, combines and projects all available data on the strategic decision at hand.

16 Supports any strategic decision.

17 Detects the vital few factors that influence the outcomes of decisions the most.

The transition to a circular economy inevitably implies a paradigm shift. The Responsible Business Simulator can be used as a tool to accelerate that shift. Businesses working towards ameliorating social goals, such as shifting towards a circular economy, need incentives. Sustainability for the environment and people has, however, traditionally been regarded as merely representing a corporate philosophy; a charitable corporate strategy that is often seen as just a burden and a necessity for marketing. As opposed to this, increase in profit typically functions as the largest incentive for any business, sometimes indeed at any cost when it comes to environment and people. Not surprisingly, the most important barriers to implementation of circular economy practices are high upfront investment costs and risks for businesses (Preston, 2012). The Responsible Business Simulator, however, converges these two seemingly contradicting doctrines – environmental/social and economic benefits – operating within the framework of shared values (People, Planet and Profit). In this respect, the Responsible Business Simulator makes the complexity of the value chains in a circular economy more transparent. Sustainability in the long term is more beneficial to a company's profit than short-term destructive use of resources and disregard for the social dimension. Reports by the McKinsey group state there is an economic potential of €250–500 billion per year within the EU in the next decade for the durable products and solutions industry (Ellen MacArthur Foundation, 2012).

The importance of shared values for the company's long-term continuity is affirmed with the strategic decision-making process and the use of the Responsible Business Simulator, and profit is inherently connected as such. The Responsible Business Simulator concretely considers stakeholders' interests in attaining strategic goals. The stakeholders' interests can be found in the three Ps, which in turn find their expression as performance indicators in the model. This brings us one step closer to attaining the goals of a circular economy by getting the biggest players in the field, businesses, on board the train to circularity: no negative effects on human life, People, or the ecosystem, Planet.

References

AkzoNobel (2016) *Report 2015*. Retrieved from https://www.akzonobel.com/for-investors/all-reports/annual-report-2015

Austin, J and Reficco, E (2009) Corporate social entrepreneurship: a new vision for CSR, in *The Accountable Corporation*, ed M Epstein and K Hanson, Praeger Publishing, New York, pp. 237–47

BMA Ergonomics (2015) *BMA Ergonomics Sustainability Report 2015*, BMA Ergonomics

Ceres/Sustainalytics (2014) *Gaining Ground: Corporate progress on the Ceres roadmap for sustainability*, Ceres/Sustainalytics, Boston

Dow Jones Sustainability Indices (2017) Dow Jones Sustainability Index industry group leaders. Retrieved from http://www.sustainability-indices.com

Dutch Sustainable Growth Coalition (2015) Circular Economy: DSGC companies on their journey of implementing circular business models. Retrieved from http://dsgcpublication.online-magazine.nl/nl/magazine/7551/791725/the_circular_economy.html

Eggers, W D and Macmillan, P (2013) *The Solution Revolution: How business, government, and social enterprises are teaming up to solve society's toughest problems*, Harvard Business Review Press, Boston

Elkington, J (1997) *Cannibals With Forks: Triple bottom line of 21st-century business*, Capstone Publishers, Mankato, MN

Ellen MacArthur Foundation (2012) *Towards the Circular Economy 1: Economic and business rationale for an accelerated transition*. Retrieved from https://www.ellenmacarthurfoundation.org/assets/downloads/publications/Ellen-MacArthur-Foundation-Towards-the-Circular-Economy-vol.1.pdf

Ellen MacArthur Foundation (2013) The circular economy applied to the automotive industry. Retrieved from https://www.ellenmacarthurfoundation.org/circular-economy/interactive-diagram/the-circular-economy-applied-to-the-automotive-industry

Ellen MacArthur Foundation (2015) Ellen MacArthur Foundation. Retrieved from www.ellenmacarthurfoundation.org

European Commission (2014) *Communication from the Commission to the European Parliament, the Council, the European Economic and Social Committee and the Committee of the Regions Towards a Circular Economy: A zero waste programme for Europe*. Retrieved from http://eur-lex.europa.eu/legal-content/EN/ALL/?uri=CELEX:52014DC0398R(01)

Heineken (2016) *Sustainability Report 2015: Brewing a better world*, Heineken, Amsterdam

KLM (2016) *2015 Annual Report*. Retrieved from https://annualreports.klm.com/

Mair, J, Battalina, J L and Cardenas, J (2012) Organizing for society: a typology of social entrepreneuring models, *Journal of Business Ethics*, 11, pp. 353–73

McDonough, W and Braungart, M (2002) *Cradle to Cradle: Remaking the way we make things*, North Point Press, New York, NY

Meadows, D H et al (1972) *The Limits to Growth*, Universe Books, New York, NY

Nidumolo, R, Prahalad, C K and Rangaswami, M R (2009), Why sustainability is now the key driver of innovation, *Harvard Business Review*, 87 (9), pp. 56–64

PGGM (2015) *PGGM N.V. Annual Report 2014*. Retrieved from https://www.pggm.nl/wie-zijn-we/jaarverslagen/Documents/pggm-nv-annual-report_2014.pdf

Philips (2014) *Transitioning to a Circular Economy*. Retrieved from https://www.usa.philips.com/c-dam/corporate/about-philips-n/sustainability/sustainabilitypdf/philips-circular-economy.pdf

Philips (2016) *Philips Annual Report 2015*. Retrieved from https://www. annualreport.philips.com/downloads/pdf/en/PhilipsFullAnnualReport2015_English.pdf

Porter, M E and Kramer, M R (2011) Creating shared value: how to reinvent capitalism – and unleash a wave of innovation and growth, *Harvard Business Review*, **89** (1/2), pp. 62–77

Preston, F (2012) *A Global Redesign? Shaping the circular economy*, Chatham House, London, pp. 1–20

Puma (2011) Environmental profit and loss account. Retrieved from http://about.puma.com/en/sustainability/environment/environmental-profit-and-loss-account

Raworth, K (2017). *Doughnut Economics. Seven Ways to Think Like a 21st-Century Economist*. Random House Business Books, London.

Rogers, K and Hudson, B (2011).The triple bottom line: the synergies of transformative perceptions and practices for sustainability, *OD Practitioner*, **43**, pp. 3–9

Short, J C, Moss, T W and Lumpkin, G T (2009) Research in social entrepreneurship: past contributions and future opportunities, *Strategic Entrepreneurship Journal*, **3**, pp. 161–94

Stahel, W (1982) *The Product-Life Factor*, Product Life Institute, Geneva

UN Global Compact (2015) *Impact: Transforming business, changing the world*. Retrieved from https://www.unglobalcompact.org/library/1331

WECD (1987) *Report of the World Commission on Environment and Development: Our Common Future*. Retrieved from http://www.un-documents.net/our-common-future.pdf

Wheeler, D, Colbert, B and Freeman, R E (2003) Focusing on value: reconciling Corporate Social Responsibility, sustainability and a stakeholder approach in a network world, *Journal of General Management*, **28**, pp. 1–26

The Responsible   02
Business Simulator
at the heart of the
strategic decision-
making process

Making strategic decisions to benefit people, the planet and profits is an interactive process with stakeholders that addresses both financial and non-financial aspects. The interactive process comprises a seven-step process that leads to a clear strategic choice based on data and dialogue (Roobeek, A. and de Swart, J. (eds), 2013). The process is empowered by unique modelling software named the Responsible Business Simulator. With the help of this software, broad-based decisions are taken around balancing the People, Planet and Profit (PPP) objectives of an organization by investigating multi-dependencies between these objectives. Which aspects are weighted up, why, and with what impact?

The seven-step decision-making process can be broken down into three phases. The first phase is about unleashing collective intelligence to specify the strategic challenge that requires a decision. The setting of this phase is an explorative dialogue with stakeholders and experts from multiple disciplines. The second phase is the research phase in which additional data is collected via desk research and – optionally – field research, and the simulation model is constructed. Although various experts preferably participate to disclose and combine existing knowledge, the setting of this phase focuses less on dialogue. The third phase is about analysing output from the simulation model such that the decision-making process results in a well-balanced strategic choice. The setting of this phase is strategic dialogue in the boardroom of the organization.

Figure 2.1 The decision-making process broken down into three phases and seven steps

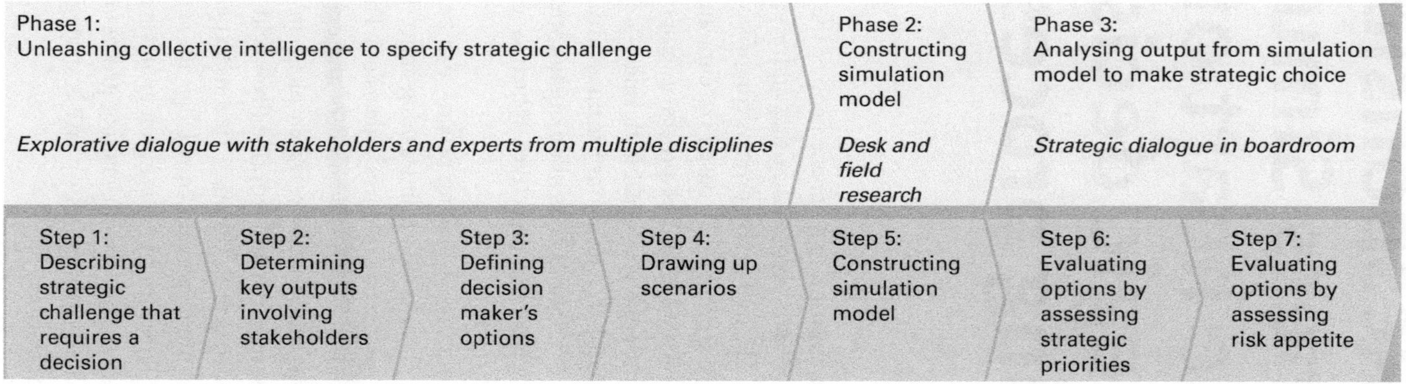

Phase 1:
Unleashing collective intelligence to specify strategic challenge

Phase 2:
Constructing simulation model

Phase 3:
Analysing output from simulation model to make strategic choice

Explorative dialogue with stakeholders and experts from multiple disciplines

Desk and field research

Strategic dialogue in boardroom

Step 1:
Describing strategic challenge that requires a decision

Step 2:
Determining key outputs involving stakeholders

Step 3:
Defining decision maker's options

Step 4:
Drawing up scenarios

Step 5:
Constructing simulation model

Step 6:
Evaluating options by assessing strategic priorities

Step 7:
Evaluating options by assessing risk appetite

The Responsible Business Simulator has three objectives: first, it facilitates the decision-making process by capturing all its elements in a structured way. Second, it allows for an easy implementation of the simulation model specified in the research step. Third, it helps to analyse the output from the simulation model in a graphical and interactive way. We named this the Responsible Business Simulator because it calculates the future financial and non-financial effects of potential decisions on the basis of a simulation model in a business context. Putting the Responsible Business Simulator at the heart of the decision-making process gives decision makers in organizations a tool that they can use, with the aid of strategic dialogue, to make clear and well-founded choices. This makes the transition from a vague 'gut feeling' to clear strategic decision making a far simpler step than we often imagine.

Making strategic decisions to benefit people, the planet and profits uses an approach that is advanced, yet transparent at the same time. Advanced, because the software that is used is based on a complex computational program. Econometric formulas are not, however, everyday fare for the average employee, manager or even director. It is therefore not necessary that they fully understand the underlying calculations, let alone be able to carry them out: we have specialists for that. What, on the other hand, must be made transparent for the participants of round-table sessions in dialogue form, are non-trivial assumptions underlying the simulation model and the mutually interdependent importance of performance in the domains of People, Planet and Profit.

We have applied and fine-tuned the methodology in a variety of organizations during multiple sessions. This form of action research formed the basis of this seven-step decision-making process in which Q&Q (Quantitative and Qualitative) aspects are combined, thereby giving realistic estimates of the values around the themes of People, Planet and Profit. This finally leads to strategic choices based on shared value.

We also tested the developed methodology during MBA lectures for a variety of participant groups at Nyenrode Business Universiteit. It may be interesting to note that it is possible to learn how modelling works through the medium of workshops as interactive round-table sessions in which the participants are guided through the decision-making process.

In this chapter we elaborate on the seven-step decision-making process depicted in Figure 2.1. For simplicity we have presented a sequential stepwise approach here. However, in practice several feedback loops and iterative actions take place during the decision-making process.

Chapter 7 describes the supporting software, the Responsible Business Simulator, more extensively. In the chapters that follow, we illustrate the use of the developed methodology in practical situations using a number of case studies. Therefore, we restrict ourselves here to a brief general description of each of the seven steps, because further elaboration can be found in the cases described later in this book, and this will give the reader a much clearer impression.

Step 1: Describing strategic challenge that requires a decision

The first step in the decision-making process is to describe the strategic challenge that requires a decision. In this step questions such as 'What is the decision about?', 'Who is the decision maker?', and 'Which stakeholders should be accounted for?' are discussed. In addition, a high-level qualitative assessment is performed regarding the impact of potential decisions on the decision maker and the stakeholders. The essence of the methodology is that this impact is considered beyond Profit only. Finally, the stakeholders and other experts who need to be involved in the first phase are listed. Examples of descriptions of strategic challenges that may result from this step are 'How to sustain employability', impacting the financial result and employee well-being, or 'How to source energy', impacting the financial and environmental bottom line. Examples of stakeholders that may be listed in this step are regulators, clients, opinion leaders, shareholders, employees and local residents.

Step 2: Defining key outputs

After the strategic challenge of the decision has been described, it is now crucial to involve the stakeholders listed in Step 1. Together with the decision maker, they determine the outputs upon which the decision maker will base his decision, the so-called key outputs. Key outputs can be thought of as the basis for decision criteria. Note that a key output does not have to be a decision criterion yet, since such a criterion typically needs a target value for the key output as well. For example, if payback period is a key output, then 'payback period should not be longer than 1.5 years' may be a decision criterion.

Step 2 of the decision-making process normally takes place by first formulating a longlist of outputs which will then be reduced to a shortlist of key outputs, again in an interactive setting. A group of participants working under guidance can quickly learn how to pinpoint outputs and then place them in order of priority. Progressing from a longlist to a shortlist of key outputs is also a way to focus attention: in which areas the organization needs to achieve success or concrete results; which areas should be given priority; who are the key stakeholders whose interests should be taken into account. Hence, when defining key outputs, it is of crucial importance to take into account the views and standpoints of all stakeholders as formulated in Step 1. Chapter 7 will clarify that there are more types of outputs than key outputs. However, key outputs matter to the boardroom. These are often referred to as Key Performance Indicators or KPIs. An existing Integrated Report, the GRI framework (Global Reporting, nd), or other documents of an organization containing KPIs may be important sources for key output definitions.

Often, key outputs together cover the three Ps. There might be cases where not all three Ps are relevant, but key outputs together should preferably address at least two Ps in order to exploit the potential of the Responsible Business Simulator concept. However, even if all key outputs belong to just one P, but have been defined such that they are hard to compare because they have different units, for example Internal Rate of Return next to payback period and Net Present Value, this strategic decision-making methodology may be useful to study the multi-dependencies between these key outputs and find the right balance. Examples of key outputs addressing People and Planet are change in employee commitment and change in percentage of energy consumption from sustainable resources. In practice, most of the time it suffices to work with the themes People, Planet and Profit, but the user of the Responsible Business Simulator can specify the themes himself. For example, in Chapter 12, the People aspect has been broken down into three themes: Cohesion, Health and Nurture.

Step 3: Determining decision maker's options

In order to define the options a decision maker has, we first introduce the concept of internal variable inputs. Internal variable inputs are in the hands of the decision maker. Within Operations Research, a discipline within econometrics that focuses on the application of analytical methods to support operational decision making, these are known as endogenous or in-control inputs (Pintér, nd). The values of these internal inputs are adjusted during the decision-making process. Each internal variable input can be thought of as a single aspect on which a sub-decision needs to be made. First we need to determine the internal variable inputs by answering the question, 'What actions can the decision maker possibly take?' A decision maker's option can then be formulated by assigning a single value to all internal variable inputs. It assumes that every option within the scope of the decision can be completely described by one value per internal variable input. Since there is typically more than one internal variable input, a decision maker's option can be thought of as a set of potential sub-decisions, where each potential sub-decision is represented by choosing a single value for the corresponding internal variable input. For example, when a municipality decides on a new waste collection system, it may not only need to select a supplier, but also decide whether the service will be outsourced or not.

It is important, in this step, that any participant who wants to submit a proposal for an alternative option is given the opportunity to do so, so that this alternative can be added to the collection of options to be evaluated. This can often be effected during the workshop, by selecting a new combination of values for the internal variable inputs and saving them as a new option. As soon as there are more than three options to be evaluated, it is recommended that the options are given names that illustrate the nature of the option clearly, so that it is not necessary to inspect the values of each of the internal variables.

In many cases, it helps to include a 'nil option'. This nil option boils down to not making a decision, and leaving everything as it was. Formulating a nil option provides a good check on the formulation of the key outputs. Just as in a normal business case assessment, the outputs may illustrate the incremental effect of the decision. Quite often this means evaluating all outputs in the nil option at zero, but that is not always the case. Take, for example, the decision of whether or not to insulate the leaking roof of a science centre (Chapter 9). The nil option would mean doing nothing to the roof. Consider now the key output reflecting the energy saving to be achieved by insulating the roof. This output should, in principle, reflect the energy saving in comparison to maintaining the present situation. If the roof is still leaking, however, the option of doing nothing may cause the leaking to become even worse, thereby leading to an even higher energy consumption than the actual energy consumption. Normally, insulating the roof would automatically remedy the leakage. In that case, the output for energy saving can be given a negative value for the nil option, as is the case in Chapter 9.

Step 4: Drawing up scenarios

In order to define scenarios, we first introduce the concept of external variable inputs. External variable inputs are the inputs that are not in the hands of the decision maker and hence also known as exogenous variables or out-of-control inputs. The values of these external inputs are adjusted during the decision-making process. Each external variable input can be thought of as a single aspect of external uncertainty affecting the outcome of the decision in scope. A scenario is defined by assigning a single value to all external variable inputs. It assumes that every possible future outcome of all external uncertainty with respect to the scope of the decision can be completely described by a single value per external variable input. Since there is typically more than one external variable input, a scenario can be thought of as a coherent combination of future developments, where every single aspect of external uncertainty is represented by choosing a single value for the corresponding external variable input. For example, both the future interest rate and the future price of solar panels may have to be set when designing a scenario in the context of an energy sourcing decision.

Just as formulating the decision maker's options consists of multiple rounds of filling in data for the internal variable input, so the drawing up of scenarios consists of filling in data for the external input several times. Since the external input cannot, by definition, be influenced by the decision makers, the challenge of the latter task is many times greater than that of the former step. During the workshop some basic scenarios will be formulated by the participants, and these – together with the key outputs and internal variable inputs – will be further investigated, updated and completed outside of the workshop. The data to fill in the scenarios is collected from a combination of existing research, historical data, expert opinions and simulation. The objective of the exercise is not per se to fill out the scenarios as realistically as possible; it is more important to gain access to the sources that can be made available within a reasonable amount of effort, and to make the remaining uncertainty more transparent.

It is desirable to draw up at least three scenarios at this stage: a base-case or neutral scenario (in which all external output is given a 'most plausible' value), along pessimistic and optimistic scenarios to represent the most negative and most positive reactions of the environment to the decision. Once again, all participants in the workshop must feel that they are free to add or adapt scenarios. This might include adding specific stress scenarios so as to test extreme settings of external input, or adding alternative base-case scenarios if there is a difference of opinion among the experts as to what the most probable values actually are.

As the Responsible Business Simulator is uncommonly patient, and the addition of a scenario is a simple task, there is no limit to the number of scenarios that can be considered. Therefore, it is important to ensure that the names of the scenarios reflect the intention clearly, at first sight, without the need to inspect the individual values of the external input.

Typically, not all values needed to define scenarios can be produced on the fly in this step. Desk and even field research may be needed to complete scenario definitions. Historical data may be involved, and/or other experts may be consulted. Since these activities are too time consuming to perform in the explorative dialogue setting in the first phase of the decision-making process, these are postponed until the next phase: the construction of the simulation model.

Step 5: Constructing simulation model

The primary objective of Step 5 is to specify the simulation model in the form of a set of formulas that compute key outputs based on the decision maker's options and scenarios. Constructing this simulation model typically involves more than just writing down as many formulas as there are key outputs. First, the model may become more transparent by breaking down formulas in a number of steps, thereby generating a set of intermediates. For example, instead of calculating the Total Cost of Ownership (TCO) of a new asset, it may be wise to break down TCO into capital expenditure, capital charges and operational costs, calculate these components separately and then aggregate them. Second, more inputs than just the internal variable input and external variable input defined in Steps 3 and 4 are often needed to model the relationship between these inputs and key outputs. Since there is less focus on understanding the dependency of key outputs on the changes in these additional inputs, we call these fixed inputs. For example, in order to calculate maintenance costs, the cost per hour of a maintenance operator has to be known. Third, besides key output it may be useful to compute additional output to create additional insights and/or simple validation possibilities. For example, besides the decrease in energy usage, the new level of energy usage might be communicated as well.

The secondary objective of Step 5 is to complete all input data needed to feed the simulation model. As explained in the previous section, Steps 3 and 4 take place in a boardroom setting and focus on defining the decision maker's options and scenarios respectively. These only require setting the values of the internal and external variable inputs. However, data needs to be collected for all additionally defined fixed input as well. This is typically done using desk research and – if no useful secondary data is readily available – using primary data collection, historical data, expert opinions and/or Monte Carlo simulation. From the point of view of efficiency it is, of course, preferable to use existing research that is directly applicable to the situation being modelled. A great deal of relevant quantitative data is often already available from previous research, somewhere. Nonetheless, non-statisticians often find it difficult to access such results and relate them to the results of other existing research. It can also be considered difficult to superimpose the results of this research onto the situation in hand. Our experience has been that the Responsible Business Simulator provides an excellent aid to accessing, disclosing and combining existing research, and translating that combination of research to the business context of the organization at hand. The use of historical data that has a direct relevance to the decision-making process comes in a well-deserved second place. In practice, however, such relevant historical data is rarely available. First, data of this nature cannot always be made readily accessible. Second, we need data that describes the future, not the past, and extrapolating historical data realistically into the future is not a particularly trivial task. Third, sustainable decision making often has an innovative character and this more or less precludes the possibility that historical data will be applicable. In the latter case, it can still help to collect historical data of vaguely similar situations. In all cases it is recommended that historical data, as a source, is combined with expert opinions. This can be effected by giving experts the opportunity to adjust the historical data (up or down) to make it more representative for the future. In credit risk modelling, this method became known as 'judgmental overlay'. Conversely, experts can also arrive at more reliable estimates if these are based on historical data rather than on guesstimation. At the same time, experts might forfeit their impartiality if they allow themselves to be unduly influenced by historical data that has only a limited relevance. This effect – known as 'anchoring' – is one of the pitfalls of decision making processes (Hammond, Keeney and Raiffa, 2006). The final source of data for the external input is simulation. This source can be considered a last resort in the event that there is absolutely no relevant previous research, no historical data is available and/or the experts are reluctant to make any rigorous estimates.

We use the Monte Carlo simulation method for this purpose. This technique entails estimating a probability distribution for each external input so that each possible future end result corresponds with a draw from each of the distributions. Historical data and expert opinions can, of course, help to determine the type of probability distribution and its parameters. Subsequently, we ask the software to compute, say, 50,000 draws of future end results for each highly uncertain input. Ultimately, therefore, we have 50,000 observations for each output and these are then aggregated into the most plausible value. A 95 or 5 percentile of those 50,000 observations can also be calculated as output. By 'promoting' the parameters of the probability distribution to the status of external inputs, and allowing them to vary per scenario, it is possible to obtain the desired level of variation in the environment being studied. The process of investigating, updating and completing scenarios is often rather time-consuming, because the members of the modelling team need to speak to co-workers and to external experts to obtain the data. It is therefore sensible to do this in the intervals between modelling sessions; besides that, it is an instructive intervention to request reports and information from others within the organization, and from suppliers and customers as well. Not infrequently, informal knowledge is thus brought to light that can be used to refine the definition of key outputs and the decision maker's options.

Reaching these two objectives is supported by two sub-steps in the Responsible Business Simulator: specifying the formulas encompassing the simulation model, and collecting data. More details on these-sub steps will be given in Chapter 7.

After the simulation model has been constructed, all the information gathered in the foregoing steps of the decision-making process has been processed within the model, and the simulation model has been validated, the Responsible Business Simulator calculates the key output scores and we can proceed to the selection of the best strategic choice. For that, two steps are remaining: assessing the strategic priorities (Step 6) and the risk appetite of the decision maker (Step 7), which will be discussed in the next sections.

Step 6: Evaluating options by assessing strategic priorities

Strategic priorities are discussed by assigning weights to key outputs. This discussion is the start of phase 3 and takes the form of a strategic dialogue in the boardroom. The Responsible Business Simulator also allows for assigning weights to themes instead of key outputs. Since every key output is linked to one or more themes, weights per theme can be transformed to weights per key output and vice versa. It depends on the situation at hand whether it is preferable to work with weights per theme or per key output. Irrespective of this choice, weights depend on the mission and vision of the organization that is making the decision. This mission and/or vision should in fact reflect how the equilibrium of its performance in terms of the three Ps is perceived. An organization that is primarily profit-driven, but wants to show its customers that it also has an eye for People and Planet, will assign more weight to (key outputs attached to) Profit than will a charitable institution that sees financial performance as little more than a peripheral condition. Changing the weights assigned to the key output enables the decision maker to get a feeling for the relationships between inputs and key outputs and also shows the decision maker to what extent his mission and/or vision are aligned with the decision he is about to take.

An organization that wants to be sustainable will need to score on all the three Ps, or at least two of them, but there can be large discrepancies between different organizations in the proportionality of the scores on the individual Ps. A construction company that is devoting its efforts to enhancing the sustainable employability of its staff will assign a greater weight to People-related outputs than a tomato grower whose objective is to operate an energy-efficient greenhouse. The tomato grower will value Planet-related aspects more highly. It is a no-brainer that the maturity of an enterprise – in terms of sustainability – influences the proportionality of the importance assigned to the different Ps. An organization that is just beginning to make its production chain sustainable will be different from an enterprise that has been high in the rankings of sustainable businesses for many years. Using this strategic decision-making process, it is possible for employees and management to work together to find a balance that is appropriate to the situation, context and possibilities of the organization.

Even more important than the current sustainability status is the fact that there is a vision and a desire at the top of the organization to have the corporate strategy and operational management practices calibrated objectively against values determined by employees and management alike. By visualizing the proportionality between People, Planet and Profit in various constellations, everyone can gain insight into the consequences of potential choices. The Responsible Business Simulator brings shared value creation to life in a strategic dialogue with all relevant stakeholders. As discussed in Step 2, key outputs may well have been linked to these stakeholders. Often, stakeholders link directly into the themes reflecting the different aspects of the impact of a decision. As such, weights assigned to key outputs are also weights assigned to stakeholders. The more weight one assigns to a stakeholder, the more one tends to 'listen' to that stakeholder when making decisions.

A dialogue to establish strategic priorities thus leads to the assignment of weights to each key output or theme. The Responsible Business Simulator uses these weights to aggregate the three-dimensional set of scores per key output per decision maker's option per scenario into a two-dimensional set of scores per decision maker's option per scenario. Before key outputs can be aggregated, the Responsible Business Simulator transforms the different units that key outputs typically have into one, unitless, scale by means of appreciation functions. In this context, appreciation means the value induced per key output. This valuation concept will be further explained in Chapter 7, but should for now be considered as the instrument to ensure that key outputs can be compared even though they have different base units (eg euros or kWh). Now, that the key outputs are comparable, the Responsible Business Simulator calculates the weighted sum of the appreciation per key output for each combination of options and scenarios. Figure 2.2 shows how placing 50 per cent weight on the key output relating to Planet and dividing the remaining 50 per cent evenly between the People- and Profit-related key outputs produces an overall score per decision maker's option for three possible contextual scenarios: pessimistic, neutral and optimistic. The attractiveness per option depends on the scenario: option A is to be preferred in the optimistic and pessimistic scenarios, whereas B is the prevailing option in the neutral scenario.

Interestingly, as we will see in the case studies, the outcomes are often unexpected. Experience has shown that in many cases an initial focus on sustainable objectives in terms of People and Planet often leads to better

Figure 2.2 Input of strategic priorities leads to scores per option per scenario

KPI	Weight
People	25
Planet	50
Profit	25

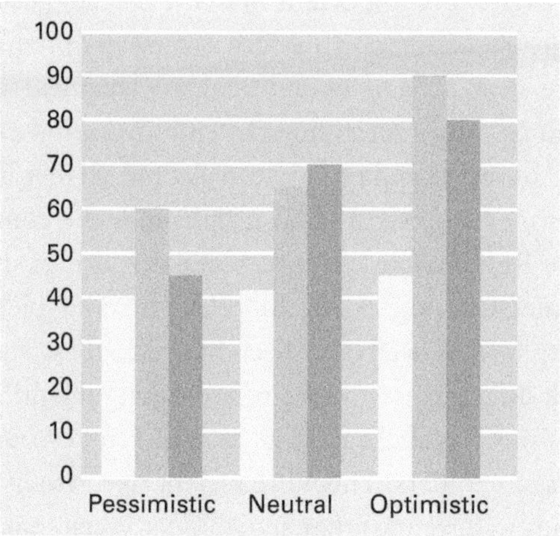
100
90
80
70
60
50
40
30
20
10
0
Pessimistic
Neutral
Optimistic
Strategy
No investments
Investment package A
Investment package B

Profit results in the longer term. The assumption is often that sustainability is expensive, but better educated personnel can be more effective in their work and need less management, as a result of which savings can be made. Sustainably produced goods often last longer and need less maintenance or repair. We have also seen that the overall costs can actually be reduced significantly by adding a time factor to the equation.

Step 7: Evaluating options by assessing risk appetite

Risk appetite is discussed by assigning weightings to scenarios. The weights depend on the risk appetite of the organization, which might be risk loving, risk averse or risk neutral. The risk appetite should in fact reflect how the organization perceives the equilibrium of its performance in terms of risk aversion. An organization that is risk averse will assign more weight to a pessimistic scenario than one that is risk neutral. Once the weightings of the scenarios have been set, the Responsible Business Simulator has sufficient information to be able to express the desirability of each strategy in numerical terms. This is done by taking the weighted sum of the scores per scenario for each strategy. The option with the highest score corresponds with the decision that the organization should take, taking into account all the assumptions made throughout the seven-step decision-making process.

In Figure 2.3 we see how a relatively low risk appetite is translated into weights that result in one overall score per option.

Figure 2.3   Processing risk appetite leads to one score per option

KPI	Weight
Pessimistic	50
Neutral	25
Optimistic	25

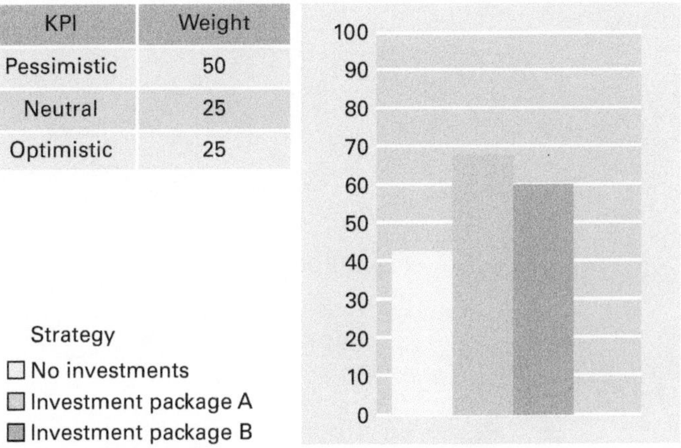

Strategy
☐ No investments
☐ Investment package A
☐ Investment package B

On the basis of the chosen strategic priorities and the risk appetite, as translated into weights for key outputs and scenarios, the enterprise would therefore choose option A. This analysis makes it clear what the assumptions are to finally choose one of the available options. By establishing these assumptions in a dialogue setting together with all relevant stakeholders and experts from all relevant disciplines, a 'black box' experience can be avoided. Instead there is a hands-on process of weighing up the options that is a perfect fit for the specific situation in which the organization finds itself.

References

Global Reporting (nd, accessed 22 November 2015) GRI Standards. Retrieved from https://www.globalreporting.org/standards

Hammond, J S, Keeney, R L and Raiffa, H (2006) The hidden traps in decision making, *Harvard Business Review*, **84** (1)

Pintér, J (nd, accessed 23 November 2015) Operations Research, *Mathworld*. Retrieved from www.mathworld.wolfram.com/OperationsResearch.html

Roobeek, A and de Swart, J (eds.) (2013) *Sustainable Business Modeling*, Academic Service, The Hague

Shared value as a framework for shaping strategy

It is interesting to see how concepts have been developed in recent decades so as to achieve a better balance between the interests of enterprises and shareholders on the one hand and the interests of society and stakeholders on the other. Over the years, various articles from Michael Porter and Mark Kramer have provided fuel for the debate from the perspective of business administration (2002, 2006, 2011). In this chapter, we will first introduce the concept of shared value as introduced by Porter and Kramer (2002). They elaborated the concept in practice with first moving companies like Nestle. Thereafter, we will outline Porter and Kramer's arguments as to why there does not necessarily have to be tension between economic and social goals and the role the Responsible Business Simulator can play to integrate social and economic goals in the decision-making process.

The concept of shared value

In 2002 Porter and Kramer wrote that companies could well use their philanthropic efforts to improve their competitive context within the business environment that shapes their productivity. The intellectual development path illustrated by these authors is a good reflection of current thinking within the field of sustainability. The frontrunners are becoming quite adept; they are attracting disciples and a real movement is emerging. The core of the development is shifting towards integrating societal objectives into corporate strategy, previously the exclusive domain of purely commercial economic objectives. Porter and Kramer (2002) describe the development of the concept of philanthropy or charity from what was merely a peripheral consideration to one that shapes Corporate Social Responsibility (CSR), but they do express some criticism.

In their later article, Porter and Kramer (2006) move on to Corporate Social Integration (CSI) as a way to explain that CSR must not become a discrete activity for a small group within a company, but must be directly and firmly connected to the enterprise's commercial economic objectives. From CSI they go on to speak of how important it is for businesses to create social value. Some radicalization is discernible in their most recent articles (2011), in which they advocate a redefinition of capitalism with shared value as the underlying principle. It is precisely commercial enterprises that can offer an answer to today's major social questions by being innovative and sustainable, and showing respect for people, the planet and the social environment. It is the ultimate amalgamation of societal interests and a reinvented form of entrepreneurship that arises from the common values, the shared value, being pursued.

Even though the concept of creating shared value has received a lot of attention among management scholars and within the business community, there have also been some critics. Crane et al (2014) published an assessment on the topic at the end of 2014 outlining both the strengths and weaknesses of shared value creation. The strength of their approach, according to these authors, mainly lies in the fact that Porter and Kramer elevate social goals of enterprises to a strategic level as well as including the role of the government in the social initiatives of companies. The main weakness these authors put forward is that Porter and Kramer focus too much on corporate self-interest in a sense that enterprises only engage in socially responsible behaviour if it serves the economic purpose of the company. The authors state that Porter and Kramer neglect the possibility that companies can have a social purpose, and that they also neglect the possible tension between economic and social goals. However, Crane et al do acknowledge that the concept of shared value does add value to the debate on the role of business in society, and it may well contribute to the rise of business practices that are beneficial to society.

For this book, we take shared value as a framework for the shaping of corporate strategy and the decision making that underlies that strategy. Pinpointing what exactly the shared value in a company is, and the importance of that shared value for the company's long-term continuity, can be simplified and made more transparent using the Responsible Business Simulator.

No conflict between societal and economic objectives

When a company is socially active within its own competitive context, the effort it puts into achieving a particular charitable objective will have a social dimension, and economic benefit can often be derived at the same time. Porter and Kramer (2002) suggest that in the longer term, far from causing conflicts, this instead leads to an amalgamation of societal and economic objectives. They suggest, quite correctly, that at the point where social and economic benefits converge, focus on corporate strategy is of great significance. After all, if you can 'do good' and achieve the commercial objectives of your company at the same time, you can draw multiple objectives into the scope of the same strategy.

This argument by Porter and Kramer is supported by meta-analytic findings (over 35 years of empirical data) in studies by Orlitzky, Schmidt and Rynes (2003) and Margolis, Elfenbein and Walsh (2007). These findings suggest that Corporate Social Performance (CSP) is likely to pay off, thus being positively correlated with Corporate Financial Performance (CFP). Above all, it becomes clear that market forces do not penalize companies that have high CSP levels. Rather, the market rewards corporations for incorporating sustainability into their corporate strategy. In addition, social audits, which often result in receiving public endorsements from federal or international agencies, can have a positive effect on CFP (Porter and Kramer, 2006).

Moreover, it has been found that bad environmental performance has a negative effect on the market value of publicly traded companies. A study by Konar and Cohen (2001) has shown that the emission of toxic chemicals generally has a negative effect on the intangible asset value of companies, and that reducing these emissions increases market value. A more recent investigation into the effect of corporate sustainability compared 180 US companies grouped as either *High Sustainability* or *Low Sustainability* companies (Eccles, Ioannou and Serafeim, 2014). The high sustainability companies were characterized as being early adopters of sustainability policies. Evidence showed that these companies outperformed the others, especially over the long term, both in accounting and stock market performance.

Another, more internal way in which social and economic benefits converge, is illustrated by the following example: at first sight, investing in better-qualified personnel means increasing the wage costs. But that same personnel can provide the basis from which to develop more sophisticated products or services and thus create more added value for the company. If we take this example a stage further, and the company invests actively and deploys its employees in activities to raise the level of education in disadvantaged areas, that investment not only has value in terms of the reputation of the company but also ensures that more people are encouraged to continue to learn and therefore to have a better chance of finding work and generating income. This in turn creates new consumers and – at the same time – reinforces the self-sufficiency of the local community. 'When corporations support the right causes in the right ways – when they get the where and the how right – they set in motion a virtuous circle' (Porter and Kramer, 2002, p. 66).

In their article titled 'Strategy and Society' (2006), Porter and Kramer take this positive image of philanthropy a step further. By 2006, Corporate Social Responsibility was well established. Porter and Kramer argue that CSR should not exclusively be seen as an expense, but that it can also be the source of new opportunities, innovation and competitive advantage. They were quick to see that sustainability fits so well into the P for Planet in the triple bottom line of People, Planet and Profit. However, integrating sustainability into an organization demands a sense of stewardship from that organization. To give substance to the concept of sustainability is to show respect for the natural environment and it is the moral duty of enterprises to do so in such a way that future generations will be able to fulfil their own needs (Porter and Kramer, 2006). People, Planet and Profit have to be seen as equal partners in this process of integration. It is extremely short-sighted that often People and Planet are only used in the service of Profit, or only used to bring about Profit. The critical note that the authors sound in their 2006 article is that enterprises frequently use CSR to obtain a 'licence to operate' and to uphold stakeholder satisfaction in the short term. In this context, Porter and Kramer specifically mention the power and chemical industries, both of which are pragmatically engaged with CSR but nonetheless have not allowed it to penetrate to the core of their strategy. The authors argue that in the case of companies such as Ben & Jerry's, Patagonia and The Body Shop, cited as prime examples of long-term commitment, social responsibility and CSR did find their way into the core of corporate strategy. They can be said to have achieved true integration between the three Ps of People, Planet and Profit.

In terms of our positioning of strategic decision making and the Responsible Business Simulator, it is interesting to note that Porter and Kramer state that 'The essential test that should guide CSR is not whether a cause is worthy, but whether it presents an opportunity to create shared value – that is a meaningful benefit for society that is also valuable to the business' (Porter and Kramer, 2006, p. 85). But a further step is necessary to integrate corporate objectives and societal needs. This entails creating different relationships both within and outside the organization, creating transparency in operational management about objectives and how they are achieved, being explicit about values and, finally, accounting candidly in reports. According to the authors, CSR should no longer be perceived as a separate discipline; a progression needs to be made from CSR to CSI (Corporate Social Integration). Corporate Social Integration is far more than a simple name change. In their view, social responsibility should be seen as creating shared value. And that calls for more than simple damage control or the organization of public relations campaigns with a short-lived result (Porter and Kramer, 2006).

A good example of non-integrated CSR is illustrated by the following example. The International Organization for Standardization (ISO), as one of the world's largest developers for voluntary International Standards, has published guidelines for incorporating CSR in business practices. These guidelines, the ISO 26000, were launched in 2010 and aim at clarifying what CSR is, as well as helping businesses and organizations translate these principles into effective actions. CSR is defined according to seven generic principles: accountability, transparency, ethical behaviour, respect for stakeholder interest, respect for the rule of law, respect for international standards of conduct, and respect for human rights. These principles are then to be implemented within different CSR subject areas such as the environment and human rights. The ISO 26000 guidelines for implementing CSR principles in core subject areas are expressed in a complex body of definitions and rules that reflect the mentality of CSR as a separate discipline. The implementation of rules does not lead to a CSI result, as the guidelines are too fragmented and do not have the potential to maximize creation of shared value by leaving out corporate profit, for example (International Organization for Standardization, 2010).

Opting for sustainable business practices is a strategic choice

Where sustainability was seen for a long time as 'doing good' or at least observing a minimum set of rules (compliance), it is now seen as a strategic choice that touches the essence of business practices. And that applies just as much to the private as to the public sector. A government that opts for sustainability, circularity and social inclusion, will take decisions about the design of public spaces, drinking water quality, mobility, or the purchasing process for the apparatus of government quite differently than one for which sustainability has a low priority.

The double political standard – saying one thing but doing the opposite – has never prevented some countries (such as Germany, the Scandinavian countries, Italy and Austria) and some multinational enterprises (those that want a high ranking on the Dow Jones Sustainability Index) from purposefully taking up the baton. They do so not only because it is better for the climate, but because they realize that sustainability is a strategic choice for the long term. A strong draught of persistence is called for if the necessary institutional changes are to be implemented in either a country or an enterprise. Countries can create the necessary conditions by means of regulation, legislation, an appropriate tax regime and institutional adaptation. In doing so, they also create a stimulating investment climate for businesses. Businesses can look upon opting for sustainability as a necessary investment to enhance their competitiveness. They choose to distinguish themselves through sustainable, innovative products, production chains and stakeholder management.

As a strategic choice, sustainability calls for a rational analysis that goes far deeper than responsible business practices or CSR. It also goes further than eco-efficiency (Dyllicki and Hockerts, 2002). It hinges on a strategic choice that is fundamental to the management and direction of the enterprise, to investments, to the internal working processes and the competences of the employees, to the enterprise's interaction with its environment, its accommodation, the input of raw materials and the chosen combination of power sources, the processing methods (throughput), and to the output of the enterprise.

It goes without saying that such a complicated assemblage of steps will be fraught with uncertainty. So much can go wrong, and well-intended efforts might not amount to much. If a successful strategy for sustainability in the management of an enterprise is to be achieved, the operational implementation of that strategy will need to be given due consideration in the decision making from the earliest stages. More often than not, that will be seen as an extra layer of complexity, but if sustainable practices are to be put in place it will be desirable to ensure the involvement of the entire organization and of the stakeholders.

Towards shared value

In 2011, Porter and Kramer published an article about creating shared value which was very well received by companies that already had some experience with CSR (Porter and Kramer, 2011). In this article, the authors take the line set out in previous publications one step further still. They speak about 'rethinking capitalism'; Michael Porter makes it clear that he advocates a radical change. The tenor of the article is that the concept of shared value has the potential to release a new wave of global growth – a growth that is characterized by innovation and that can be beneficial to both business and society as a whole. There are three ways by which shared value opportunities can be created:

- reinvention of products and markets;
- redefinition of productivity in the value chain;
- creating local clusters.

Such a drastic change will require businesses to make some fundamental strategic decisions. A switch from short-term to long-term vision, for example, from relocating production facilities because of lower wages to investing in high-tech production processes which are closer to the customer, from waste mountains to recycling and reprocessing waste and 'left-over' material. The impact of the crisis we have been experiencing since 2008 will certainly be a factor in the radical approach advocated by Porter and Kramer. Another factor is their observation that although businesses pay lip service to CSR it doesn't seem to be getting them anywhere because the impact remains inconsequential. The authors realize that creating social value unlocks enormous potential to develop new products and satisfy societal needs and challenges. According to the authors, businesses that can identify societal needs and respond to them with innovative products and services will enjoy competitive advantage over businesses that are unwilling to stray beyond the well-known boundaries of capitalism. They recommend a different business model, based on the needs of the enterprise and society, that can create value for both the enterprise and society by using the resources of the enterprise to address society's challenges.

'Value' is defined in the following chapters as benefit in relation to costs, not just as benefit in isolation. What matters is that businesses not only seek to make a profit, but also seek to create shared value. According to Porter and Kramer (2011), this is the ultimate legitimization of an enterprise. Business is given an opportunity to offer society innovative business solutions in the domains of healthcare, housing, healthy eating, ageing, sustainable energy and many other environmental issues. These are major challenges that society is struggling with, and ones to which businesses could (or perhaps even should) align their strategic compasses, specifically when striving for circularity.

Rolling out shared value through the Responsible Business Simulator

The route that Porter and Kramer have taken from philanthropy, via CSR to Corporate Social Integration, and from there to shared value, is fairly consistent. In the course of their research, they have observed that increasing numbers of enterprises want to 'do good', but more often than not that wish is translated into short-term opportunistic intentions, ways of keeping stakeholders happy, avoiding reputation damage, supporting good causes at random, etc. From that perspective, CSR will continue to be sidelined, while social challenges continue to increase and call for precisely the corporate approach the authors describe. Bringing the two sides together is what leads to shared value.

In Europe, the concept of B Corporations (B Corps) has an enormous take-off. B Corps are for-profit organizations that meet rigorous standards of environmental and social performance, as well as the corresponding accountability and transparency (B Lab, nd). These companies are certified by the non-profit B Lab. Moreover, there are currently many social enterprise start-ups, of which Amplino (case study, Chapter 14) is an excellent example. This movement shows that an increasing number of conscious entrepreneurs and companies want to do more than average.

In their argument for shared value, Porter and Kramer give a number of examples of businesses who are indeed thinking along these lines, but they give no indication of what the potential value could be in terms of actual outcomes for People, Planet and Profit. They do contend that these considerations should have a place in any major decision taken in or by a business. To achieve this, they say that concrete and tailored metrics are needed for each business unit in each of the three areas (Porter and Kramer, 2011).

The concept of strategic decision making in combination with the Responsible Business Simulator builds further on this premise and shows that strategic objectives can be achieved with due observance of the three Ps, that then find expression in the principal key outputs.

References

B Lab (nd, accessed 12 August 2015) What are B Corps? *B Corporation*. Retrieved from https://www.bcorporation.net/what-are-b-corps

Crane, A et al (2014) Contesting the value of 'creating shared value', *California Management Review*, 56 (2), pp. 130–53

Dyllicki, T and Hockerts, K (2002) Beyond the business case for corporate sustainability, *Business Strategy and the Environment*, **11**, pp. 130–41

Eccles, R G, Ioannou, I and Serafeim, G (2014) The impact of corporate sustainability on organizational processes and performance, *Management Science*, **60** (11), pp. 2835–57

International Organization for Standardization (2010) ISO 26000: 2010 guidance on social responsibility. Retrieved from https://www.iso.org/obp/ui/#iso:std:42546:en

Konar, S and Cohen, M A (2001) Does the market value environmental performance? *Review of Economics and Statistics*, **83** (2), pp. 281–89

Kramer, M R (2015) Who Are the Top Companies Changing the World? Retrieved from: https://www.sharedvalue.org/groups/who-are-top-companies-changing-the-world

Margolis, J D, Elfenbein, H A and Walsh, J P (2007) Does it pay to be good? A meta-analysis and redirection of research on the relationship between corporate social and financial performance, Working Paper

Orlitzky, M, Schmidt, F L and Rynes, S L (2003) Corporate social and financial performance: a meta-analysis, *Organization studies*, **24** (3), pp. 403–41

Porter, M E and Kramer, M R (2002) The competitive advantage of corporate philanthropy, *Harvard Business Review*, **80**, pp. 56–69

Porter, M E and Kramer, M R (2006) Strategy and society: the link between competitive advantage and corporate social responsibility, *Harvard Business Review*, **84**, pp. 78–92

Porter, M E and Kramer, M R (2011) Creating shared value: how to reinvent capitalism – and unleash a wave of innovation and growth, *Harvard Business Review*, **89** (1/2), pp. 62–77

Innovation and sustainability as catalysts for responsible growth

04

Sustainable operations need not mean extra expense. It can in fact be the leverage to achieve cost savings and an incentive to find new sources of income. This is the main message set out by the late management guru Prahalad and his co-authors Nidumolu and Rangaswami in their 2009 article titled 'Why Sustainability Is Now the Key Driver of Innovation'. In this article, the authors argue that sustainability should be the touchstone for innovation. They contend that any business that sees sustainability as an objective will have a competitive edge. It does, however, demand adaptation of business models, products, technology and processes, and such far-reaching interventions can take many years to implement. The authors suggest a step-by-step approach to take on the challenge of sustainable operational management, to acquire the necessary new competences and to identify innovative opportunities. In this chapter, the step-by-step approach introduced by Nidumolo, Prahalad, and Rangaswami is further elaborated upon. Moreover, we will discuss the importance of innovation in moving towards responsible growth. The approach we developed for the Responsible Business Simulator seamlessly follows the suggestions made by Prahalad and his co-authors.

No alternative to sustainability

According to Nidumolo et al (2009) there is no alternative to sustainability. Businesses may well complain about the extra costs and compartmentalize sustainability along with CSR, but just like Porter and Kramer (2002, 2006, 2011), Nidumolo et al contend that by doing this they are missing opportunities and their competitive power will decline.

Social and financial objectives do not have to cancel each other out, but they can go hand in glove. Research among 30 major corporations showed that '... sustainability is a motherload of organizational and technological innovations that yield both bottom-line and top-line results' (Nidumolo et al, 2009, pp. 57–58). By using fewer raw materials, applying recycling and energy-saving measures, using sustainable energy and making logistic processes more efficient, costs can be reduced and the quality of products can increase (Nidumolo et al, 2009). Sustainability is a catalyst for innovation, and that could mean new possibilities for further growth for many businesses (Ellen MacArthur Foundation, 2015).

This is a powerful argument to persuade us to take a closer look at overall operational management and the existing business models. The authors recommend looking for those links in the business chain where internal adjustments can be made, and similarly where opportunities can be found for sustainability interventions in the external network.

Interestingly enough, this causes external developments such as legislation, standards and regulation in the domain of sustainability to be seen as positive factors. Strategically, it is smarter to be a forward thinker, to adapt operational management and change production processes, rather than simply complain and delay the inevitable. The first-mover advantages become greater as soon as change is linked to innovation with a positive social impact. Sustainability is the driver for far-reaching renewal and rethinking of business models. The enterprise, the employees, the customers, the suppliers and even society can profit from these innovative impulses (Nidumolo et al, 2009).

Sustainability as an incentive for the economy

The financial crisis of 2008 affected a great number of enterprises in subsequent years. Now, a decade later, the economic tide looks brighter and many technology based companies explore and exploit new business models. The challenge is finding a new fit between technological change, changing working environments and an ecological balance. We are living in an exciting era, a time of a transition from a global mass-production model to a flexible decentralized quality model based on principles of the circular economy and social inclusion. Good examples of the 'old' quantitative model can be found in the traditional energy producers (coal, gas, oil, nuclear power). The mass production of foodstuffs also falls into this category, with the concentrated production of deep-frozen ready meals as a prime example. The regional, sustainable food-stuffs producers, and certainly the producers of renewable energy (from solar, wind, water and biomass sources) have a place in the 'new' qualitative model.

During the past century, an extensive infrastructure with accompanying logistics systems was set up for the mass production model, but an entirely different infrastructure is needed for the new model. For example, the development, construction and implementation of a new smart grid for decentralized sustainable power generation and distribution to end users would in fact provide an excellent impetus for the economy.

The 2011 study titled 'A New Growth Path for Europe' – written by Jaeger et al and commissioned by the German Federal Ministry for the Environment, Nature Conservation and Nuclear Safety (BMU) – sets out how raising the emission reduction target for 2020 from 20 per cent to 30 per cent could give Europe a tremendous growth impulse with an increase in employment opportunities as a result (Jaeger et al, 2011). The view put forward in the study is that the financial crisis has had a detrimental effect on European growth, and when we think in terms of 'business as usual', there will indeed be less growth in Europe than there was before the crisis. As a consequence, European unemployment will remain at a high level, with major disparities between the various regions. A more ambitious goal setting is necessary, according to the authors. As long as Europe continues to aim for a 20 per cent reduction in emissions, to meet the climate targets, there will be no incentive for innovation simply because this target is already within reach thanks to the lower economic growth and corresponding lower use of raw materials, energy and power (Jaeger et al, 2011). And this is precisely the reason the authors say that we should jack up our ambitions a notch or two. They advocate directing innovation efforts at a different growth model, one in which the focus is not on keeping wage costs down but on learning by doing: seeking large-scale innovation in high-tech, high-spec products, new technologies and low-carbon materials. They feel that raising the emission reduction target to 30 per cent would lead to the following outcomes(Jaeger et al, 2011, pp. 6-10):

- an increase of the European economy's growth to 0.6 per cent per annum;
- the creation of up to 6 million extra jobs in Europe;
- an incentive for European investment to around 18–22 per cent of GDP;
- an increase of the European GDP to around US $842 billion (based on the value of the dollar in 2004);
- an increase of 6 per cent growth in the GDP in both the 'old' European member states (EU15) and in the 'new' states (EU12).

This argument for sustainable growth in a reviving economy finds its origins in the climate issue. It is not without reason that the authors repeat a quote from Josef Ackermann, until 2013 the CEO of the Deutsche Bank: 'Make no mistake: a new world order is emerging'. The race for leadership has already begun. For the winners, the rewards are clear: 'innovation and investment in clean energy will stimulate green growth; it will create jobs; it will bring greater energy independence and national security' (Jaeger et al, 2011, p. 5).

At this moment Germany is in many ways ahead of other countries with regard to sustainability. Germany has started multiple ambitious environmental programmes since 2002 which have significantly increased its resource, energy and carbon efficiency. According to the OECD Environmental Performance Review of Germany, they achieved one of the highest levels of resource productivity and were able to reduce their absolute greenhouse gas emissions (OECD, 2012). Even more promising, these achievements were all reached while the German economy continued to grow robustly for most of the 2000s, showing a remarkable resilience during the 2008 crisis.

Furthermore, the 2015 United Nations climate change conference in Paris was largely successful and the largest three polluters, the United States, China and India, committed to join the agreement. In April 2016 it was ratified, which was a unique moment in history. Although President Trump has announced his intention to withdraw the United States from the 2015 Paris Agreement, it might have very little effect on the goals of the accord and the impact on markets and investors. According to Morgan Stanley's sustainability specialist Eva Zlotnicka in a recent paper (Zlotnicka, 2017) an exit from the agreement will take several years and would not be an easy path for the United States. In the meantime, other countries are stepping up and doubling their efforts in the light of global climate concerns. In the same report it is mentioned that companies have been stepping up, too, arguing for competitiveness, job creation and business risk management. In addition, local governments within the United States, together with companies and investors, have supported the initiative 'We Are Still In'. Hence, huge investments are expected to contribute to sustainable economic growth.

The impact of sustainability on neoclassical business models

The one thing that makes sustainability fundamentally different from other challenges faced by businesses is that changes need to be made at each and every level of the organization. Moreover, sustainable business practices call for a reassessment of the values underlying the entire business. Sustainability calls for sharing actual experiences, beyond the borders of organizations, economic sectors and even countries. After all, sustainability issues are unfettered by borders and demand a communal, holistic approach. For that reason it is prudent to switch from a purely competitive model to a model in which collaboration and networking can take place. In the literature, this is often referred to as a 'co-opetitive model' (ie simultaneously competing and collaborating in the market), whereby enterprises and organizations join together to tackle the pressing issues surrounding sustainability (Brandenburger and Nalebuff, 1996). Organizations in which sustainability has permeated through all layers develop new business models, create an open work culture and develop initiatives based on sustainability. Instead of seeing sustainability as simply an 'add-on', it is perceived to be an integral part of the business. Profit becomes a result and the facilitator of environmentally friendly and socially sustainable activities. Ideally, sustainability should be a goal from both an ethical and an economic perspective (Bansal and Roth, 2000). In other words: it is the 'right' thing to do and the 'smart' thing to do.

The dominant business models are based on neoclassical theories: maximization of profit for the shareholders is taken as the principle on which an enterprise is founded (Brenner and Cohrane, 1991; Stormer, 2003). In this perspective, social and ecological goals are seen as minor considerations, or perhaps not considered at all. This classic paradigm is therefore less suitable as a backdrop to the achievement of social and ecological goals. We therefore need to seek out new business models and management paradigms to help us look beyond 'the organization as an economic entity' (Dunphy, Griffiths and Benn, 2003; Shrivastava, 1995). The neoclassical model cannot simply be supplemented with social and ecological objectives. The entire model must therefore be transformed into a model in which sustainability plays an essential role in both determining the mission or driving force of the organization and decision making (Wicks, 1996; Raworth, 2017). In the neoclassical model, sustainable objectives are only pursued if they are in the interests – usually the short-term interests – of the organization, if required by legislation (compliance), under pressure from shareholders, or to achieve greater corporate legitimacy (Bansal and Roth, 2000). In the neoclassical model, organizations must constantly be competitive in order to acquire the best 'resources' (in terms of both human capital and raw materials). The production cycle of a business is often based on a linear 'take–make–waste' approach, without any consideration being given to – let alone responsibility being taken for – the element of 'waste' (McDonough and Braungart, 2002). Given what we now know, it is clear that such models are no longer tenable and that different priorities need to be set.

The consequences of sustainability and innovation for a circular economy and inclusive economy

We hear from various disciplines in the academic world about the systemic changes that are occurring as a result of the progression towards a circular economy. The philosophies and frameworks within which production processes and operational management have been organized until very recently are no longer working effectively; you could in fact say that they are proving to be a hindrance to the revival that is just around the corner.

Each era has its challenges, but at the moment it seems that we are faced with an unusual level of concurrence of factors. Just consider the possibilities that IT and the internet are offering for services and products that we could not even have imagined just a few years ago, and see Figure 4.1 for possible future scenarios. The stream of new applications is only possible because of the mobile internet infrastructure. That same infrastructure has brought drastic changes to education, for example. Where education at top-level universities was previously only accessible to a small number of people who could afford the fees or earn one of the few available scholarships, it is now possible to disseminate parts of that same knowledge 'for the few' to millions of people around the world via e-learning, blended learning and 'massive open online courses'. As a result, the revenue model of universities is undergoing a dramatic change, as will the activities that are still going to be on offer at the universities themselves. Changes in education have a far-reaching impact on the economy, on social structures, and on the way we live and interact. Where revenue models were previously built around the products that were delivered, they are now increasingly oriented to the services that keep the economy afloat, towards 'performance-based contracting' and business models based on Service as a Product (SaaP). This is a transaction of service production and delivery model in which a productized service is sold via sellers or vendors on websites or platforms. In Chapter 1 we mentioned a few companies, like Philips and BMA Ergonomics, who are using this type of revenue model.

Another disruption can be found in the drastic changes that are occurring in the way we work. In the past 15 years, there has been a shift from a homogenous working population towards a population of highly differentiated expert professionals, who are just as likely to use their expertise as a self-employed person as they are to work for a major company. Where it used to be almost inconceivable that someone would work from multiple

Figure 4.1 Innovative technological scenarios (Diana, 2015)

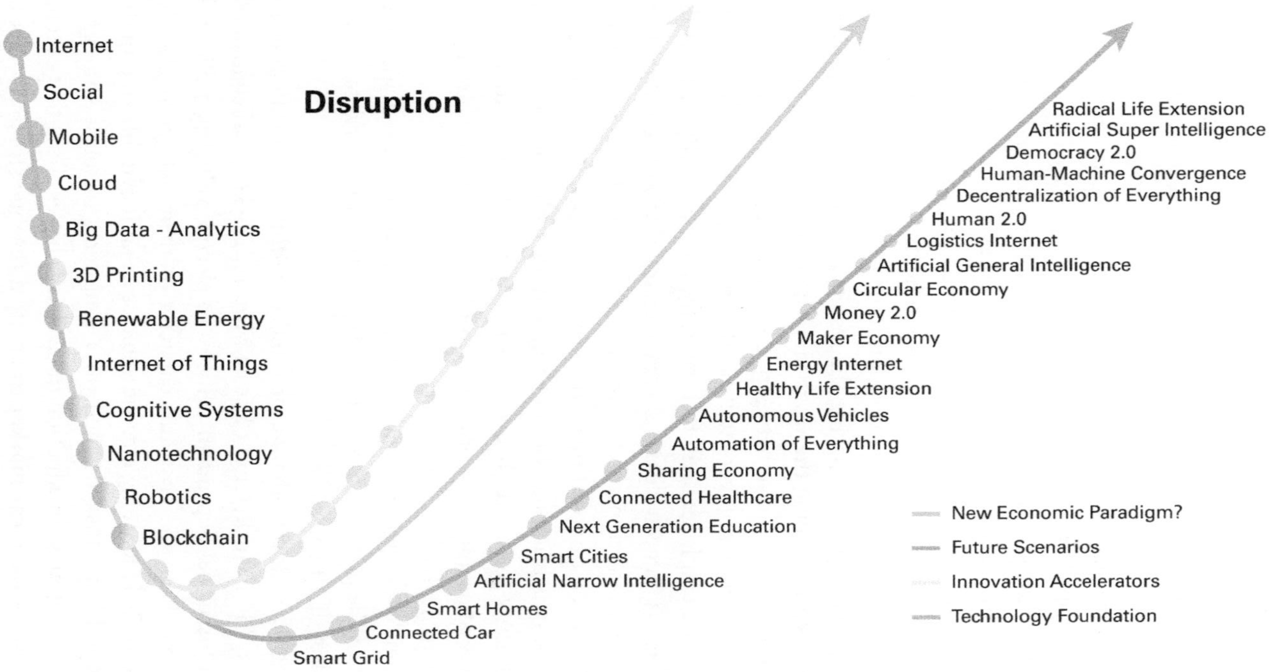

Internet
Social
Mobile
Cloud
Big Data - Analytics
3D Printing
Renewable Energy
Internet of Things
Cognitive Systems
Nanotechnology
Robotics
Blockchain

Disruption

Smart Grid
Connected Car
Smart Homes
Artificial Narrow Intelligence
Smart Cities
Next Generation Education
Connected Healthcare
Sharing Economy
Automation of Everything
Autonomous Vehicles
Healthy Life Extension
Energy Internet
Maker Economy
Money 2.0
Circular Economy
Artificial General Intelligence
Logistics Internet
Human 2.0
Decentralization of Everything
Human-Machine Convergence
Democracy 2.0
Artificial Super Intelligence
Radical Life Extension

New Economic Paradigm?
Future Scenarios
Innovation Accelerators
Technology Foundation

locations, these days millions of people can work from their homes or a meeting place and still connect and collaborate with others. The main technology behind this connectivity is the ever-growing 'Internet of Things'. These days everything from thermostats to cars, from buildings to refrigerators, is collecting and exchanging data through a network. This trend has had sweeping consequences for logistics and transportation, for offices and real estate.

Along the same lines, the Organization for Economic Co-operation and Development (OECD) reached the conclusion based on their data that there is a correlation between shorter working hours and greater productivity. Working fewer hours, meaning employees get more time off to focus on their life outside work, apparently leads to a more committed and stable workforce. In the Swedish city of Gothenburg, the municipality decided to start an experiment by cutting an hour in the daily work hours of a group of employees and comparing the results to a control group working regular hours. While keeping the wage in both groups the same and considering the data on the correlation between fewer working hours and greater productivity, it is likely employers will be able to save money when cutting working hours and employees will feel mentally and physically better (OECD, 2015).

There is an even clearer systemic character to the combination of climate change and the transition to sustainable energy. The transition from a power system based on fossil fuels to a system in which sustainable energy sources hold sway is bringing about changes in the techno-economic system of society. Energy forms the bedrock of the system. Every company, every home, every gymnasium or workplace will be affected. The business models that apply to nearly every product or service will be affected. It is precisely these systemic challenges that call for innovative business activities and an adjustment of the present government regulatory framework, tax systems and the mindset of all concerned.

Showcasing this change of mindset within the sustainable energy paradigm is Elon Musk, CEO of Tesla Motors. The key challenge in transitioning from fossil fuel-dependent vehicles to electric vehicles, a disruptive innovation, has been the cost and capacity of their battery packs (Nykvist and Nilsson, 2015). Seeing electric vehicles as an inevitable step in the evolution of cars, Elon Musk decided on a long-term business strategy that would bring about mass production of electric vehicles. Tesla first entered the high-end, low-volume car market to create a revenue stream to invest in electric charging infrastructure, cheaper and higher-capacity battery packs, and to develop a medium-end car. The success of the high-end Tesla electric car has been a challenge for the German luxury car market. With the Tesla Model

3 first tested by its own employees and company insiders, and with more than 400,000 reservations since 2016, Tesla shows it is a gamechanger in the car market. Even in the used car market, high premiums are paid for the first Model 3 vehicles. Here, again, sustainability and profitability go hand in hand. Tesla is years ahead of the competition. BMW plans to launch a Model 3 competitor in 2021 and Mercedes plans a full electric SUV in 2019 (Lambert, 2018). The global electric vehicle market was valued at US $103.342 million in 2016, and is projected to reach $350.963 million in 2023, according to an industry forecast for 2017–2023. China surpassed the United States as the largest market for electric cars in 2015, with over 200,000 new registrations (Allied Market Research, 2017).

These trends will disrupt the current economic systems in place and demand innovative business models, and as we will explain in the following chapters the Responsible Business Simulator is a useful tool in quantifying all financial and non-financial benefits of the investment in new business models.

Industrial and service sectors transition differently towards a sustainable situation. The global food market started a slow transition towards organic foods decades ago, but has been picking up pace in recent years, especially in North America and Europe. In contrast to 10 years ago, we now find organic food and beverages in almost every supermarket. This market has grown by more than 15 per cent each year and it is projected that this growth will continue for another five years. Worth US $84 billion in 2014, the organic food and beverages market is forecasted to grow to US $212 billion by 2020 – a huge expected growth that indicates the tipping point for sustainable food production and hence large opportunities for businesses. FrieslandCampina, the world's largest dairy cooperative, is one of the companies capitalizing on this transition to sustainability. Their motto is the very fitting 'Nourishing by Nature'. FrieslandCampina has introduced a new separate price system for organic milk due to increasing demand, incentivizing farmers to switch towards organic farming (FrieslandCampina, 2016).

The end result of these systemic shifts, prompted as much by sustainability as by technological opportunities, is that it will become ever more relevant for businesses and organizations to take a long and critical look at their present business models. The approach that we call strategic decision making towards a circular economy with the use of the Responsible Business Simulator can take all this into account: from the changing circumstances and environment, disruptive innovations, the expectations of employees, customers and stakeholders, to all the other demands that sustainable growth imposes on a business.

References

Allied Market Research (June 2017) Report on global opportunity analysis and industry forecast, 2017-2023. Retrieved from https://www.alliedmarketresearch.com/electric-vehicle-market

Bansal, P and Roth, K (2000) Why companies go green: a model of ecological responsiveness, *Academy of Management Journal*, **43**, pp. 717–36

Brandenburger, A and Nalebuff, B (1996) *Co-opetition*, Doubleday, New York, NY

Brenner, S and Cohrane, P (1991) The stakeholder theory of the firm: implications for business and society theory and research, *IABS Proceedings*, pp. 449–67.

Diana, F (2015) An interview with Gerd Leonhard. Retrieved from http://thefuturesagency.com/2015/02/20/an-interview-with-gerd-leonhard/

Diana, F (2015) Expanding disruptive scenarios. Retrieved from https://frankdiana.net/2015/06/26/expanding-disruptive-scenarios/

Dunphy, D C, Griffiths, A and Benn, S (2003). *Organizational Change for Corporate Sustainability: A guide for leaders and change agents of the future*, Routledge, London, UK

Ellen MacArthur Foundation (2015) *Towards a Circular Economy: Business rationale for an accelerated transition*. Retrieved from https://www.ellenmacarthurfoundation.org/assets/downloads/TCE_Ellen-MacArthur-Foundation_9-Dec-2015.pdf

FrieslandCampina (2016) *Annual Report 2015*. Retrieved from https://www.frieslandcampina.com/app/uploads/sites/2/2016/03/FrieslandCampina-annual-report-2015-English-A4.pdf

Jaeger, C C et al (2011) *A New Growth Path for Europe: Generating prosperity and jobs in the low-carbon economy*. Retrieved from https://www.pik-potsdam.de/members/cjaeger/a_new_growth_path_for_europe__synthesis_report.pdf

Lambert, F (2018) Tesla Model 3 vehicles spotted on their way to Germany, presumably to be reverse-engineered, *Elektrek*. Retrieved from https://electrek.co/2018/01/27/tesla-model-3-germany-reverse-engineered/

McDonough, W and Braungart, M (2002) *Cradle to Cradle: Remaking the way we make things*, North Point Press, New York, NY

Nidumolo, R, Prahalad, C K and Rangaswami, M R (2009) Why sustainability is now the key driver of innovation, *Harvard Business Review*, **87** (9), pp. 56–64

Nykvist, B and Nilsson, M (2015) Rapidly falling costs of battery packs for electric vehicles, *Nature Climate Change*, **5** (4), pp. 329–32

OECD (2012) *Environmental Performance Reviews: Germany 2012*. Retrieved from https://www.oecd.org/env/country-reviews/50418430.pdf

OECD (2015) *OECD Employment Outlook*. Retrieved from http://www.oecd-ilibrary.org/employment/oecd-employment-outlook-2015_empl_outlook-2015-en

Porter, M E and Kramer, M R (2002) The competitive advantage of corporate philanthropy, *Harvard Business Review*, **80**, pp. 56–69

Porter, M E and Kramer, M R (2006) Strategy and society: the link between competitive advantage and corporate social responsibility, *Harvard Business Review*, **84**, pp. 78–92

Porter, M E and Kramer, M R (2011) Creating shared value: how to reinvent capitalism – and unleash a wave of innovation and growth, *Harvard Business Review*, **89** (1/2), pp. 62–77

Raworth, K (2017) *Doughnut Economics. Seven Ways to Think Like a 21st-Century Economist.* Random House Business Books, London

Shrivastava, P (1995) Ecocentric management for a risk society, *Academy of Management Review*, **20**, pp. 118–37

Stormer, F (2003) Making the shift: moving from 'Ethics Pays' to an inter-systems model of business, *Journal of Business Ethics*, **44**, pp. 279–89

The Tesla Team (2016) The week that electric vehicles went mainstream. Retrieved from https://www.teslamotors.com/nl_NL/blog/the-week-electric-vehicles-went-mainstream

Wicks, A C (1996) Overcoming the separation thesis: the need for a reconsideration of business and society research, *Business & Society*, **35**, pp. 89–118

Zlotnicka, E (2017) The path ahead after U.S. leaves Paris Agreement. What is the real impact of President's Trump move to pull the U.S. out of the global accords to combat climate change? *Morgan Stanley*. Retrieved from https://www.morganstanley.com/ideas/us-path-after-paris-agreement.

Stakeholder management and interactivity in the decision-making process

05

In the strategic decision-making process with the use of the Responsible Business Simulator, advanced econometric calculation techniques are combined with interactive sessions with employees, management and external stakeholders. It is the interactive and iterative use of evidence from data and interpretation via dialogue that creates the value of the Responsible Business Simulator for the decision making process. This qualitative and quantitative combination is unique because – during the progression towards a strategic decision – it brings transparency to the identification and linkage of the hard, financial objectives and the non-financial objectives. This interaction takes place during the action learning sessions that are held within the businesses and organizations, and during sessions held with external stakeholders. By bringing together true cross-sections of employees, management and stakeholders, thereby guaranteeing a diversity of knowledge, experience and latest insights, the process becomes an active exercise and not a 'black box', as can be the case when advisors are allowed to conjure statistics from Excel files like rabbits out of a top hat. In this chapter we discuss the concept of action learning and its applicability to the strategic decision-making process with the use of the Responsible Business Simulator.

Integrating stakeholder management into the business process

To manage the transition towards sustainability and social inclusion, we need new business models that do justice to the complexity of that transition. This includes making allowance for a long-term timeline, assessing uncertainties, and ensuring that the opinions of stakeholders are taken into account (Loorbach et al, 2010). To put innovation and more sustainable business practices into operation, an enterprise needs to reinvent itself; organizations must learn to see themselves as actors in a much larger societal system and think about their own interactions with that system. Organizations no longer exist in isolation, but have become open, dynamic systems that operate in constant interaction with their environment. The advancement of business ecosystems with interlinking networks of networks is an indication of this. Good practices regarding business ecosystems can be found at Deloitte, specifically in their report *Business Ecosystems Come of Age* (2015).

It is in this environment that the term 'stakeholder' plays a pivotal role. We also saw this element in Porter and Kramer's concept of shared value (Porter and Kramer, 2011). The aim of organizations that apply the Responsible Business Simulator is not only to realize a profit and create a good working environment for their employees, but also to improve the sense of well-being of the stakeholders. These can be widely diverse parties, from local residents to NGOs, suppliers, customers and in a circular economy all actors related to the same material chains. Sustainable companies adjust their perspective from one that focuses exclusively on shareholders to one that also includes other stakeholders. The stakeholder concept was traditionally limited to people or groups with a particular political or economic impact; people or groups that were in a position to help – or hinder – organizations.

Businesses, however, operate in a particular natural environment; some are even dependent on that environment. That is manifestly the case for businesses in the agricultural and energy sectors, but it actually applies to any business. Businesses have long ceased to be isolated entities, static systems that have no need to take account of various other external parties or of their possible dependence on such parties. Stakeholders should not be perceived as 'the others' or simply 'external' to the organization, but as partners whose future and interests are closely interwoven with those of the organization. In this way, the concept of 'stakeholder' acquires not only a politico-economic meaning, but also an element of moral legitimacy whereby the 'parties' – the people and the environment on which you, as a business, can exercise some influence – are also perceived as stakeholders in that business (Carroll, 1993).

The importance of dialogue and interactivity in decision-making processes

In commerce, sustainability is often expressed as 'the triple bottom line' (TBL), whose central themes are social, ecological and economic objectives, in other words People, Planet and Profit objectives. This TBL model, coined by John Elkington in 1997, emphasizes the relationships between the three elements and all three objectives are, ideally, pursued equally, in an effort to create a 'triple-win' situation. Nonetheless, tension can arise between these three objectives. The aim is therefore not to treat the three objectives as individual goals, but as a single unified goal. However, decision making on sustainability issues is often complex, especially when this initial tension is evident. According to Rogers and Hudson (2011), decision making on sustainability issues should therefore take place at a higher level of systemic abstraction. In other words, decisions need to be taken in a far broader societal context. This is obviously not 'business as usual', since managers must be thinking beyond the confines of their own organization. It could even be argued that experts who are not part of the upper echelon of an organization but who see themselves as part of a far greater social totality, are in a better position to embrace this broader approach than the members of the upper echelon themselves. It is therefore important to involve employees in this shift towards sustainability. After all, employees of an organization are also members of society. The encouragement and empowerment of employees helps to create a sustainable mindset within the organization. It is not simply a matter of change. What is called for is a far-reaching transformation or revitalization, as it is termed by Pascale, Millemann and Gioja (1997): 'Providing a permanent impetus for individual creativity and responsibility, an enduring transformation of the internal and external relationships of the organization, and a lasting behavioural change within the organization'.

Conversely, it is also the case that employees of an organization where socially responsible business practices are the norm are generally more satisfied in their work and also feel that they are treated more fairly. This is because sustainability satisfies their desire for honesty and justice (Aguilera et al 2007; Tziner et al, 2011). It also exerts a positive influence on the way employees perceive their organization, making them prouder to work for that organization (Galbreath, 2010), which in turn has a positive influence on the commitment of the employees (Peterson, 2004). Getting employees involved in sustainable business practices will therefore not only help to actually achieve the sustainability objectives, but it will help create a workforce that is passionate about and committed to the business. This is precisely the reason why we use a 'round table' format and conversations when applying strategic decision making and the Responsible Business Simulator, so that employees and management alike are involved in working towards a sustainable strategy that does justice to the triple bottom line.

Interactive determination of key outputs

Once a corporate team gets started on strategic decision making with the use of the Responsible Business Simulator, the first priority is to establish the main hard (financial) and not-so-hard (non-financial) key outputs. In this action learning setting, knowledge is exchanged over the course of several sessions, and at the same time incremental decision making takes place about the principal key outputs that serve to achieve the enterprise's strategic objective. The choices for particular financial and non-financial objectives can be adjusted during the sessions once the outcomes of the computational process show what effect that choice of key outputs and the value that team members ascribe to them will have on a possible strategy. The fact that this computational model shows the outcomes in a graphic form is an important factor for the team sessions, because even the less mathematically minded can immediately see what could be the impact of applying certain values and weightings to the financial and non-financial objectives.

The interesting thing is that the process is completely transparent, and adjustments can immediately be made visible. This clears the way for a decision-making process towards finding a sustainable business model that is free of subjective values ('we believe in sustainablity' or 'we believe in social inclusion'), while the action learning sessions nonetheless provide an opportunity for the expression of subjective opinions. The combination of tweaking the input in a team session and learning in an informal setting what the impact of possible choices might be, makes this a sophisticated, yet low-threshold method. One important advantage is that strategic choices can be made, on the basis of the objective outcomes of the computational model, that go hand in hand with the phase in which the enterprise finds itself in terms of the triple bottom line (People, Planet, Profit). By incorporating the time dimension into the simulator, any enterprise – whether it is just starting to become sustainable or has already progressed some way along the route – can make the strategic choices that best suit its current situation. It can pinpoint where investments in the coming years are going to pay off, and how the enterprise or organization could evolve.

Complex issues require an interdisciplinary approach

It follows from the above that sustainable business practices take place within a highly complex framework. We can call this the 'management of complexity'. Sustainable management covers a wide spectrum of aspects, and can be approached from a variety of different angles. The subject as seen from the accountancy and finance angle will differ from the subject as seen from the business administration or human resources angle. Looking from an ethical perspective, different facets will be considered than from the perspective of operational research, risk management, strategy or climate science. Each discipline looks at the matter through its own spectacles, and adds its own specific knowledge. In this context, Pojasek (2007, pp. 81–82) mentions the creation of an 'interdisciplinary body of knowledge' that will ultimately lead to a framework for business sustainability.

Businesses do not operate in isolation but in a social context, one in which technology, economy, culture, biological and technological material chains and institutions play a leading role. To be able to understand the transition to sustainability, we need to take a systemic approach in which the roles played by and the interrelationships between government, commerce and society are explained (Loorbach et al, 2010; Rotmans et al, 2000). Eamonn Kelly re-introduced the concept of business ecosystems in a highly accessible study with practical insights on shaping business environments for innovation with highly diverse public and private actors (Kelly, 2015).

Limiting sustainability to the level of the enterprise gives an imperfect view of the complexity and the persistent institutional problems that hinder the transition towards sustainability. 'The complexity and persistent nature of sustainability issues pose new challenges on business, which requires new conceptual models for researching in relation between firms and the natural environment' (Loorbach et al, 2010, p. 134). In the same article, Loorbach et al argue – on the basis of articles by Porter and Kramer (2006), Korhonen and Seager (2008), and Seager (2008) – that it is necessary to include knowledge about sustainability in strategic decision making. That knowledge is still, however, badly fragmented and more needs to be done to create cohesion between commerce and the social context. If we add the principles of the triple bottom line, do justice to Porter and Kramer's principle of shared value, and envision the transition to a circular economy and inclusion, it will quickly be clear that we need to approach sustainable business practices in a much wider social context and from an interdisciplinary perspective (Elkington, 1998, 2006; Ellen MacArthur Foundation, 2012).

Collaborative research for new insights and actionable results

The desire to do more than draw conclusions from the perspective of individual disciplines is reflected in a 'collaborative research' approach taken in our research into sustainability and social inclusion with the Responsible Business Simulator as a tool for strategic decision making. At the heart of this research approach is the fact that we concentrate on specific issues, bridging and blending knowledge from academic disciplines into the Responsible Business Simulator. This yields new insights, based on well-founded academic theories, knowledge and practical experience.

This unique combination of academic and practical knowledge has been put to good use in exploring, explaining, applying and testing the Responsible Business Simulator in real-world business environments. The members of the team reflected on the intermediate outcomes in iterative sessions. During the course of the research, we held various reflection and discussion sessions in an academic setting with the businesses and stakeholders involved in the action research projects. This way, we made best efforts to replicate the complexity surrounding sustainable business practices. At the same time, we also realized the necessity of ensuring that our research had practical applicability for businesses and organizations. A significant reciprocal benefit was gained from the combination of on-site action research, modelling using sophisticated calculation programs, and the reflection sessions with the academic staff.

We also presented the results of our research on the Responsible Business Simulator to students in bachelor's, master's and MBA programmes and to participants in executive programmes at various business schools, universities and at conferences with business professionals. We have examined whether modelling using the Responsible Business Simulator can be made more comprehensible, and whether it is something that can be picked up fairly quickly. Thanks to the interdisciplinary approach and the iterative research method used – the testing, reflection and modification – the modelling has been given extra depth. The Responsible Business Simulator has made complexity manageable. It can now be put to practical use in the decision-making processes within businesses and organizations. In the next chapters a series of case studies will be described giving a real-life context to the application of the Responsible Business Simulator.

References

Aguilera, R V et al (2007) Putting the S back in corporate social responsibility: a multilevel theory of social change in organizations, *Academy of Management Review*, **32**, pp. 83–45

Carroll, A B (1993) *Business and Society: Ethics and stakeholder management*, South-Western Publishing, Cincinnati

Deloitte (2015) Business ecosystems come of age. Retrieved from https://www2. deloitte.com/content/dam/insights/us/articles/platform-strategy-new-level-business-trends/DUP_1048-Business-ecosystems-come-of-age_MASTER_FINAL.pdf

Elkington, J (1998) *Cannibals with Forks: Triple bottom line of 21st-century business*, Capstone publishers, Mankato, MN

Elkington, J (2006) Governance for sustainability, *Corporate Governance: An International Review*, **14** (6), pp. 522–29

Ellen MacArthur Foundation (2012) *Towards the Circular Economy 1: Economic and business rationale for an accelerated transition*. Retrieved from https://www. ellenmacarthurfoundation.org/assets/downloads/publications/Ellen-MacArthur-Foundation-Towards-the-Circular-Economy-vol.1.pdf

Galbreath, J (2010) How does corporate social responsibility benefit firms? Evidence from Australia, *European Business Review*, **22**, pp. 411–31

Kelly, E (2015) *Introduction: Business ecosystems come of age*, Deloitte University Press, Westlake, Texas

Korhonen, J and Seager, T P (2008) Beyond eco-efficiency: a resilience perspective, *Business Strategy & the Environment*, **17** (7), pp. 411–19

Loorbach, D et al (2010) Business strategies for transitions towards sustainable systems, *Business Strategy and the Environment*, **19**, pp. 133–46

Pascale, R, Millemann, M and Gioja, L (1997) Changing the way we change: how leaders at Sears, Shell, and the U.S. Army transformed attitudes and behavior – and made the changes stick, *Harvard Business Review*, **75**, pp. 126–39

Peterson, D K (2004) The relationship between perceptions of corporate citizenship and organizational commitment, *Business and Society*, **43**, pp. 296–319

Pojasek, R B (2007) Quality toolbox: a framework for business sustainability, *Environmental Quality Management*, **15**, pp. 81–88

Porter, M E and Kramer, M R (2006) Strategy and society: the link between competitive advantage and corporate social responsibility, *Harvard Business Review*, **84**, pp. 78–92

Porter, M E, and Kramer, M R (2011) Creating shared value: how to reinvent capitalism – and unleash a wave of innovation and growth, *Harvard Business Review*, **89** (1/2), pp. 62–77

Rogers, K and Hudson, B (2011) The triple bottom line: the synergies of transformative perceptions and practices for sustainability, *OD Practitioner*, **43**, pp. 3–9

Rotmans, J et al (2000) *Transities en Transitiemanagement: De casus van de emissie-arme energievoorziening*, International Centre for Integrative Studies (ICIS), Maastricht

Seager, T P (2008) The sustainability spectrum and the sciences of sustainability, *Business Strategy & the Environment*, **17** (7), pp. 444–53

Tziner, A et al (2011) Corporate social responsibility, organizational justice and job satisfaction: how do they interrelate, if at all? *Review of Psychology of Work and Organizations*, **27**, pp. 67–72

Using the Responsible Business Simulator

07

Making strategic decisions to benefit people, the planet and profits is an interactive process with stakeholders that addresses both financial and non-financial aspects. It comprises a seven-step process that leads to a clear strategic choice. The process is empowered by unique modelling software named the Responsible Business Simulator (tRBS). The seven-step process has been described extensively in Chapter 2 and is illustrated in Figure 7.1. This chapter focuses on the practical use of the Responsible Business Simulator to execute these steps.

The Responsible Business Simulator has been developed in the software package AIMMS. For the simulation model to work, in each step of the process relevant information needs be stored into a database. We allow the user to provide the data in an SQL Server database, an MS Access database, a text file, an MS Excel sheet or tRBS's internal database that can be filled via the Graphical User Interface (GUI). For each strategic decision-making case, a new database with case-specific information has to be provided. Just like in previous chapters, we will follow the stepwise process to explain what information needs to be inserted into the Responsible Business Simulator. Figure 7.2 displays the tables that are part of the database. In every step, one, two or three database tables are filled. After completing the first two phases of the decision-making process, the database will be imported into the Responsible Business Simulator. In the third phase, only the weights of the key outputs and scenarios will be altered in previously created database tables when these weights are modified by the user in the GUI of the Responsible Business Simulator. In case the user wants to optimize their decision, the decision maker's option settings will be overwritten in this phase as well.

Within the GUI the database tables can be inspected via various dispalys. As well as providing a description of the information that needs to be inserted into these tables, this chapter will highlight some examples of the many graphical visualizations designed to create transparency around the

Figure 7.1 The decision-making process broken down into three phases and seven steps

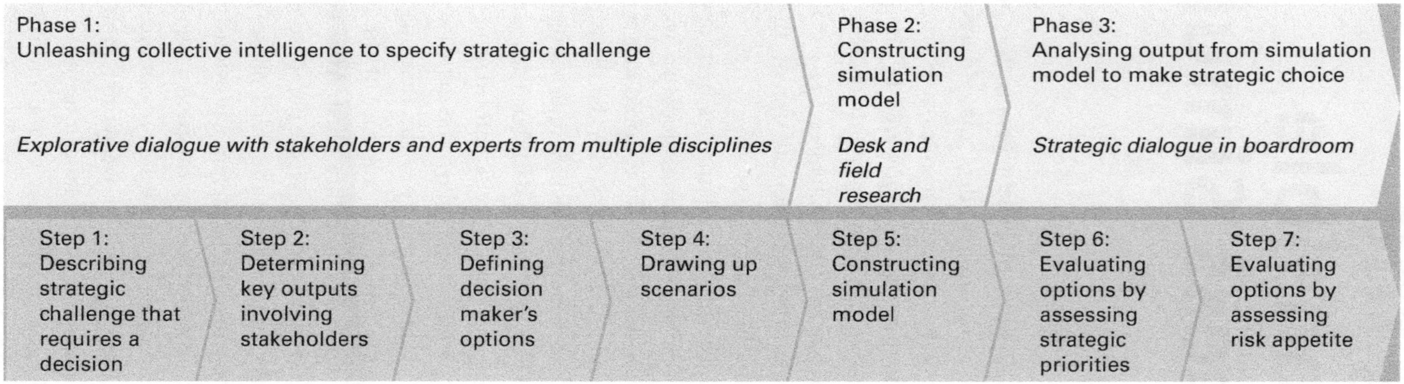

Phase 1: Unleashing collective intelligence to specify strategic challenge				Phase 2: Constructing simulation model	Phase 3: Analysing output from simulation model to make strategic choice	
Explorative dialogue with stakeholders and experts from multiple disciplines				*Desk and field research*	*Strategic dialogue in boardroom*	
Step 1: Describing strategic challenge that requires a decision	Step 2: Determining key outputs involving stakeholders	Step 3: Defining decision maker's options	Step 4: Drawing up scenarios	Step 5: Constructing simulation model	Step 6: Evaluating options by assessing strategic priorities	Step 7: Evaluating options by assessing risk appetite

Figure 7.2   The database tables in the database connected to the steps of the decision-making process

Step 1: Describing strategic challenge that requires a decision	Step 2: Determining key outputs involving stakeholders	Step 3: Defining decision maker's options	Step 4: Drawing up scenarios	Step 5: Constructing simulation model	Step 6: Evaluating options by assessing strategic priorities	Step 7: Evaluating options by assessing risk appetite
Table 1a: General Information	Table 2a: Themes	Table 3a: Internal Variable Input	Table 4a: External Variable Input	Table 5a: Fixed Inputs	Table 2b: Key Outputs (column Weight only)	Table 4b: Scenarios High Level (column Weight only)
Table 1b: Colors	Table 2b: Key Outputs	Table 3b: Decision Makers Options High Level	Table 4b: Scenarios High Level	Table 5b: Intermediates	Table 3c: Decision Makers Options Detailed (only for optimisation)	
Table 1c: Language		Table 3c: Decision Makers Options Detailed	Table 4c: Scenarios Detailed	Table 5c: Additional Outputs		
				Table 5d: Dependencies		

simulation model. There will also be some attention paid to the mathematics within and reasoning behind the model.

For the purpose of explaining the use of the Responsible Business Simulator in a consistent way, we have formulated the following fictional case that will be used through each step of the process.

Suppose that we are a decision maker at Australian beer brewery Beerwiser. Just like other brewers we use a lot of water during the heating process as well as in the cleaning of bottles and kegs. On average our brewery uses five pints of water to produce one pint of beer. We are outperformed by competitors like Heineken and Carlsberg who respectively were using 4.8 and 3.3 pints of water per pint of beer in 2012 (Appleyard, nd). At the same time, injuries amongst people working on brewery shop floors, which are reported to the Bureau of Labour Statistics, have been on the rise, increasing from 160 in 2011 to 530 in 2014 (Roth, 2016). This is also an issue at our brewery. Therefore, our strategic challenge is to know which investments we need to make for a more sustainable brewing process. We want to create transparency towards our most important stakeholders around the potential value to our organization of reducing water consumption and safety accidents.

Step 1: Describing strategic challenge that requires a decision

The first step of the decision-making process is to describe the strategic challenge that requires a decision. The strategic challenge for us as decision maker

Table 7.1 The three database tables completed after Step 1 for Beerwiser case

Table name	Description
1a General information	Scalar information to tailor generic settings to the strategic decision-making case at hand, such as the name of the organization ('Beerwiser'), the strategic challenge ('How to brew more sustainably'), the pathname to the organization logo ('Beerwiser.jpg') and the date of analysis ('22 July 2016'). Some advanced settings are stored in this table as well.
1b Colours	Organization-specific colours to align the GUI to the organization making a decision.
1c Language	Text to be displayed per keyword in the user interface. This gives the user the opportunity to add their own language to the user interface. Currently, the user interface supports the following languages: Dutch, English, German, Italian and Spanish.

is how to brew more sustainably. The main stakeholders to be accounted for in this specific case are the board of the organization – as every decision needs their approval – the employees, and the customers.

The information collected in this step is restricted to three database tables, which are described in Table 7.1

Step 2: Determining key outputs involving stakeholders

Before we can determine the best possible decision, we need to define what good looks like in the eyes of the stakeholders. Therefore, in this step we shortlist all important stakeholders and ask them by means of which measurable outcomes of the decision they can determine whether they are satisfied.

Once the strategic challenge of the decision maker and organization-specific information have been inserted, the key outputs on which the decision maker will base their decision and corresponding themes are formulated. This boils down to completing two database tables. In this simple example case, the key outputs are water use reduction, safety accidents reduction, and unit production cost reduction.

Database table 2a: Themes

Recall that in the context of strategic decision making towards a circular economy, it may be important that not only the financial effects (Profit) of the decision are made visible, but also any non-financial effects, such as the effect on society (People) and on the natural environment (Planet). In this table the themes relevant to the decision maker are formulated. People, Planet and Profit are the default themes, but of course it is also possible to use just two themes, to add themes, or to alter the default themes. For example, the healthcare organization in Chapter 11 focusing on sustainable employability only uses the themes People and Profit, while in the research executed for the Dutch Football Association as outlined in Chapter 12, four themes have been formulated: Economy, Cohesion, Health and Nurture. For the example case, the applicable themes are the default themes.

Database table 2b: Key outputs

Next, the defined key outputs are to be inserted into the database. The first column in Table 7.2 shows the key outputs that result from the explorative dialogue with stakeholders for the Beerwiser case. To each key output

Table 7.2 Database table 2b completed for Beerwiser case

Key output	Theme	Weight	Unit	Automatic	Monetary	STB	Linear	Min	Max
Water use reduction	Planet	1	hl/year	√			√		
Accidents reduction	People	1	#/year	√			√		
Production cost reduction	Profit	1	%	√					100%

characteristics such as corresponding theme, relevant stakeholders, unit of measurement, whether or not a key output is monetary, and how each key output is appreciated need to be assigned. There are three ways for the user to appreciate key outputs, all by means of an appreciation function. Appreciation functions translate what a particular score on a key output means to the decision maker, such that the key outputs can be compared. The easiest and most commonly used option is the option to let the Responsible Business Simulator estimate the appreciation functions automatically. Another option is that the user controls all characteristics per appreciation function manually, and last but not least, the user has the option to specify their own function indicating the simultaneous appreciation of key outputs. This will require some programming outside of the database and is part of Step 5.

For the first two options, the decision maker should indicate whether a key output is Smaller The Better (STB) or not. Key outputs that are labelled STB are those the decision maker wants to minimize, like total investment in the example case. Key outputs that are not categorized as STB are those that the decision maker wishes to maximize, such as safety accidents reduction and unit production cost reduction. The user can also indicate whether they want a key output to be appreciated in a linear fashion or not. In the non-linear case the Responsible Business Simulator uses an appreciation function that employs the law of diminishing marginal gains. It is important to realize that in case multiple key outputs are set to monetary, all monetary key outputs are appreciated the same way. The euro, dollar or pound of every monetary key output is appreciated equally. Additionally, the user can insert thresholds on the key outputs via inserting minimum and maximum values. For example, since we know in the current case that unit production cost reduction cannot exceed 100 per cent, the maximum value of this key output is 100 per cent.

For the Beerwiser example case we have decided to use the option to let the Responsible Business Simulator estimate the appreciation functions automatically. This is indicated in the corresponding database table, which is displayed in Table 7.2.

The weight per key output as displayed in Table 7.2 is initially set to one, but may be altered during Step 6.

In case of automatic appreciation, the Responsible Business Simulator calculates the appreciation functions based on the characteristics described in previous table. The extremes of the key outputs over all the decision maker's options and scenarios are calculated as the so-called Start and End points of the appreciation functions. These points are connected with each other via a straight line when a key output type is set to monetary or linear, or via a (transformed) sinusoid when a key output's type is set to non-linear.

Figure 7.3   Example of a non-linear (non-monetary) non-STB appreciation
function for Beerwiser case

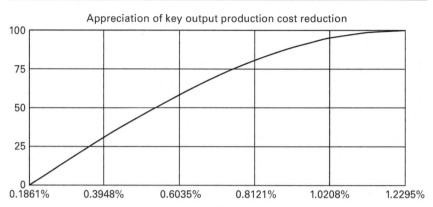

The automatically generated appreciation function for key output production cost reduction is depicted in Figure 7.3.

In this figure, the horizontal axis displays the minimum and maximum attainable value of the key output and every value in between, and the vertical axis displays the appreciation. Start is displayed in one of the left corners, while End is displayed in one of the corners on the right-hand side. If key outputs are modelled manually, the user needs to define a Start and End point. Using automatic or manual estimation of the appreciation functions, all key outputs are at all times appreciated independently. This may not always be realistic, since the appreciation of one key output may depend on whether another output has reached a certain level as a bare minimum. For these cases, the user has the option to specify their own functions indicating the simultaneous appreciation of key outputs. In that case they should switch off the setting of independent appreciation in the database and program the appreciation functions in Step 5.

Step 3: Determining decision maker's options

When selecting the best possible decision, of course there should be a choice in potential decisions. In this step, we define the options the decision maker has. We do this by first defining all degrees of freedom for the decision maker and then attaching values for these degrees of freedom per decision maker's option.

Now that general information on the strategic challenge and characteristics of the key outputs are inserted into the first five database tables, data regarding the options a decision maker has will be inserted. In this step we fill three additional database tables.

Database table 3a: Internal variable inputs

Internal variable inputs are inputs to which the decision maker can assign values, the so-called endogenous input. The pieces of information that are captured in database table 3a are the names of the internal variable inputs and – optionally – information on saturation points, accessible populations and probabilities of success in case the internal variable inputs represent investments. In practice, values of the latter three optional characteristics of the internal variable inputs are often collected during the fifth step in the decision-making process, when more detailed information is specified via desk research.

As can be seen in Table 7.3 below, the internal variable inputs for the Beerwiser example case do represent investments, namely those in training of employees and those in water recycling. Investing in the training of employees refers to educating the employees on the safety regulations regarding beer production, with the purpose of diminishing the number of accidents that occur. Investing in water recycling refers to investing in systems like membrane filtration or reverse osmosis systems. For simplicity, all investments in this case are assumed to be annual expenditures.

The saturation point indicates the maximum effective investment, or the ceiling above which further investment has no additional effect. In other words, it indicates to which maximum value an internal variable input can be increased in order to remain effective. For example, if a decision maker decides to invest a total amount of $350,000 in the training of employees and the saturation point is $300,000, then the last $50,000 does not have additional impact and can be better invested differently. The accessible population is the part of the population on which the investment will have an effect. In the case of a decision maker wanting to invest in training employees, this intervention will only reach those employees that are capable of following the training. The probability of success is the likelihood that the investment will prove to be successful. From the employees that form part of the accessible population, not everyone will experience the intended impact. The probability of success determines which percentage will be impacted as intended by the training. We consider the values entered

Table 7.3 Database table 3a completed for Beerwiser case

Internal variable input	Saturation point	Accessible population	Probability of success
Invest in training of employees	$300,000	95%	90%
Invest in water recycling	$275,000	100%	100%

Table 7.4   Database table 3c completed for Beerwiser case

Decision maker's option	Internal variable input	Value
Focus on water recycling	Invest in water recycling	$250,000
Focus on water recycling	Invest in training of employees	$50,000
Focus on training	Invest in water recycling	$50,000
Focus on training	Invest in training of employees	$250,000
Equal spread	Invest in water recycling	$150,000
Equal spread	Invest in training of employees	$150,000

in this table to be fixed inputs, inputs that do not change throughout the decision-making process.

Database table 3b: Decision maker's options high level

A combination of internal variable inputs is called a decision maker's option and these are formulated in database table 3b. It is recommended that the names of the decision maker's options reflect what combination of internal variable inputs forms each option.

For the example case, we have formulated three options:

- 'Focus on water recycling', where a decision maker invests $250,000 in water recycling and $50,000 in training.

- 'Focus on training', where a decision maker invests $50,000 in water recycling and $250,000 in training.

- 'Equal spread', where a decision maker invests $150,000 in water recycling and $150,000 in training.

Database table 3c: Decision maker's options detailed

Database table 3c is linked to database tables 3a and 3b: for every decision maker's option in 3b, all the non-zero internal variable inputs in 3a will be assigned a value. Table 7.4 illustrates how this database table looks for the options defined above.

Step 4: Drawing up scenarios

Next to the degrees of freedom the decision maker has, there are also a lot of external factors that influence the outcome of the decision. In this step we structure these factors by defining scenarios that contain coherent settings for these external factors. In order to be able to draw up scenarios, three additional database tables have to be filled with data, in a way that is analogous to Step 3, but the internal variable inputs are now replaced by external variable inputs and the decision maker's options by scenarios.

Database table 4a: External variable inputs

External variable inputs are the inputs that are not in the hands of the decision maker and hence also known as exogenous variables or out-of-control inputs. Each external variable input can be thought of as a single aspect of external uncertainty affecting the outcome of the decision in scope.

For Beerwiser the external variable inputs are the cost of a safety accident and the effectiveness of the water recycling investments. The latter represents a factor of conservatism by which the expected effect of investing in water recycling on the use of water is multiplied.

Database table 4b: Scenarios high level

A scenario is defined by assigning a single value to each external variable input. Since there is typically more than one external variable input, a scenario can be thought of as a coherent combination of future developments, where every single aspect of external uncertainty is represented by choosing a single value for the corresponding external variable input. Thus, scenarios are used to account for a decision maker's risk appetite. It is recommended that the names of the scenarios reflect what the values of the external variable input imply. Typical names for scenarios are:

- 'Base case', representing the scenario reflecting most likely outcomes for the external variable inputs. A risk-neutral decision maker may want to put most weight on this scenario.

- 'Optimistic', representing the scenario reflecting potential outcomes for the external variable inputs that are deemed to have a positive effect on the key outputs. A decision maker with a relatively high risk appetite may want to put most weight on this scenario.

- 'Pessimistic', representing the scenario reflecting potential outcomes for the external variable inputs that are deemed to have a negative effect on the key outputs. A risk-averse decision maker may want to put most weight on this scenario.

To create robust decisions, the decision maker may want to give equal weights to all these scenarios.

Table 7.5   Database table 4c completed for Beerwiser case

Scenario	External variable input	Value
Base case	Cost of accident	$15,000
Base case	Effectiveness water recycling	98%
Optimistic	Cost of accident	$12,000
Optimistic	Effectiveness water recycling	100%
Pessimistic	Cost of accident	$20,000
Pessimistic	Effectiveness water recycling	90%

It is possible to alter the default scenario names as well as to add or delete scenarios. Typical scenarios that may be added on top of the three scenarios listed above are stress scenarios in which severe shocks are applied to one or more external inputs or scenarios reflecting the personal view of one of the stakeholders or experts taking part in the explorative dialogue. The scenario names are stored in database table 4b. For the example case we stick to the three default scenario names.

Database table 4c: Scenarios detailed

Database table 4c is linked to database tables 4a and 4b: For every scenario in 4b, all non-zero external variable inputs in 4a will be assigned a value.

Table 7.5 shows what the scenarios look like for the Beerwiser example case.

Recall from Chapter 2 that additional desk and field research may be needed in Step 5 to complete the scenario definitions. Historical data may be involved, and/or other experts may be consulted. In this example case we used expert opinions to determine the values of the external variable inputs per scenario.

Step 5: Constructing simulation model

Constructing the simulation model consists of specifying as well as validating the simulation model. It typically involves more than taking into account internal variable inputs, external variable inputs and key outputs. Additional model elements may be required. These are extra inputs in the form of fixed inputs, intermediates in order to create more transparency in the modelling process, and additional outputs for supplementary insights.

Figure 7.4 Calculation flow within the Responsible Business Simulator. The arrows indicate the formulae describing dependencies

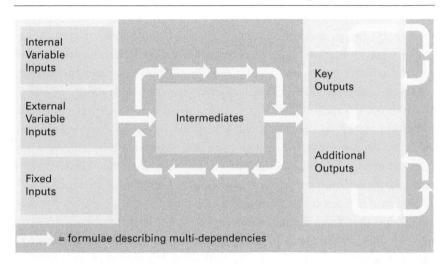

After specifying the additional elements, all model elements are linked by specifying so-called dependencies. The calculation flow looks as displayed in Figure 7.4.

We see that intermediates may depend on internal variable inputs, external variable inputs, fixed inputs and other intermediates. Similarly, key outputs may depend on internal variable inputs, external variable inputs, fixed inputs, intermediates and other key outputs. Finally, additional outputs may depend on all model elements. From Figure 7.4 we can also infer that key outputs can be input into the calculation of additional outputs, but the reverse is not allowed, because in that case these additional outputs would be labelled as intermediates. Also, key outputs cannot be used in the calculations of intermediates. Model elements from which arrows originate we refer to as drivers, while model elements to which arrows are directed, are referred to as destinations.

Specifying simulation model

All necessary information to specify the simulation model that is additional to the information specified in previous steps is provided through four database tables. We will first discuss the contents of these database tables and then explain the Responsible Business Simulator's functionality to validate and visualize the simulation model.

Database table 5a: Fixed inputs

Fixed inputs are inputs additional to previously defined internal and external variable inputs and are often needed to model the relationship between the variable inputs and key outputs.

For brewery Beerwiser these are the water unit cost, number of employees, the current water use, the current production cost and the current number of safety accidents. Their values are listed in Table 7.6.

Although the term 'fixed' suggests that these inputs can have only one value, in practice we see that it can sometimes be difficult to get a reliable value for certain inputs. One way of dealing with this is to consider this input as external variable input and try out several values. However, this means that the number of trials is limited to the number of scenarios.

Within the Responsible Business Simulator it is therefore also possible to indicate that fixed inputs should be generated by Monte Carlo simulation. Monte Carlo simulation, ascribed to Stanislaw Ulam (Ulam, Richtmyer and Neumann, 1947), is a sampling method that can be used to simplify a complex reality. It involves the random sampling of a probability distribution such that a specified number of trials (or scenarios or iterations) are produced that together form the shape of a new distribution. Based on this resulting distribution, the probability that a value occurs can be determined. The higher the number of trials, the higher the level of precision (Vose, 2000). By using Monte Carlo simulation, one can use large numbers of trials. Whether one should use scenarios or Monte Carlo simulation to deal with uncertain input also depends on the sensitivity of the key output for this input. Later in this chapter we will discuss how sensitivity can be analysed graphically.

Monte Carlo simulation has been applied in the Rimetaal case described in Chapter 10. A commonly used process in Monte Carlo simulation is a Poisson process, which is a random counting process that is memoryless as there is a constant and continuous opportunity for an event to occur

Table 7.6 Database table 5a completed for Beerwiser case

Fixed input	Unit	Value	Source
Water unit cost	$/hl	0.050	(Every little drop, nd)
# employees		500	Company information
Current water use	hl/year	15,000,000	Company information
Current production cost	$/year	7,500,000	Company information
Current # accidents	#/year	51	Company information

(Kingman, 1992; Mikosh, 2008). The Poisson distribution is often used to model accidental breakdowns (Vose, 2000).

Database table 5b: Intermediates

The model will become more transparent by breaking down complex formulas in a number of steps, thereby generating a set of intermediates. For example, instead of calculating the production unit cost reduction, it may be wise to first break this key output down into the decrease in production cost due a decrease in water use and the decrease in production cost due to a decrease in safety accidents, then to calculate these components separately and finally aggregate them. All intermediates are stored in database table 5b.

For the example case the intermediates are the relative reduction in accidents, the relative water use reduction, and the production cost reduction in $.

Database table 5c: Additional outputs

Besides key outputs it may be useful to compute additional outputs in order to create complementary insights and/or simple validation possibilities. The additional outputs are stored in database table 5c.

In the example case, besides the decrease in water consumption, the decision maker is interested in the new number of safety-related accidents, the new water consumption and the cost of training per employee.

Database table 5d: Dependencies

Dependencies refer to the relations that the six types of model elements (three types of inputs, intermediates and two types of outputs) mutually have. Many of the simulation models that we have developed do not require any programming by the user but can be specified via this database table. Recall from the description of Figure 7.4 in the previous section that model elements from which arrows originate we refer to as drivers, while model elements to which arrows are directed are referred to as destinations.

Filling out database table 5d is the most technical part of the whole process and here a data science expert may be required. However, users with only limited modelling expertise but some experience in working with formulas will be able to specify relatively simple simulation models themselves based on the following guidance.

Let us first look at simulation models in which every destination can be written as the sum of the product of two model elements that are either inputs or destinations that have already been computed. In that case no programming is required. We will now explain how a user can specify these simulation models via database completion:

1 Let x be the vector containing p elements that stacks the three types of inputs in any order. Let y denote the vector containing q elements that stacks all destinations (intermediates and two types of outputs) in the following order:

   a First, as all model elements that are used in a formula need to be calculated before they can be used as input into this formula, all intermediates are sorted such that every intermediate appears after the intermediates on which it depends.

   b Second, all key outputs, again are sorted such that every key output appears after the key outputs on which it depends.

   c Third, all additional outputs, again – *mutatis mutandis* – are sorted in the same way as the intermediates and key outputs.

2 Then the formula for y_1, the first destination, may be written as follows:

$$y_1 = \sum_{i=1}^{p} x_{l(1, i)} * x_i \, ,$$

where $1 \le l(1, i) \le p$.

3 The formula for y_j, where $2 \le j \le q$, looks somewhat more complicated:

$$y_j = \sum_{i=1}^{p} x_{l(j, i)} * x_i + \sum_{k=1}^{j-1} x_{m(j, k)} * y_k + \sum_{l=1}^{j-1} y_{n(j, l)} * y_l \, ,$$

where $1 \le l(j, i) \le p$, $1 \le m(j, k) \le p$ and $1 \le n(j, l) \le j - 1$.

4 Based on this notation, database table 5d can now be specified. This table has five columns: Driver, Destination, Slope, Operator and Maximum effect. Every term in the formulas above is specified by one row in database table 5d as follows: the model elements x_i, y_k and y_l are drivers, y_j is the destination and the model elements $x_{l(j, i)}$, $x_{m(j, k)}$ and $y_{n(j, l)}$ serve as slope. When completing the database, keep in mind that the order of the model elements inserted into the vectors is crucial for correct calculations, as can be seen from the ranges for $l(j, i)$, $m(j, k)$ and $n(j, l)$.

5 If the destinations can be calculated by the formulas above, then the operator simply reads '*'. However, the Responsible Business Simulator also supports expressions for destinations that take the same form as the formulas above, but use other operators than '*', such as '–*', '/', 'min' or 'max'. In those cases, the corresponding operator is put in the operator column of database table 5d. Table 7.7 allocates the model elements in the formulas above into database table 5d and – for illustrational purposes – contains various types of operators and some example values for maximum effects.

Table 7.7 Database table 5d columns completed with vectors, matrices and columns

Destination	Driver	Slope	Operator	Maximum effect
y_j	x_i	$x_i(j,i)$	*	100
y_j	y_k	$x_m(j,k)$	$-*$	10
y_j	y_l	$y_n(j,l)$	$/$	0.5

Note that in many cases, the formulas for y_j will contain a lot of terms in which the slopes are simply 1, thereby simplifying the specification of dependencies considerably.

If the calculation of the destination is more complicated than this, the user will have to do some programming. In the operator column of database table 5d they can then specify 'Other', and program the corresponding expression manually in AIMMS.

For the Beerwise example case, there is no need for additional programming regarding the dependencies.

Note that the column named 'Maximum effect' in database table 5d has not been explained yet. A maximum effect can be seen as the limit of or the capping on the effect a driver has on a destination. These effects communicate closely with saturation points, accessible population and probabilities of success as defined in database table 3b. Together they form the inputs to the calculation of effects of drivers on destinations. When this type of capping is applied, the operator column in database table 5d needs to be set to 'Squeezed *'.

Direct effects are calculated in case the dependency operator inserted in database table 5d is 'Squeezed *'. In that case the following formula is applied, where i refers to the driver that affects destination j:

$$\text{Direct effect}_{ij} = \text{Accessible population}_i * \text{Probability of success}_i$$

$$* \frac{\min(\text{Investment amount}_p, \text{Saturation Point}_i)}{\text{Saturation Point}_i} * \text{Maximum effect}_{ij}$$

A capped or squeezed effect in the Beerwiser example case is the effect that can be attained on water consumption reduction by investing in water recycling systems. We learned that with the right device, 50 per cent of the waste water can be recycled (Appleyard, nd). We also learned that investing in training can decrease safety-related incidents by a maximum of 48 per cent (Burke et al, 2006).

For the Beerwiser case, we have filled database table 5d according to the aforementioned recipe, which has resulted in Table 7.8. Note that water use reduction and accidents reduction appear both as intermediate and as key outputs.

Table 7.8 Database table 5d columns completed for Beerwiser case

Destination	Driver	Slope	Operator	Maximum effect
Accidents reduction %	Invest in training of employees	1	Squeezed *	0.48
Water use reduction % when effective	Invest in water recycling	1	Squeezed *	0.5
Water use reduction %	Water use reduction % when effective	Effectiveness water recycling	*	
Accidents reduction tmp	Current # accidents	Accidents reduction %	*	
Water use reduction tmp	Water use reduction %	Current water use	*	
Production cost reduction $	Invest in training of employees	1	-*	
Production cost reduction $	Invest in water recycling	1	-*	
Production cost reduction $	Water use reduction tmp	Water unit cost	*	
Production cost reduction $	Accidents reduction tmp	Cost of accident	*	
Production cost reduction	Production cost reduction $	Current production cost	/	
Accidents reduction	Accidents reduction tmp	1	*	
Water use reduction	Water use reduction tmp	1	*	
Cost of training per employee	Invest in training of employees	# employees	/	
New # accidents	Current # accidents	1	*	
New # accidents	Accidents reduction	1	-*	
New water use	Current water use	1	*	
New water use	Water use reduction	1	-*	

Validating simulation model

After the simulation model has been constructed via storing and processing all the information gathered in the foregoing steps of the decision-making process within the model, the simulation model can be validated. The Responsible Business Simulator has several (visual) functionalities that help the user to accommodate this. There is the option to review the dependencies as they are programmed in general. The user can also evaluate key output scores visually as well as investigate sensitivities.

Checking dependencies

Since Table 7.8 may look a bit technical, we have created dependencies graphs. This figure is produced by the Responsible Business Simulator to visualize dependencies as programmed in the simulation model. Figure 7.5 shows the dependencies for the Beerwiser case. The thick arrows refer to links between drivers and destinations, and the thin arrows refer to links between slopes and destinations. Along the arrows it is stated which operator is used. The user has the possibility to select a specific dependency graph for one single driver or destination as well, by clicking on the node corresponding to the output or intermediate of interest. Clicking on an arrow results in an overview of all data involved in the corresponding dependency.

The user may also perform a dependency check on circular definitions and to see whether all model elements inserted into the database tables are used somewhere in the simulation model and – vice versa – whether all model elements needed to compute other model elements are inputs or calculated from inputs.

Comparing key outputs

A spider plot as displayed in Figure 7.6 for the Beerwiser case supports the decision maker to compare the performance of the different key outputs for each decision maker's option visually. Each axis of the plot represents one key output. The better a decision maker's option scores on a key output, the further away it is from the center of the spider plot where all axes intersect.

Analysing sensitivities

Sensitivities can be used to understand graphically how a destination reacts upon changes in a driver via a so-called sensitivity curve. In this curve, the horizontal axis displays the driver value and the vertical axis displays the destination value. The curve itself indicates the sensitivity of the destination to changes in the driver.

Figure 7.5 Dependencies as displayed in Step 5 of the strategic decision-making process for Beerwiser case

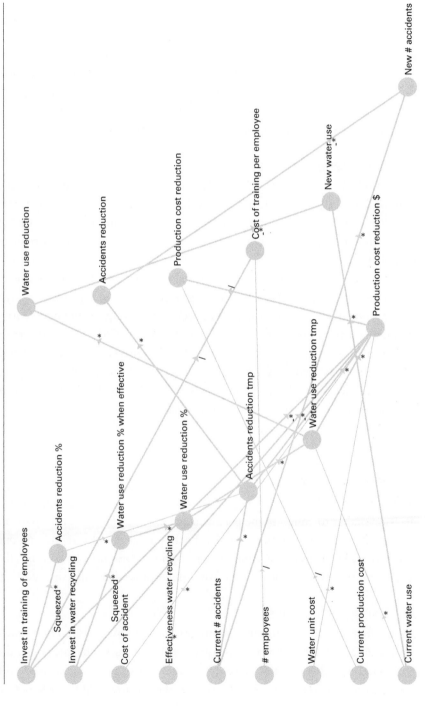

Figure 7.6   Key output scores compared for different decision maker's options for Beerwiser case

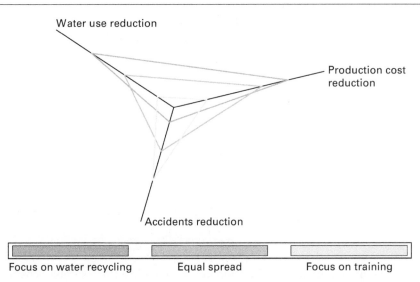

To illustrate this, let us consider again our Beerwiser example. Suppose that we as a decision maker decided to invest in water recycling systems and that we want to know the direct effect of our investment on the water consumption reduction. In Step 3 we learned that the accessible population and the probability of success are both 100 per cent. In Step 5 we learned that with the right device, 50 per cent of the waste water can be recycled. The direct effect of our investment in water recycling systems therefore causes a reduction of water consumption of $100\% * 100\% * 50\% = 50\%$. This implies that the water consumption can be decreased by 50 per cent via this intervention.

This, however, is only the case if a decision maker invests the maximum effective amount or the saturation point. Based on company-specific information we learned that the saturation point of investing in water recycling is $275,000. In this case, all Beerwiser's available water is recycled. Let us assume now that we only have an available budget of $250,000. The direct result would then be: $50\% * \left(\dfrac{250,000}{275,000}\right) \approx 45\%$. This is exactly what can be inferred from Figure 7.7, which shows this sensitivity curve for the Beerwiser example case. On the horizontal axis the invested amount in water recycling is displayed. On the vertical axis the attainable reduction of the water consumption is shown without the factor of conservatism. The water consumption reduction varies from 0 per cent up to 50 per cent, and

Figure 7.7   Sensitivity of 'Water consumption reduction' to changes in 'Invest in water recycling' for Beerwiser case

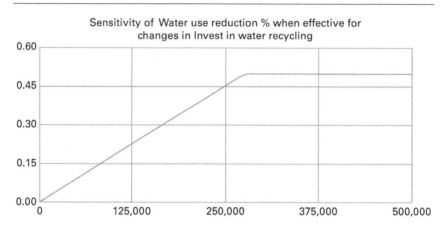

takes its maximum at the saturation point. Of course this example sensitivity curve is a fairly simple one because we specified it ourselves directly via the maximum effect and the saturation point. However, when one selects, for example, a fixed input as driver and a key output that is computed through a sequence of intermediates, the sensitivity curve often turns out to be non-linear. For large sensitivities one might rethink whether one is really sure about the value of this fixed input. If not, one might 'promote' the fixed input to an external variable input to test its effect on the optimal decision maker's option. The opposite may also happen: if one selects an external variable input as driver, and the sensitivity is quite flat for all key outputs, then one may 'demote' the external variable input to fixed input.

The minimum value and the maximum value as well as the number of points plotted in the sensitivity curve may be changed via database table 1a or via the GUI for Step 5.

The sensitivity plot discussed so far allows the user to select one driver and one destination. It is also possible to inspect the sensitivity of the appreciations of all key outputs simultaneously for one selected driver. This functionality makes it easy to find out which drivers primarily drive the key outputs.

Now that the Responsible Business Simulator is specified and validated, the key output scores can be calculated and we can proceed to the selection of the best strategic choice. For that, two steps are remaining: assessing the strategic priorities (Step 6) and assessing the risk appetite of the decision maker (Step 7), which we will discuss in the coming sections.

Step 6: Evaluating options by assessing strategic priorities

Now that we have a validated simulation model that converted all inputs to outputs, we can study these outputs to compare the decision maker's various options and select the best out of these.

Now that the simulation model has been completed, strategic priorities can be indicated by assigning weights to key outputs. The Responsible Business Simulator also allows for assigning weights to themes. This depends on the set-up chosen when starting the modelling process. For NEMO and KNVB we have chosen to set priorities based on themes, while for the other cases we have decided to prioritize via key outputs. In case of assigning weights to themes, all key outputs within one theme are weighted equally. As described earlier in this chapter, key output weights can be altered in database table 2b or in the GUI for Step 6 within the Responsible Business Simulator. Extra information on the contribution of each output's appreciation to the overall appreciation per decision maker option is available in the GUI as well. Note that Step 6 focuses on comparing the decision maker's options for one selected scenario. By default this is the base-case scenario, but this can be changed via database table 1a or via the GUI for Step 6.

Optimization is an additional feature that enables the decision maker to let the Responsible Business Simulator, under a specified scenario and given his strategic preferences, determine an optimal combination of settings for internal variable inputs. The pre-programmed (constrained) optimization engine currently only works when all internal variable inputs represent investments. All the decision maker needs to do is to insert the maximum amount of total investment. The optimization engine will then search for a breakdown of this maximum investment over the internal variable inputs such that the total appreciation is maximized. The decision maker's option in which this breakdown is stored is called 'Optimal' by default, but this can be changed via database table 1a. Logs of this optimization engine are available for inspection via Step 6 -> Solver details. Here, parameters for the optimization engine can be calibrated as well.

For the Beerwiser case, Figure 7.8 shows the comparison of the three decision maker's options that we defined ourselves, plus the Optimal option calculated by the Responsible Business Simulator for the neutral scenario when the weights assigned to reduction of safety accidents, reduction of water use and reduction of production costs are 2, 1 and 1 respectively. In this case the optimal decision maker's option slightly outperforms the

Figure 7.8 Comparison of decision maker's options when more focus is put on reduction of safety accidents in the base case scenario for Beerwiser case

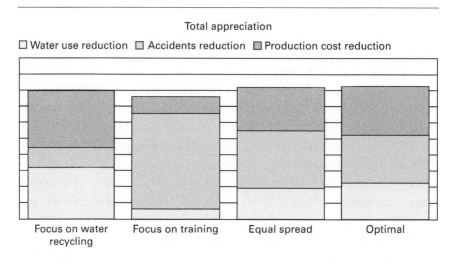

Total appreciation

☐ Water use reduction ☐ Accidents reduction ☐ Production cost reduction

| Focus on water recycling | Focus on training | Equal spread | Optimal |

integrated approach, by spending $124,170.70 on training and $175,829.30 on water recycling. This setting is only optimal for this specific strategic priority setting and in the base-case scenario. How it performs under other scenarios will be subject of the next section.

Step 7: Evaluating options by assessing risk appetite

In the previous step, we kept all external factors fixed in one scenario. Now we want to go one step further and understand the impact of different scenarios, which allows us to compare the decision maker's options, including variations in external factors.

Analogous to Step 6, in which weights are assigned to key outputs to reflect strategic priorities, risk appetite can be indicated by assigning weights to scenarios. The scenario weights depend on the risk appetite of the decision maker, who might have a high or low risk appetite, or may be neutral in this respect. As described in Step 4, scenario weights can be altered in database table 4c or via the GUI for Step 7 within the Responsible Business Simulator. The best decision maker's option depends on his risk appetite.

Figure 7.9 illustrates this for the Beerwiser case. In the optimistic scenario, the focus on water recycling option scores best, because in that scenario less

Figure 7.9   Comparison of decision maker's options when more focus is put on reduction of safety accidents for all scenarios for Beerwiser case

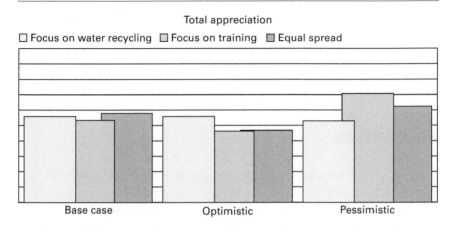

Figure 7.10   Comparison of decision maker's options when all scenarios have equal weights for Beerwiser case

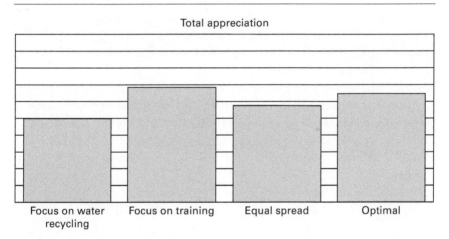

cost for accidents is expected, and therefore the return on investment in training to avoid accidents is smaller. In this scenario, the effect of water recycling is also deemed higher. In the pessimistic scenario it is better to focus on training followed by the equal spread option. Here, the effect of training is higher because of the high expected costs of accidents.

In order to determine a robust scenario, the decision maker has the possibility of searching for a decision maker's option that performs well when accounting for all scenarios. The decision maker can assign weights to the scenarios and let the Responsible Business Simulator calculate one aggregated score per decision maker's option over the scenarios. This means that we aggregate the scenarios based on the weight that is assigned to them and then conclude what the best decision maker's option is.

For the Beerwiser case, if the decision maker looks for a robust option in the sense that they put equal weights to all three scenarios, then it turns out that the focus on training would be the winning option, as shown in Figure 7.10.

References

Appleyard, D (nd) Brewing up change in water treatment technology, *Waste & water international*. Retrieved from http://www.waterworld.com/articles/wwi/print/volume-29/issue-1/technology-case-studies/industrial-water-treatment/brewing-up-change-in-water-treatment-technology.html

Burke, M J et al (2006) Relative effectiveness of worker safety and health training methods, *American Journal of Public Health*, **96** (2), pp. 315–24.

Every little drop (nd, accessed 11 July 2016) The Cost of Water. Retrieved from http://everylittledrop.com.au/knowledge-center/the-cost-of-water/

Kingman, J F (1992). *Poisson processes*, Claredon Press, Oxford

Mikosh, T (2008) *Elementary Stochastic Calculus with Finance in View*, World Scientific Publishing, Singapore

Roth, B (2016) As safety accidents increase, so do conversations about safety, *All About Beer Magazine*. Retrieved from http://allaboutbeer.com/brewery-safety/

Ulam, S, Richtmyer, D and Neumann, J v (1947) Statistical methods in neutron diffusion, *LAMS-551*

Vose, D (2000) *Risk Analysis: A quantitative guide*, John Wiley & Sons Ltd, West Sussex

Strategic decision making based on data and dialogue via the Responsible Business Simulator 06

Strategic decision making with the use of the Responsible Business Simulator is a communal activity, one in which employees and management both play an active role in providing input; the advisor stimulates the strategic dialogue and renders that input transparent in the computational model. During the sessions, all participants are on an equal footing. Entering into a dialogue with each other about the direction a business or organization should take, or about the interests that particular stakeholders have in realizing a specific strategy, is an important part of the strategic decision-making process. Everyone is able to speak openly to one another during the sessions, and in between sessions, reports, figures, comparative studies, data and other information is collected. These documents, for instance consulting or engineering reports, which are often already available at various locations within the business, are frequently found to contain important hints for constructive dialogue. The process brings a large volume of existing information to the surface, avoiding the usual tendency to reinvent the wheel. For example, a firm of consulting engineers might already have produced a report with hard facts about what is needed for the repair of a roof (see the NEMO case in Chapter 9). Such details can then be included in the computational model.

Even more important is the identification of unsubstantiated assumptions, which can sometimes prove vital to altering the way the strategy is looked at. In the NEMO case, what proved to be an important hint was found in a casual comment in the report about the roof at the Science Museum. The engineers suggested that a sustainable roof could well have a positive effect on visitor numbers; our research team then had these effects calculated in the

Responsible Business Simulator. For the engineers, this was barely relevant information; they had after all been called in to look at the technical side of the options for the roof repairs. But the Responsible Business Simulator encompasses all the factors that provide information about People, Planet and Profit. From the holistic perspective, this comment about visitor numbers was an important factor that brought together various strategic objectives, namely a sustainable roof that was attractive to visitors and the city alike and that would generate more revenue in terms of admissions tickets sold and an even better reputation in the city of Amsterdam. This example also demonstrates why the Responsible Business Simulator is not the introvert activity of a lone calculator sitting at a computer, but precisely an interactive activity between employees and management so as to bring extra dimensions into the equation and to appraise them in terms of their value for a sustainable, widely supported strategy instead of just taking a decision on a single aspect and losing sight of all the rest.

Action research as method

The method that we used in the development of the Responsible Business Simulator and its application in real-world corporate environments can best be described using the action research concept. Action research can be defined as a process that is suitable for situations in which you simultaneously wish to realize change ('action') and acquire academic insight ('research') (Dick, 2002). Since our research had a strong practical and pragmatic component, we contend that it is impossible to achieve a thorough understanding of the Responsible Business Simulator without having practical experience of its application on the one hand, and a fundamental knowledge of current practice within the participating organizations on the other. For a more extensive overview of the action research method and related theories than we present here, see the *Handbook of Action Research* by Reason and Bradbury (2001).

Dick (2002) explains that action research can be 'cyclical' or 'spiral', whereby action and critical reflection continually alternate. You begin by studying either the present practices or the policy currently pursued in the organizations. This is an exploratory phase, which is carried out from an unbiased perspective. A setting is subsequently created in which key persons within the organization can arrive at new insights that help to improve the current organizational processes. Action research can be described as progressing through cycles of intervention, reflection and investigation. With the unprecedented development of information systems and IT, the role of action research proved to be very relevant. Particularly the practitioner/

researcher interaction, as well as the group dynamics among practitioners themselves, lead to much more personal investment in the research than with traditional research methods.

Action research is a form of research that takes place outside experimental laboratories and is common practice at universities, corporate consultancies and knowledge-intensive companies in domains such as pharmaceuticals and IT. Action research is carried out in living laboratories with the people from businesses or organizations. The research is carried out under 'real-life' conditions as far as possible, so that the true impact of interventions can be determined. The researchers are conscious of the interventions that they are implementing, and they communicate about them. This introduces a form of subjectivity, something that is considered to be impure science within traditional scientific circles.

However, not every issue is suitable for dissection in the unnatural environment of a technical laboratory, simply because the input needed to arrive at the heart of the matter cannot be poured out of a test tube but has to be delivered in collaboration with the real actors involved. Baskerville (1999) states that the key assumptions of the action researcher are that (1) the social settings cannot be reduced for study, and (2) action brings understanding. These assumptions are clearly valid for corporate strategic decision making. Although scientists are sometimes reticent about action research, the phenomenon has existed for a long time and it is applied in practice on a large scale in the social sciences and in the world of corporate consultancy. Lewin (1946, p. 35) already defined action research as 'A spiral of steps that proceeds from planning to action to observation and finally to reflection'.

Society also has a great need for research which is connected to a concrete action element, especially in the transition to a circular economy, as timely action is required. The unknowns in this transition are widespread and plentiful, such that most strategy decisions made will involve some of these unknown factors. Learning by doing fits this scenario. The action research paradigm suits research into sustainability and social inclusion while the economy is in such an unprecedented transition because knowledge acquired can be directly utilized in the next iteration of the research cycle.

Action research to unleash collective intelligence

In the Responsible Business Simulator approach we unleash the 'collective intelligence' of a group of highly diverse experts for strategic decision making. As shown by Woolley et al (2010) it is this collective intelligence that explains the performance of a group, not the individual intelligence of group members. Moreover, Woolley et al found evidence that group intelligence does not correlate strongly with the average intelligence of group members, but that it is correlated with the 'average social sensitivity of group members and the equality distribution of conversational turn-taking', which affirms the importance of using a round-table format (Woolley et al, 2010, p. 686). Specifically, collective intelligence has been found to be crucial in settings that incorporate research (Buecheler et al 2010) and the use of computer applications to support human interaction and decision making (Gregg, 2010). This evidence illustrates that the Responsible Business Simulator and its interactive setting are very effective in dealing with complex issues.

Action research forms a counterbalance to the so-called 'extractive research', whereby researchers extract knowledge from a group of subjects while no changes are brought about in the situation of the subjects investigated (Tromp, 2006). Action research's iterative method of working allows participants to learn informally and ensures that new insights fall into place as the research progresses.

This is a highly desirable situation when developing well-supported strategy and processes of change, because it only strengthens the outcome. From a steady state perspective, however, it is disturbing that living actors live up to their epithet and continually switch tracks during the process on the basis of those new insights, instead of continuing on the original track. This is a fundamentally different perspective from that taken in a physics laboratory; it is impossible to return to the starting situation of the initial experiment, because the actors have already undergone change. In the context of the social environment, however, this is self-evident, and appropriate to this research method (Roobeek, 1996). Action research can be distinguished from conventional research in two ways: first, there is close collaboration with key persons within the organization. In other words, the organizations are not merely the subject of the research: they actively participate. According to Boonstra (2012), the underlying principle here is that insight, reflection and perspective lead to actions, and that sustainable change can only be achieved through participation. Knowledge is acquired because people reflect on their actions. The second distinguishing characteristic is that 'action' is the aim of the research. The goal is to achieve a positive change, not simply to describe present state findings. One comment that describes the core of action research really well is: 'Practice follows theory, theory follows practice' (Boonstra, 2012).

Action research places itself outside the realm of the paradigm that is otherwise dominating science at the moment, namely that of logical empiricism. That movement centres around a model in which the researcher as an 'objective and value-free' observer tries to understand the object of his research as well as possible. Action research, on the other hand, is set up as a communal learning process involving researcher and investigated subjects in which all parties jointly decide which objectives and values are to be achieved by the research. Participative research is based on the principle that there is a close relationship between the development of theory and the search for practical solutions. This does not, however, mean that action research is not objective. Wilmsen (2006) indicates that the most successful projects are those characterized by reciprocity: relationships that are characterized by open communications, trust and exchange between the researchers and the investigated subjects. This situation maximizes the use of the group's collective intelligence, as mentioned earlier in this chapter. According to Tromp (2006), this form of research actually has the potential to enhance objectivity, because there are extra control opportunities. An open attitude and controllability increase reciprocal confidence, and this in turn increases openness. In this way, reciprocity enhances the effectiveness of knowledge; Tromp suggests that this can be seen as an alternative way of interpreting conventional reliability and validity criteria.

Action research entails trying to 'reframe' the problems that have been identified so that they can be viewed in a different light. It is based on a systematic dialogue rooted in factual data which fits perfectly with the way we have designed our research. Existing knowledge is used, combined and tested by means of an econometric simulation model. Before such complex simulation models were possible it was already recognized by Baskerville and Wood-Harper (1996) that the action research method is ideally suited to the study of information systems and technology in its human context. Our research is specifically aimed at this. The goal is improving theory and technology, the Responsible Business Simulator, in order to support the interactive processes that integrate sustainability into all layers of the organization.

Although the transition towards a circular economy and social inclusion can currently be considered to be a hot topic, in research, policy and practice, insights from the organization itself are often not put to good use and organizations are not yet able to place sustainability and social inclusion strategically within their decision-making processes. The aim of our action research is explicitly to move sustainability from the sidelines into the heart of the organization. To this end we have collaborated actively with businesses and organizations; in applying the model in the real world we have ourselves learned a great deal and been able to introduce improvements. In addition, we invited various parties to join us at the university so that we could all reflect critically on our findings. The results served as input for the further refinement of the model, and also helped to enhance our understanding of the obstacles that are inherent in business strategies. Collaborative research proved its worth through the process of cyclical reflection and through providing tips for the further research process. Making maximum use of each participant's expertise – the mathematician, the financial expert, the organizational expert, the strategist – we were able to develop a simulation model that enhances insight into which interventions carried out at what juncture would have the greatest impact on sustainability and profit objectives alike. The ultimate aim was to create sustainable interventions based on hard data rather than on intuition and assumptions. The results of the action research proved that this is a feasible method, and strengthened the content of the process of strategic decision making with the use of the Responsible Business Simulator.

Data science in strategic decision making

The interest in data science has increased enormously over the past years. According to the *Economist* (2010), 'A new kind of professional has emerged, the data scientist, who combines the skills of software programmer, statistician and storyteller/artist to extract the nuggets of gold hidden under mountains of data'. Davenport and Patil called data scientist 'The sexiest job of the 21st century' in the title of their article in the *Harvard Business Review* (2012). In this and the following paragraphs we look at some obstacles when applying data science in practice and focus on how the Responsible Business Simulator offers a practical way of creating business impact by applying data science in strategic decision making.

The challenge of applying data science in practice lies not so much in having enough statistical modellers, or data managers, or professional strategists who have the ability to present their views with impact in the boardroom, but rather in the combination of these three capabilities. This combination is what that truly creates business and social impact.

In our business practice, we have seen many examples of organizations who could combine only two out of these three when making decisions. Just IT and analytics together typically lead to advanced models on real data that cannot, however, be used in a suboptimal way in boardrooms. For decisions with impact, a collective interpretation is necessary from the data experts and statistical modellers (internal or external), in combination with the (interactively operating) strategists and the participants in the company.

This is confirmed by Accenture's study showing that only 24 per cent of companies feel that they excel in what is called decision science (Hernandez, Berkey and Bhattacharya, 2013). It is interesting to see that their study claims that the number of companies excelling in data management and statistical modellers is higher (44 per cent and 33 per cent respectively), confirming that the combining various expertise when it comes to decision making is key.

Avoiding the pitfalls of spreadsheet modelling

We often see companies making decisions based on spreadsheet models. These models typically implement a discounted future cash flow analysis, leading to a Net Present Value (NPV) and Internal Rate of Return (IRR) that pass the hurdle rate set by the company. Although in principle it is possible to create a transparent spreadsheet model doing much more than such a cash flow analysis, there are a number of fundamental limitations to this approach:

- *Risk of goal reasoning.* A spreadsheet reporting an NPV or IRR not meeting the hurdle rate will probably not make its way to the boardroom. This automatically creates some pressure to set so-called fudge factors (uncertain inputs to the model having high impact on NPV and/or IRR) to values that favour the decision preferred by the author of the spreadsheet. This confirmative, deductive reasoning is actually deeply embedded in many forms of practical analytics. One of the promises of big data is to be more open for explorative, inductive insights as well as confirmative insights. In other words, data should not only be used to find answers to predefined questions, but also to pose new ones. Figure 6.1 displays the conceptual difference between the two approaches.

- *Proneness to errors.* Spreadsheet models can easily introduce errors. Many examples of this can be found in the horror stories section on the website of the European Spreadsheet Risks Interest Group (European Spreadsheet Risks Interest Group, 2016).

- *Non-transparency.* The complexity of spreadsheets is often measured by counting the number of distinct formulas; spreadsheets supporting big decisions often contain thousands of these. On the one hand this should not be a problem, as there are many ways to structure these spreadsheets

Figure 6.1   Many spreadsheets for decision making still follow confirmative reasoning (Tuthil, 1990)

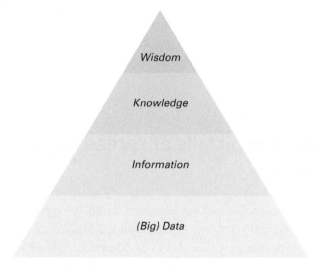

adequately. Microsoft's Excel has functionality to trace precedents and dependents and there are also many good add-ons available to create more transparency around spreadsheets, such as OAK and Spreadsheet Professional (Audit Excel, 2013; Operis Analysis Kit, nd). On the other hand, however, these mitigating measures are not always used and even if they are, it may still be hard for non-experts to get a grasp of what is really going in these large spreadsheets. We encounter many spreadsheets that are unattractive for those who want to challenge or learn from the model.

- *Focus on traditional business functions.* Spreadsheets are typically used by business professionals. However, for decision making towards a circular economy, there is a *mer à boire* of key insights from other disciplines, eg environmental impact and human behaviour, that are not automatically disclosed via spreadsheets. This also explains why a lot of spreadsheets still tend to focus on financial effects.

- *Inefficiency.* In our experience, many organizations spend lots of time on creating spreadsheets for decision making. Although spreadsheets allow for automatic interfacing with databases, this functionality is typically used more for reporting purposes than for decision making. Also, for many decisions, a new spreadsheet is built from scratch, although many elements are the same in all these spreadsheets, such as a discounted future cash flow analysis.

- *Two-dimensionality.* Spreadsheets try to capture a complex world in a two-dimensional world of rows and columns. Ways of increasing the number of dimensions to more than two by using multiple sheets or blocks typically increase the error count.

- *Inflexibility.* The addition of an extra product, time period, region or cost category to a dimension within a data structure which already contains more than two dimensions is often cumbersome.

- *Suboptimal access to more advanced statistical techniques.* Although there are many good add-ins available such as @Risk (Palisade Corporation, nd) for – amongst others – decision trees and Monte Carlo simulations, many powerful algorithms – such as solvers for Mixed Integer Problems – are still not easily accessible. As an example, the Goal Seek function in Microsoft Excel is one-dimensional and may have difficulty in solving non-linear problems.

- *Lack of handling large data sets.* Although the number of rows and columns has been increased significantly over the past years (up to 1,048,576 and 16,384 respectively in Microsoft Excel 2016), opportunities offered by big data may require more. Also, spreadsheets are not primarily designed to handle sparse data sets. If a two-dimensional data set has 20 million rows and 20,000 columns, but only contains 1 million non-zeros, then it will not be straightforward to work with in Microsoft Excel.

Strategic decision making based on data and dialogue via the Responsible Business Simulator

We developed the Responsible Business Simulator to overcome the obstacles encountered by spreadsheet models for strategic decision making. Just like a spreadsheet model is built within a spreadsheet software environment – typically Microsoft's Excel – the Responsible Business Simulator has been programmed in a mathematical modelling software environment called AIMMS. The main advantages of AIMMS over a spreadsheet environment are that AIMMS has been designed to create graphical user interfaces around multidimensional models and offers access to advanced mathematical techniques such as optimization and Monte Carlo simulation. AIMMS can also handle large datasets efficiently by exploiting sparse data structure. There is also a web-enabled server version of AIMMS. The disadvantage of AIMMS may be that it has a high enter barrier for non-mathematicians. To overcome this handicap, the Responsible Business Simulator offers a shell around AIMMS' mathematical programming language that closely follows the seven-step strategic decision-making process. The user just has to capture what is said during the stakeholder dialogue and the strategic dialogue in a number of non-technical screens. Simple simulation models can be specified by non-experts via one database table, without the need to make any programming effort in AIMMS. When the importance of the decision at hand justifies an investment in a more advanced model, a data scientist may be needed. To quote Einstein, things should be made as simple as possible, but not simpler. Even then, the focus in our approach is to create transparency around the assumptions behind the more advanced parts of the simulation model by a number of preprogrammed visual displays.

It may still happen that the simulation model becomes so complex that the decision maker does not have a solid grasp of the main assumptions in the model. In this case, we see two possible solutions. First, the expert responsible for these complex model parts should reduce complexity by breaking down the calculations in smaller sub-steps, for which it is possible to communicate the main assumptions to the decision maker. Again we quote Einstein: 'Complexity is a lack of understanding'. Second, a less complex model should be preferred in order to mitigate the risk that a decision is purely taken based on a black box and thus not thoroughly understood by the decision maker. One should also realize that – no matter how complex the simulation model becomes – every model is a limited representation of reality. In our view, it is better to have a business dialogue around assumptions that are well understood, as well as risk appetite, by using a number of comprehensive scenarios than to be in the hands of the designer of the black box.

In summary, the Responsible Business Simulator reveals the power and beauty of mathematics to the business world by combining and disclosing analytical insights from various disciplines and putting these in the context of the decision at hand.

The added value of combined research methodologies

The method we propose, combining advanced computational techniques with interactive action learning sessions, removes the vague assertions and false choices about sustainability from strategic decision making and from the accompanying investments.

By assigning values and weightings to both financial and non-financial key outputs during the interactive sessions, and thereby indicating how important a particular key output is in comparison with any other, the input for the strategy becomes transparent. Even more importantly, the entire process helps create support for the strategic choices. That is an important factor, because experience shows that strategies that are imposed from the top down hardly ever work. Interaction is important to people, particularly to professionals, so that they feel they have had some say in bringing the strategy about. If people, not only from within the organization but also stakeholders from outside, have been able to provide an active contribution, and that contribution is visible in the strategic choices, the strategy is far more likely to be accepted. The chance that the strategy is actually going to be implemented increases in equal measure. The return on the explicit involvement of employees and management alike in interactive action learning sessions will be a greater flexibility during the implementation of the strategy. This is one important benefit of the Responsible Business Simulator approach.

Besides recruiting support as the foundation of the strategic decision-making process, the Responsible Business Simulator also ensures that the input is objectified. It quantifies the key outputs and visualizes the weightings that are chosen by the team members. Repeating the sessions a couple of times allows fine-tuning to be effected on the basis of data and dialogue. This just serves to reinforce the probability of the outcomes. As far as the decision making in the board of an organization is concerned, this means that a proposal for sustainable investments or for a strategic choice can be tabled that is not only 'hard' in terms of outcomes but also well supported by all concerned. For decision making, it also means that the software makes the outcomes of the process crystal clear. It becomes clear whether an enterprise is only pursuing Profit and ignoring the other Ps, or whether it is making efforts to ensure a well-chosen balance between the Ps of People, Planet and Profit. This avoids the phenomenon known as 'greenwashing': acting as if the enterprise is really sustainable while, in reality, sustainability is being used as a marketing tool to portray the enterprise as greener and more social than it really is.

The strategic decision-making process allows no scope for manipulating sustainability or social factors in a Triple P context. This is relevant in the context of the evolution towards fully integrated reporting. In recent years, we have seen that businesses are increasingly supplementing their mandatory annual reports with a social and sustainability annual report. An ever growing group of pioneers is turning to fully inclusive reporting, a concept that revolves around transparency, ensuring that what is expressed in the enterprise's strategy is also put into practice (Eden and Huxham, 1996). The Responsible Business Simulator puts sustainability to the litmus test and enterprises and organizations can use the method to arm themselves proactively.

References

Audit Excel (2013) Spreadsheet testing tool. Retrieved from http://www.auditexcel.co.za/download/spreadsheet-testing-tool/#.V5ILscKKBp8

Baskerville, R L (1999) Investigating information systems with action research, *Communications of the AIS*, **2** (3), p. 4

Baskerville, R L and Wood-Harper, A T (1996) A critical perspective on action research as a method for information systems research, *Journal of Information Technology*, **11** (3), pp. 235–46

Boonstra, J (2012) *Actie-onderzoek, leren en veranderen*, Presentatie Sioo/ Universiteit van Amsterdam. Amsterdam

Buecheler, T et al (2010) Crowdsourcing, open innovation and collective intelligence in the scientific method: a research agenda and operational framework, *ALIFE*, pp. 679–86

Davenport, T H and Patil, D J (2012) Data scientist: the sexiest job of the 21st Century, *Harvard Business Review*, October

Dick, B (2002) Action research: action and research. Retrieved from http://www.aral.com.au/resources/aandr.html

Economist (2010, 25 February) Data, data everywhere, *The Economist*. Retrieved from http://www.economist.com/node/15557443

Eden, C and Huxham, C (1996) Action research for management research, *British Journal of Management*, **7**, pp. 75–86

European Spreadsheet Risks Interest Group (2016) EuSpRIG Horror stories, *European Spreadsheet Risks Interest Group*. Retrieved from http://www.eusprig.org/horror-stories.htm

Gregg, D G (2010) Designing for collective intelligence *Communications of the ACM*, **53** (4), pp. 134–38

Hernandez, J, Berkey, B and Bhattacharya, R (2013) Building an analytics-driven organization, *Accenture*. Retrieved from https://www.accenture.com/dk-en/~/media/Accenture/Conversion-Assets/DotCom/Documents/Global/PDF/Industries_2/Accenture-Building-Analytics-Driven-Organization.pdf

Lewin, K (1946) Action research and minority problems, *Journal of social issues*, **2** (4), pp. 34–46

Operis Analysis Kit (nd, accessed 22 July 2016) Operis Analysis Kit. Retrieved from http://www.operisanalysiskit.com/

Palisade Corporation (nd, accessed 22 July 2016) The future in your spreadsheet. Retrieved from http://www.palisade.com/risk/

Reason, P and Bradbury, H (2001) *Handbook of Action Research: Participative inquiry and practice*, SAGE Publications Ltd, Thousand Oaks, California

Roobeek, A J M (1996) Strategic management from the bottom up, in *Beyond Theory: Changing organizations through participation*, ed S Toulmin and B Gustavsen, John Benjamins Publishing Company, Amsterdam/Philadelphia

Tromp, C (2006) Action research als relevante vorm van interventieonderzoek, *Sociale Interventie*, 4

Tuthil, S (1990) *The Data Hierarchy*, 3M, Minesota

Wilmsen, C (2006) Participation, reciprocity, and empowerment in the practice of participatory research, *University of California, Berkeley*. Retrieved from http://nature.berkeley.edu/community_forestry/Workshops/2006/WCAR%20 2006%20final%20draft%20Wilmsen.pdf

Woolley, A W et al (2010) Evidence for a collective intelligence factor in the performance of human groups, *Science*, **330** (6004), pp. 868–88

Reducing greenhouse gas emissions

08

This chapter illustrates the application of the Responsible Business Simulator in the case of Koninklijke DSM N.V. or Royal DSM (DSM). Climate change, due to among other things the greenhouse gas emissions from fossil fuel combustion, calls for decarbonization of DSM's energy systems. DSM, a global frontrunner in sustainability, takes a leading role in climate action. Since some of DSM's production processes are energy intensive, it is important for DSM to improve its energy efficiency, while increasing the percentage of energy purchased from renewable sources, and making strategic choices in the area of renewable energy. The main options for DSM are generating renewable energy as an activity of DSM or sourcing renewable energy from an external supplier. However, the decision-making process is not as simple as it seems, since a decision should also take into account the country of origin where CO_2 certificates come from and whether or not an internal carbon price should be applied. The Responsible Business Simulator was able to process all required inputs and helped to give the decision makers the relevant scenarios to make a sustainable decision on energy sourcing.

We will start by introducing this global science-based company in the context of making strategic decisions to benefit people, the planet and profits.

About DSM

Royal DSM (DSM) is a global science-based company active in health, nutrition and materials. DSM operates in global markets such as food and dietary supplements, personal care, animal feed, automotive, electronics, alternative energy and bio-based materials (DSM, 2016b).

Sustainability is both a core value and a sustainable growth driver. By connecting its unique competences in life sciences and materials sciences,

DSM strives to create economic, social and environmental value. The organization has been named among the worldwide leaders in the Materials industry group in the Dow Jones Sustainability World Index, holding the number one position seven times since 2004 (DSM, 2016a), including most recently in 2015. *Fortune* magazine recently included DSM in its 2016 'Change the World' list of 50 companies worldwide that are making an important social or environmental impact through their profit-making strategy and operations (*Fortune*, 2016). By 2020, DSM aims for 65 per cent of its sales to be 'Brighter Living Solutions', products and services that, when considered over their whole life cycle, offer better social and/or environmental impacts, compared to the mainstream competing solutions.

With the aspiration to remain a frontrunner, DSM wants to continuously improve its sustainability performance simultaneously on the dimensions of People, Planet and Profit.

This chapter elaborates on the specific case where DSM wants to reduce its greenhouse gas emissions, first of all by becoming more energy efficient and secondly by sourcing renewable energy. The strategic challenge, therefore, has been formulated as how to balance various criteria used when deciding upon the sourcing of (renewable) energy, including those criteria that are hard to compare. In this chapter the focus will be on the strategic dialogue that is facilitated by the Responsible Business Simulator regarding renewable energy sourcing and how this dialogue supported the introduction of using an internal carbon price.

Since the context of the strategic challenge DSM faces around energy sourcing is quite complex, some additional background information is provided on carbon footprint, greenhouse gas emission, renewable energy, Guarantees of Origin and the internal carbon price.

About energy sourcing

During the entire process, energy sourcing terminology such as greenhouse gas emissions, renewable energy and carbon footprint plays a key role. Since there are multiple definitions of these concepts that can be interpreted in various ways, this section elaborates on how terminology is applied in the context of this study.

Carbon footprint

The definition of carbon footprint is complicated. Historically, it has been defined as the total set of greenhouse gas (GHG) emissions caused by an organization, event, product or individual, but since GHG can also be produced by natural occurrences, Wright, Kemp and Williams (2011) have proposed a more refined, though technical definition. Here, for simplicity, we will express carbon footprint in kilotons of carbon dioxide, or its equivalent of other GHGs, emitted (CO_{2e}).

Sustainability Reporting Guidelines (Global Reporting Initiative, 2013) divide energy use and emissions in three separate scope levels:

- Scope 1: Direct GHG emissions are emissions from sources that are owned or controlled by the reporting entity.

- Scope 2: Indirect GHG emissions are emissions that are a consequence of the activities of the reporting entity, but occur at sources owned or controlled by another entity.

- Scope 3: Other indirect GHG emissions such as the extraction and production of purchased materials and fuels, transport-related activities in vehicles not owned or controlled by the reporting entity, outsourced activities, waste disposal, etc.

In this case, only scope 1 and 2 CO_{2e} emissions are taken into account. In the remainder of this article, they will be referred to as GHG emission or carbon footprint. The type of energy focused on in this case is electricity.

Before we define carbon footprint, we first introduce the notions of renewable energy, Guarantees of Origin and Renewable Energy Certificates, since its definition depends on these notions.

Renewable energy

Renewable energy originally means 'Energy from renewable non-fossil sources: wind, solar, aerothermal, geothermal, hydrothermal and ocean energy, hydropower, biomass, landfill gas, sewage treatment plant gas and biogases' (European Parliament, 2009). Sometimes renewable energy is loosely referred to as 'green energy' and non-renewable energy as 'grey energy'.

Renewable energy consumption for DSM consists of two components: direct use via its own energy production, and indirect use by using energy purchased from the grid or another external supplier. For the organization's own production, it is clear how renewable electricity is produced and how much GHG emission is involved. As for the electricity that is used from the grid, this is not so straightforward since it is impossible to distinguish renewable from fossil fuel-based electricity as an end consumer (an electron is an electron).

Guarantees of Origin (GoOs) or Renewable Energy Certificates (RECs)

Since energy from a renewable source cannot physically be differentiated from electricity from fossil fuel-based power plants when supplied through the grid, an administrative solution is used, named Guarantees of Origin (GoO) (Dutch Ministry of Economic Affairs, 2010). GoOs are sometimes referred to as RECs (Renewable Energy Certificates). Several governments have introduced a system of GoOs or certificates to distinguish energy that is generated in an environmentally friendly way from conventionally generated energy. One GoO is equivalent to one MWh of energy. The system of GoO provides insights into how the power was produced: by using fossil fuels, nuclear or renewable power plants. In the Netherlands, certificates for renewable electricity are the only official proof that a retailer delivers 'green electricity' to the end user.

Certificates can be used for international trade. Installations receiving certificates are wind turbines, biomass power plants, solar systems and hydro power plants. Since 2007, it has also been possible to obtain certificates for electricity from highly efficient Combined Heat and Power (CHP) plants.

As an example, RECs in the Netherlands are issued and managed by CertiQ, a subsidiary of TenneT, the Dutch transmission system provider. Issuing occurs conform to the Electricity Act of 1998 and several ministerial regulations. Dutch Distribution System Operators (DSOs) such as Liander, Stedin and Enexis, validate whether the electricity generated in an installation can be defined as renewable energy (or energy from CHP) and whether the volumes of electricity can be clearly measured. Subsequently, the DSO sends the information to CertiQ, which converts the measured data into certificates. Many countries have a similar set-up for dealing with certificates.

It is important to realize that energy is only named 'renewable' when it originates from a non-fossil or renewable source and is accompanied by a certificate.

DSM's focus is on realizing power purchase agreements with third parties whereby long-term commitment is given to source renewable power from, for example, a wind or solar park. One such example is Windpark Krammer, announced in October 2016, where Philips, AkzoNobel, Google and DSM have teamed up with a citizens' initiative for a wind park in the Netherlands (Edelman, 2016). Ninety-five per cent of the power generated from this park will be purchased by these four companies. DSM's share is 90 GWh and will cover 50 per cent of the electricity needs in the Netherlands as of 2019, when the park will be operational. In the meantime, as a transition measure to support more renewable electricity projects, DSM is considering buying a limited number of RECs from recently initiated projects, thus stimulating the addition of more renewable power to the grid (so called 'additionality').

Using the definition of GoOs, three methods can be distinguished to calculate carbon footprint as a consequence of buying energy from a third party or the grid:

- *Uncorrected country factor* (location-based method). A country factor corrected for combined heat and power plants is used (Brander et al, 2011). This is an easy calculation, but the offtake does not take into account the allocation of GoOs, which increases the risk of double counting with parties that have claimed the GoOs. The impact of increasing the share of renewables is low since benefits are also harvested by other users of power from the grid.

- *Corrected country factor* (location-based method). A country factor is used for the residual mix, which is the amount of electricity that has not been claimed via tracking systems such as GoOs. Using this factor, the share of renewable energy is determined (Reliable Disclosure Systems, 2015). Since claimed GoOs are subtracted, the threat of double counting is mitigated. Offtake depends on contractual agreements, so using a country average will provide a deviation from an organization's actual renewable energy (RE) percentages and GHG emissions. The risk of double counting in case renewable energy is produced but not claimed through a GoO is expected to be small.

- *Supplier contract* (market-based method). An offtake contract for electricity provides, at least in the Netherlands, information about percentages of RE and GHG emissions per kWh. The information is backed up by GoOs. This approach avoids double counting since the supplier is obliged to report the percentage renewables and GHG emissions according to the GoOs used.

Country of origin, availability of data and time are all reasons for organizations to choose differently between the options listed above.

Internal carbon price

Organizations that acknowledge the process of ongoing climate change as a key relevant business factor for which they wish to be prepared often implement an internal carbon price. Addressing climate change will be both a business cost and a possible business opportunity, regardless of the regulatory environment (Carbon Disclosure Project, 2013). An internal carbon price is a price on each unit of reported CO_{2e} emission. This 'penalty' for CO_{2e} emission can be actually collected or used when evaluating business cases. DSM uses the latter approach, a so-called 'shadow carbon price' in business case evaluations. The idea of evaluating business cases with the incorporation of an internal carbon price is 'forward-looking' as pricing of carbon pollution will eventually be part of day-to-day business. The number of organizations that incorporate an internal carbon price for their decision making almost tripled from 150 in 2014 to 435 in 2015. This number grew to 1,249 in 2016 (Carbon Disclosure Project, 2016) and is expected to keep growing (Carbon Disclosure Project, 2015). Organizations such as Shell, BP, ExxonMobil, General Electric and Microsoft are well-known users of an internal carbon price. Globally, the internal carbon price varies from US $0.97 to US $357.37 for every ton of CO_{2e} emission (Carbon Disclosure Project, 2015).

The strategic decision-making process

In the case study at DSM, we collaborated with a team that represented various fields of expertise from various departments (Operations, Energy, Sourcing, Life Cycle Assessment, Finance) as well as the Sustainability department. The team members' knowledge of various parts of the organization facilitated the data collection process and resulted in a meaningful strategic dialogue. The successive outcomes of the simulation model were compared and analysed carefully. As a result, key outputs were refined and new ones were added, and factual data could be brought in in a meaningful way. We now elaborate on each of the seven steps in the decision-making process. For the purpose of this publication we have used – where necessary – fictitious data to illustrate the decision-making process so as not to disclose competitively sensitive information.

Describing strategic challenge that requires a decision

A brainstorming session between decision makers and experts finally resulted in the following formulation of the strategic challenge: 'How to source renewable energy, meeting 3P criteria'. In particular, an existing business case was selected as a case study, with the intention that any similar type of decision regarding energy sourcing could be treated in the same manner in the future. The existing business case had been set up internally for the sourcing of a US-based production facility by building a power plant consisting of solar panels. Relevant internal stakeholders were listed and approached. External stakeholders were represented via the Global Brand and Communications department. With this business case in mind, the next six steps were followed.

Defining key outputs involving stakeholders

Table 8.1 gives an overview of the key outputs, to which theme they relate and their definition.

The first three key outputs clearly address the Planet aspects of this business case. The key outputs that directly link to profit are energy cost and CAPEX, which are expressed in dollars (since the production facility is US-based). These financial – Profit-related – key outputs were also present in the existing business case. The People-related outputs can be seen as indirect effects that the type of energy sourcing may have. As such, this business case generalizes the existing financial business case to a triple bottom line business case. Productivity, financial result and revenues are not listed among the key outputs, even though literature indicates that the Planet and People aspects in Table 8.1 indirectly boost productivity (Lyubomirsky, King and Diener, 2005), financial result (Gallup, 2013) and revenue (Kossovsky, Greenberg and Brandegee, 2012). These three financial effects have been discussed and selected for the longlist of outputs. However, in order to make the decision-making process easier to manage, and because their effects could be mimicked by the employee engagement score and brand value anyway, they did not make it to the shortlist.

Determining decision maker's options

Recall from Chapter 2 that in order to formulate the decision maker's options, internal variable inputs must be formulated first. These inputs refer to the six choices that have to be made when sourcing energy:

1 *Make or buy?* The first decision awaiting the decision maker is a classical make-or-buy decision. If the decision maker makes energy, it is assumed that a solar plant is financed, set up and run by DSM, and the Renewable Energy Certificates (RECs) issued are kept by DSM in order to be able to declare the produced energy as being renewable energy (RE).

Table 8.1 Key output definitions for DSM case

Key output	Theme	Definition
RE %	Planet	Percentage of renewable electricity use of total energy usage of DSM at a specific power plant. Here, renewable electricity means that the electricity originates from non-fossil sources (renewable sources) and is accompanied by a Renewable Energy Certificate (REC).
Carbon footprint reduction	Planet	Reduction of emission of carbon dioxide, or its equivalent of other GHGs, for reporting purposes. Here, carbon footprint reduction may only be reported as such if the electricity originates from non-fossil sources and is accompanied by Renewable Energy Certificates (RECs).
Actual carbon emission	Planet	Actual emission of carbon dioxide, or its equivalent of other GHGs (tons). Here, actual means that this emission is measured regardless of whether it is accompanied by Renewable Energy Certificates (RECs).
Energy cost	Profit	Costs are expressed as energy usage (MWh) times cost of energy ($/MWh).
CAPEX	Profit	Capital Expenditure ($) for the construction of a power plant that produces RE.
Increase in employee engagement score	People	Increase in employee engagement as measured by yearly employee engagement surveys (%).
Increase in employee recommendation rate	People	Increase in the rate at which employees recommend DSM as an employer in a favourable way (%) due to an increase in employee engagement as measured by yearly employee engagement surveys.
Increase in Net Promotor Score	People	Increase in customer satisfaction as measured by the yearly Net Promotor Score (%).
Increase in brand value	People	Increase in brand value ($) due to carbon footprint reduction.

2 *Where to buy energy?* If energy is bought instead of made, it can be either bought from a partner or from the market. If a partner is involved, it is simply assumed that a partner is sought to finance, set up and run the

solar panel plant instead of DSM. This implies that the energy from a partner comes from a renewable source (RS).

3 *What type of energy to buy from market?* In case energy is bought from the market, the decision maker has the option to buy energy from a renewable source (RS) or to buy it from a non-renewable source (NRS). Energy from a non-renewable source will be referred to as grey energy or GE.

4 *How many RECs to buy?* The number of RECs to buy is limited to the number of RECs available. The decision maker may want to buy a number of RECs that does not correspond to the volume of energy from their RS.

5 *Where to buy RECs?* If the decision maker decides to buy RECs, the next question is where to buy them. The supplier can either be the partner or the market. We also included the option to optimize, ie choosing the cheapest supplier. It should be noted that in practice RECs can only be bought from a partner if energy is bought from the partner as well.

6 *What internal carbon price to use?* Finally, the decision maker can decide upon using an internal carbon price, which represents the internal charge for CO_{2e} emission.

This leads to seven internal variable inputs, which – together with their units – are listed in the first two columns of Table 8.2. Here, the unit % refers to the percentage of the total energy requirement of the production plant. The reference to the number of each choice is included as well. In the fifth choice, deciding upon where to buy RECs, there are three alternatives to choose from. This leads to two internal variable inputs, % REC partner and % REC market. The percentage of RECs that is bought according to the optimization strategy is then modelled as % REC – % REC Partner – % REC Market. By varying the settings of these internal variable inputs, we formulated six decision maker's options. The settings per option are listed in the latter six columns of Table 8.2.

Note that initially we set the internal carbon price to 0. The decision tree in Figure 8.1 displays the six choices graphically.

Drawing up scenarios

Historical prices of energy and certificates have been quite volatile. Therefore, the uncertainty in predicting these prices should be taken into account. In some territories CAPEX for RE production is incentivized by governments

Table 8.2   Specification of decision maker's options for DSM case

Internal variable input	Unit	Decision maker's options					
		No RE	No RS with REC	RS partner without REC	Market RE	Partner RE	Make RE
1. % RE make	%	0	0	0	0	0	50
2. % RS partner	%	0	0	50	0	50	0
3. % RS market	%	0	0	0	50	0	0
4. % REC	%	0	50	0	50	50	0
5a. % REC partner	%	0	0	0	0	50	0
5b. % RECs market	%	0	0	0	0	0	0
6. Internal Carbon Price	$	0	0	0	0	0	0

via subsidy and tax discount rates. These rates may vary as well. Just like energy prices, subsidies and tax discounts cannot be controlled by the decision maker. Therefore, these inputs were formulated as external variable inputs in order to account for the possible uncertainties in the outcomes of the decision. Finally, obtaining energy from renewable sources bought from the energy market instead of energy produced by the solar panel plant operated by DSM or the partner, which is located next to the production plant, is expected to have less impact on the two key outputs that refer to employees. This is because research tells us reading or hearing counts less than visual experience. Since there is a debate on the extent to which this effect applies, we defined this reduction factor as an external variable input.

Thus eight uncertainties were considered and their influence on key outputs monitored: the price of grey energy, the price of energy from renewable sources (RS) and REC prices (these both apply to the prices from the partner and from the market), the RE subsidy rate and RE tax discount rate as percentage of CAPEX, and the reduction factor that applies for a non-visual way of sourcing green energy. The prices are based on historical power purchase agreements with producers or suppliers.

Figure 8.1 Decision tree for energy sourcing in DSM case

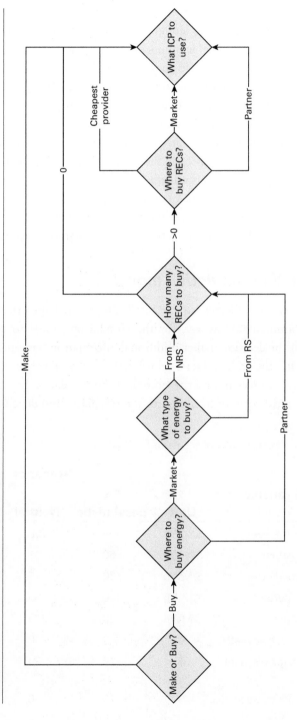

The uncertainties enabled us to draw up three scenarios. We have chosen the notions 'pessimistic' and 'optimistic' from the perspective of a decision maker that tends to use renewable energy (RE). All scenarios and corresponding values of the external variable inputs per scenario are displayed in Table 8.3.

The RE optimistic scenario may also be considered as the pessimistic scenario for a buyer that tends to use grey energy, namely that the price of grey energy becomes less attractive relative to the price of energy from renewable sources. Likewise, the RE pessimistic scenario is the optimistic scenario for the buyer of grey energy. Since the price of grey energy was initially not expected to fluctuate in this case, the comparison entails the relative difference between prices of energy from renewable sources and non-renewable sources. Even though the price of grey energy is fixed in this case, this can be different for another country and/or production plants. Therefore, this grey energy price is still considered to be an external variable input.

Constructing simulation model

The information collected so far has been inserted into the Responsible Business Simulator. However, for the simulation model to provide clear insights for the decision maker, additional information is required. In collaboration with the stakeholders, additional information has been collected from several sources in order to complete the simulation model. The information is in the form of fixed inputs, intermediates and dependencies.

Table 8.3   Specification of scenarios for DSM case

External variable input	Unit	Scenarios		
		RE pessimistic	Neutral	RE optimistic
Price NRS market	$/MWh	108	108	108
Price RS partner	$/MWh	60	51	40
Price RS market	$/MWh	130	115	90
Price REC partner	$/MWh	140	130	120
Price REC market	$/MWh	320	270	220
RE CAPEX subsidy rate	%	0	30	60
RE CAPEX tax discount rate	%	25	30	35
No visual observation reduction factor	%	70	80	90

Fixed inputs are inputs that typically remain constant during the decision-making process. Here, we distinguish internal fixed inputs from external fixed inputs depending on whether the decision maker is able to choose values for these inputs or not, respectively. Internal fixed inputs refer to the investment costs, the total energy demand and the capacity of the plant. An overview of these fixed inputs and their values, which are fictitious because of their competitively sensitive nature, are displayed in Table 8.4.

The external fixed inputs, their values and (public) sources are listed in Table 8.5.

The process of calculating key outputs from different types of inputs involves several steps. Intermediates store the results of these steps; they are used to make calculations easy and transparent and are based on inputs and/or other intermediates. Examples of intermediates are the number of certificates, the new employee engagement score and the percentage of grey energy per decision maker's option.

To illustrate a small part of the calculations, let us take a closer look at the percentage of renewable energy stored in the key output RE%. This percentage is calculated as follows:

$$RE\% = \%RE\ make + \min\ (\%RS\ partner + \%RS\ market, \%REC).$$

Table 8.4 Specification of (internal) fixed inputs for DSM case

Internal fixed input	Value	Unit	Source
Energy demand	30,000	MWh/year	(DO&RC, 2015) Note that data has been made fictitious for publication purposes.
Capacity RE make	15,000	MWh/year	(DO&RC, 2015) Note that data has been made fictitious for publication purposes.
Investment cost RE make	40,000,000	$	(DO&RC, 2015) Note that data has been made fictitious for publication purposes.
Capacity RS partner	15,000	MWh/year	(DO&RC, 2015) Note that data has been made fictitious for publication purposes.

Table 8.5 Specification of (external) fixed inputs for DSM case

External fixed input	Value	Unit	Source
CO_2 emission per MWh (uncorrected US emission factor)	0.676	tCO_2/MWh	(U.S. Energy Information Administration, 2007)
Effect of maximum carbon footprint reduction on employee engagement	1.73	%/tCO_2	(Vinerean, Cetina and Dumitrescu, 2013)
Effect of carbon footprint reduction on brand value	212	$/$tCO_2$	(Matsumura, Prakash and Vera-Muñoz, 2014)
Effect of using an internal carbon price on employee engagement	1.73	%	(Vinerean, Cetina and Dumitrescu, 2013)
Engaged employee recommendation rate	78	%	(KPMG, 2011)
Disengaged employee recommendation rate	13	%	(KPMG, 2011)
Effect of employee engagement on customer satisfaction	10	%	(Gallup, 2013)
Current employee engagement score	70	%	(DSM, 2014)
Current Net Promotor Score	36	%	(DSM, 2014)

This formula adds the percentage of the total energy demand that is sourced by DSM's own solar panel plant to the sourcing from the market and the partner. The minimum operator in the formula assures that only energy from renewable sources accompanied by certificates is counted as renewable energy.

Evaluating options by assessing strategic priorities

Having inserted all required inputs, outputs and information from desk and field research into the Responsible Business Simulator, the decision maker can easily evaluate which option is the 'best' by assigning strategic priorities. Hereby, we assume the neutral scenario. Strategic priorities are expressed by assigning weights to key outputs. From the various settings that have been considered, we will highlight three.

First, we will consider a decision maker who only assigns (equal) weights to the key outputs 'cost of energy' and 'CAPEX' and does not apply an internal carbon price. The decision maker's option 'RS partner without REC', which corresponds to buying energy from a renewable source via a partner without buying any of the associated certificates, is the best-performing option. Intuitively, one might expect that 'No RE' would be the best strategy in this case since grey energy is normally cheaper than energy from a renewable source. However, from Table 8.3 we know that the price of grey energy is higher than that of energy from the partner. The reason for this is the agreement between DSM and the partner: land is made available by DSM for the partner. Also, DSM's fixed energy demand is guaranteed to the partner. This results in a low energy price from the partner for DSM. However, when applying DSM's principles of not buying energy from renewable sources without buying the accompanying certificates, the 'No RE' option would be the best strategy from a pure cost aspect; the costs of buying RECs from the partner as well makes this option more expensive then the option to buy grey energy from the grid.

Second, we consider the situation in which there is still a focus on profit-related key outputs only, but a non-zero internal carbon price is added to the equation. In the neutral scenario it turns out that the option to source energy via the partner including RECs is beating the 'No RE' option as soon as the internal carbon price exceeds \$108.

Finally, we assume that the decision maker considers all key outputs equally important, meaning that they account for People and Planet next

Figure 8.2 Comparison of decision maker's options when all key outputs have equal weights in the neutral scenario for DSM case

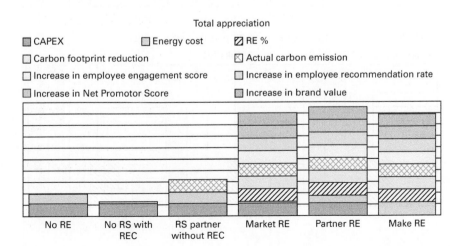

to the usual Profit aspects. Even without taking into account any internal carbon price, buying renewable energy including the certificates from a partner is the recommended strategy. This can be deduced from Figure 8.2, where the second-best strategy is buying RE from the market, followed by making RE. This should be no surprise as these are the three options that account for more than just profit aspects.

The evaluation of the three situations as described above implies that when all aspects are evaluated in a decision-making process, the decision maker is supported in making a balanced decision, weighing People, Planet and Profit dimensions. If there is only a profit-oriented business case available and time does not permit a full evaluation, then including an internal carbon price in the business case already enables the decision maker to account for more than profit-only aspects in an efficient way.

Evaluating options by assessing risk appetite

Risk appetite is indicated by assigning weights to scenarios. Figure 8.3 displays for each scenario a comparison of the decision maker's options where all key outputs are weighed equally. It can be deduced that the more weight is attributed to the RE optimistic scenario, the more attractive the Make RE option becomes. However, if all scenarios are weighted equally, representing the search for a robust strategy, the option to partner is still the preferred option.

When focusing on profit-related key outputs only, but investigating the effect of internal carbon price, it turns out that in the RE pessimistic

Figure 8.3 Comparison of decision maker's options when all key outputs have equal weights for all scenarios for DSM case

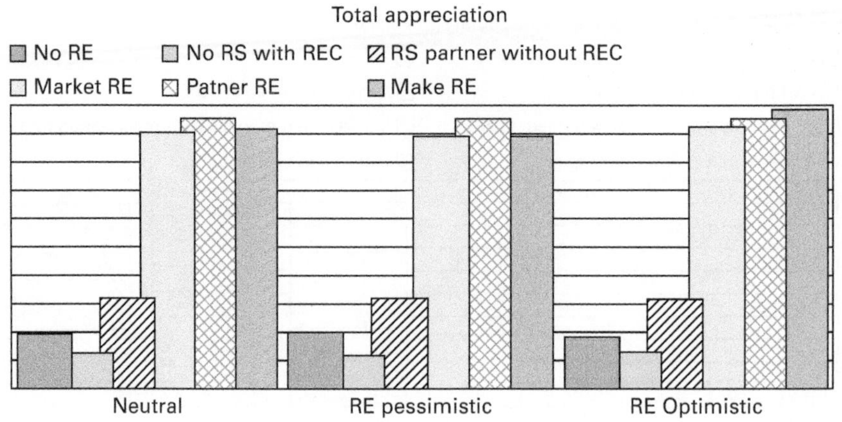

Total appreciation

☐ No RE   ☐ No RS with REC   ☒ RS partner without REC
☐ Market RE   ☒ Patner RE   ☐ Make RE

Neutral   RE pessimistic   RE Optimistic

scenario, the option to buy grey energy from the grid is the recommended strategy until the internal carbon price exceeds $137. In the RE optimistic scenario, grey energy from the grid is the recommended strategy until the price exceeds $78. Thus the minimum value of the internal carbon price to favour a more sustainable decision declines as the decision maker becomes less risk averse towards a declining trend in prices of renewable energy. This implies that when a decision maker is RE pessimistic they expect grey energy to be relatively cheaper than renewable energy. In that case there is a higher fine needed to compensate for the difference between the prices of grey and renewable energy.

Reflections

The importance of integrating sustainability into the corporate strategy has been recognized by DSM for a long time. The outcomes of the United Nations Climate Change Conference in Paris (United Nations, 2015) as well as the large amount of research and publications (McKinsey, 2011; Nidumolu, Simmons and Yosie, 2015) confirm their rationale that doing business in a sustainable way is a prerequisite for business continuity.

The execution, however, requires a mind shift for many multinational companies. Even for companies that already deal with more aspects than just Profit, like DSM, eye-openers can still be created via the Responsible Business Simulator. For the case using fictitious data described here, an internal carbon price turns out to be necessary to favour energy from renewable sources over non-renewable sources for an organization that only focuses on profit-related aspects. The fact that the internal carbon price needs to exceed values ranging from $78 to $137, depending on the risk appetite, before a more sustainable decision is made illustrates the great difference in price between grey and renewable energy.

Since the described strategic decision-making process at DSM was a multi-competency collaboration within the organization, previously described processes supported the already ongoing discussion of using an internal carbon price to evolve to a balanced and fact-based dialogue, which finally resulted in the introduction of an internal carbon price at DSM.

DSM considers the introduction of an internal carbon price as a step forward in the process of accounting for externalities in their decision-making process.

References

Brander, M et al (2011) Electricity-specific emission factors for grid electricity, *Ecometrica*. Retrieved from https://ecometrica.com/white-papers/electricity-specific-emission-factors-for-grid-electricity

Carbon Disclosure Project (2013) *Use of Internal Carbon Price by Companies as Incentive and Strategic Planning Tool*, CDP North America

Carbon Disclosure Project (2015) *Putting a Price on Risk: Carbon pricing in the corporate world*, CDP North America

Carbon Disclosure Project (2016) *Embedding a Carbon Price Into Business Strategy*, CDP North America

DO&RC (2015) *Internal documentation*. DSM Operations and Responsible Care, Heerlen.

DSM (2014) *Royal DSM Integrated Annual Report 2014*. Retrieved from https://www.dsm.com/content/dam/dsm/cworld/en_US/documents/dsm-integrated-annual-report-2014.pdf

DSM (2016a) DSM named leader in Dow Jones Sustainability World Index. Retrieved from https://www.dsm.com/corporate/media/informationcenter-news/2016/09/37-16-dsm-named-leader-in-dow-jones-sustainability-world-index.html

DSM (2016b) Markets. Retrieved from http://www.dsm.com/corporate/markets-products/markets.html

Dutch Ministry of Economic Affairs (2010) Protocol monitoring hernieuwbare energie update 2010. Retrieved from https://www.rvo.nl/sites/default/files/bijlagen/Protocol%20Monitoring%20Hernieuwbare%20

Edelman (2016) AkzoNobel, DSM, Google en Philips werken samen aan lange termijn duurzame energiedoelstellingen, *Persberichten*. Retrieved from http://www.persberichten.com/persbericht/87109/AkzoNobel-DSM-Google-en-Philips-werken-samen-aan-lange-termijn-duurzame-energiedoelstellingen

European Parliament (2009) Directive 2009/28/EC of the European Parliament and of the Council of 23 April 2009 on the promotion of the use of energy from renewable sources and amending and subsequently repealing Directives 2001/77/EC and 2003/30/EC, *Official Journal of the European Union*, **140**, Article 2

Fortune (2016) The Fortune 2016 Change the World list. Retrieved from http://beta.fortune.com/change-the-world/list

Gallup (2013) *State of the Global Workplace*, Gallup, Washington D.C.

Global Reporting Initiative (2013) *Sustainability Reporting Guidelines*, Global Reporting Initiative, Amsterdam

Kossovsky, N, Greenberg, M and Brandegee, R (2012) *Reputation, Stock Price, and You: Why the market rewards some companies and punishes others*, Apress, New York

KPMG (2011) The real value of engaged employees. Retrieved from https://www.kpmg.com/US/en/home/insights.html

Lyubomirsky, S, King, L and Diener, E (2005) The benefits of frequent positive affect: does happiness lead to success? *Psychological Bulletin*, **131** (6), pp. 803–55

Matsumura, E, Prakash, R and Vera-Muñoz, S (2014) Firm-value effects of carbon emissions and carbon disclosures, *The Accounting Review*, **89** (2), pp. 695–724

McKinsey (2011) The business of sustainability: McKinsey Global Survey results. Retrieved from http://www.mckinsey.com/business-functions/sustainability-and-resource-productivity/our-insights/the-business-of-sustainability-mckinsey-global-survey-results

Nidumolu, R, Simmons, P and Yosie, T (2015) *Sustainability and the CEO: Challenges, opportunities and next practices*. Retrieved from http://www.corporateecoforum.com/wp-content/uploads/2015/04/CFO_and_Sustainability_Apr-2015.pdf

Reliable Disclosure Systems (2015) Improving significantly the reliability and accuracy of the information given to consumers of electricity in Europe. Retrieved from http://www.reliable-disclosure.org/ Energie%20Update%20 2010%20DEN.pdf

U.S. Energy Information Administration (2007) *Voluntary Reporting of Greenhouse Gases*. Retrieved from https://www.eia.gov/oiaf/1605/pdf/ Appendix%20F_r071023.pdf

United Nations (2015) *Paris Agreement*. Retrieved from http://unfccc.int/files/meetings/paris_nov_2015/application/pdf/paris_agreement_english_.pdf

Vinerean, S, Cetina, I and Dumitrescu, L (2013) Modeling employee satisfaction in relation to CSR practices and attraction and retention of top talent, *Expert Journal of Business and Management*, pp. 4–14

Wright, L, Kemp, S and Williams, I (2011) 'Carbon footprinting': towards a universally accepted definition, *Carbon Management*, **2** (1), pp. 61–72

Putting roof renovation in a strategic context

09

This chapter illustrates the application of strategic decision making in the case of the NEMO Science Museum in Amsterdam. We will start by introducing this science museum in the context of Making strategic decisions to benefit people, the planet and profits.

About NEMO

The NEMO Science Museum (NEMO for short) aspires to be the biggest and most entertaining science centre in the Netherlands. With its five floors full of interactive, interesting things to do and discover, it is the place more than 500,000 people go to every year to be introduced to science and technology in a playful manner. For the education sector, NEMO is the biggest interactive non-school-like informal learning environment and is part of many educational programmes relating to science and engineering. NEMO also organizes training programmes for teachers and has intensive exchange programmes with an international network of science centres. The science museum is housed in a prominent building above the entrance to the IJ lake tunnel, one of the main roads into the city centre of Amsterdam. It was designed by the Italian architect Renzo Piano. He considered Amsterdam to be a 'flat city', in contrast to many other metropoles, since it lacked high and prominent viewpoints. He designed the building to look like a ship rising from the IJ lake, with the roof of the museum representing the ship's deck. The roof is accessible to the public, finally providing Amsterdam with a high viewpoint and the highest elevated square in Europe.

NEMO aims to be a sustainable cultural enterprise and is doing pioneering work to draw attention to technology and innovation in the field of sustainability. 'Walking the talk' makes NEMO eminently suitable for showcasing to the public how it is applying technology in innovative ways to make its own operational management more sustainable and work towards a circular economy. This consists of both energy-saving measures and the decision-making process in which the measures are decided upon.

About renovating NEMO's roof

Ever since the NEMO building was finished in 1997, there have been problems with the roof. As such, NEMO's roof plays a key part in this case study. Recurring leaks have required complicated and expensive repairs and the roof also falls short of the current insulation standards for this type of public building. Therefore, a few years ago, the board of directors and the supervisory board decided to build up an additional contingency fund to enable a structural solution to be found for the problems that beset the roof. Sufficient funds have been set aside and the various options for repairs were being investigated.

During this investigation, in which NEMO's own maintenance staff were being assisted by external experts from an engineering consultancy firm, the question arose whether or not it would be desirable to re-evaluate the function of the roof. The roof already housed the Splashing Water Wonder playground and people could enjoy the view of the city. The board of directors was considering the possibility of letting the roof play a prominent part in the NEMO GREEN programme. This programme is dedicated to doing everything with regards to the Triple Bottom Line that is technically, organizationally and financially possible to make NEMO the most progressive, sustainable cultural enterprise in Amsterdam.

A plan was devised to not only recoat and re-insulate NEMO's roof, but to also have it house an experimental roof garden and a power-generating system. The roof garden would have a good insulating effect; in addition, it would clean the air and rainwater and put visitors in contact with nature. In its capacity as a power generator, the roof would offer the opportunity for companies to demonstrate new developments, for visitors to learn about alternative sources of energy and, on top of that, the chance to supply the building itself with energy.

As is usual with such propositions, a business case was drawn up to see whether the required investments would yield sufficient returns. The report, which was drawn up with the help of external consultants (Hommersen and Kasteel, 2010), compared the costs required for realization and operation with the estimated savings on energy. The comparison concluded with the following remark: 'Moreover, additional revenue can be generated by attracting more visitors. The business case refrains from making any statements on this matter as it cannot be quantified.' Because of this rider, it is possible that an important aspect of the decision-making process has been ignored. This leads to the question of whether or not traditional, financially driven methods for evaluating business cases are still applicable in a world which demands more and more accountability in the domains of People and Planet next to Profit.

The purpose of strategic decision making, and the application of the Responsible Business Simulator in particular, is precisely to quantify the People and Planet aspects and make them comparable to the Profit aspects. It is of particular importance for NEMO, where profit maximization is not a primary goal, to be able to evaluate complex scenarios and compare financial and non-financial indicators with each other. The primary goal of the application of the Responsible Business Simulator was to advise the board of directors and the supervisory board as to which choice for repairing and arranging the roof would best satisfy all of NEMO's stakeholders' wishes. In other words, to give an underpinned answer to the question of 'How to renovate a roof'. The secondary goal was to gain experience in making this form of sustainable decision making more transparent, such that it can be eventually be shared with NEMO's visitors.

The strategic decision-making process

For the development of the strategic decision-making process at NEMO, we worked with a team that represented a cross-section of the personnel. With their own respective expertise, they took an active part in setting out the strategy and providing material for the simulation. Their knowledge of various parts of the organization, in combination with the active support of the directors, not only resulted in a meaningful strategic dialogue but also gathered a large quantity of useful data. The input of NEMO's team proved to be a good example of the ideal way to work. The successive outcomes of the simulation model were compared and analysed carefully. Because of this, key outputs could be refined and new ones could be entered, and factual data could be brought into the strategic dialogue in a meaningful way. By working like this, the NEMO team was surprised at how far they could go in making the roof more sustainable. The plans might have started tentatively, but they eventually ended in a completely new design from architect Renzo Piano for an advanced climate-neutral roof with an even more pronounced public function, including an overview of sustainable energy-generating methods, a sustainable stairwell that provides its own power and light, a restaurant, and a new layout for the roof's upper section. The combination of action research and strategic decision making worked out well for NEMO and resulted in a good strategic plan. At the time of writing, most parts of this plan have been realized or are in the stage of being implemented.

Describing strategic challenge that requires a decision

As mentioned in the introduction, NEMO's board of directors and the supervisory board built up a contingency fund to enable finding a structural solution for the problems that beset the roof. At the same time they considered the possibility of giving the roof a prominent role in the NEMO GREEN programme with the aim of doing everything that is technically, organizationally and financially possible to make NEMO the most progressive, sustainable cultural enterprise in Amsterdam. The hypothesis is that by investing in the People and Planet aspects, positive effects will occur as a bonus on the Profit side. The purpose of using strategic decision making has been formulated as follows: empowering NEMO to obtain insight into the optimal decision regarding a sustainable repair of their roof and sharing this insight with its stakeholders.

Defining key outputs

Even though NEMO's board made the final decision on how to repair the roof, the multiple stakeholders of this cultural enterprise were key in the decision-making process. With the objective of a sustainable repair of the roof in mind, in collaboration with NEMO's staff, we started by listing NEMO's stakeholders and their qualitative interests. We then operationalized the extent to which those interests could be served: in other words, we made them quantitatively measurable. This resulted in a list of over 30 outputs, which was subsequently reduced to a shortlist of just eight key outputs.

Table 9.1 gives an overview of the key outputs, which theme they relate to, and the stakeholders involved. Here, we have broken down the profit theme into CAPEX and other.

Determining decision maker's options

Recall from Chapter 2 that in order to formulate the decision maker's options, internal variable inputs must be formulated first. Therefore, we looked at the different sub-decisions awaiting the decision maker. We divided

Table 9.1 Key output definitions for NEMO case

Key output	Unit	Theme	Stakeholders
Increase in customer satisfaction, where customer satisfaction is measured as report mark on a scale 0-10	.	People	Customers, media and the Dutch Ministry of Education, Culture & Science
Increase in landmark value, where landmark value is measured as report mark on a scale 0-10	.	People	Local residents, the city of Amsterdam and the media; primarily involves the People aspect
Energy savings measured in kilowatt-hours per year	kWh / year	Planet	Media and suppliers
Energy savings measured in € per year	€ / year	Profit (Other)	Management
Additional revenues from admission tickets, measured in € per year	€ / year	Profit (Other)	Employees and management (in order to guarantee continuity)
Additional restaurant revenues	€ / year	Profit (Other)	Employees and management (in order to guarantee continuity)
Capital expenditure (CAPEX)	€ / year	Profit (CAPEX)	Management
Operational expenditure (OPEX)	€ / year	Profit (Other)	Management

the freedom of choice for the new layout of the roof into three types of decision. First, there is the choice of whether or not to repair the current roof. Second, there is the option to further insulate the roof. Third, a decision has to be taken about the layout of the roof. For this last decision, we split the roof into three sections: the lower roof (2,800 m²), the upper roof (1,200 m²), and the roof of the existing restaurant ('bar roof', 250 m²). Figure 9.1 shows an impression of the roof.

The visitors' terrace originally takes up most of the lower roof area. The precondition for this terrace is that its minimum area be 1,800 m². Because of the building's support structure, such a terrace can only be located on the lower roof. In accordance with the engineers' report, this leaves three possible arrangements for the roof: wind turbines (which can

Figure 9.1 NEMO's roof. The upper roof is the higher, rounded section

only be placed on the upper roof due to the wind), a garden, and solar panels. In addition to two types of wind turbines from the manufacturers Skystream and Montana, we considered the so-called PowerPlane from the manufacturer Ampyx Power. We considered the option of making a visitors' walkway on the upper roof, so that visitors could see the wind turbines, the PowerPlanes, the garden and the solar panels at close quarters. We have assumed that the garden will provide additional insulation and also offer greater recreational value.

Based on these choices, we defined 13 internal variable inputs, two of which indicate whether or not the lower and upper roofs should be repaired. Two further internal variable inputs determine whether or not these sections of the roof should receive additional insulation. A separate internal variable input determines whether or not there will be a visitors' walkway. Up until this point all internal variable inputs can be categorized as binary, implying that the decision maker has a choice between intervening or not. Two additional internal variable inputs represent the surface area (in m²) to be laid out as garden on the lower and upper roofs. Three more internal variable inputs indicate the number of square meters of solar panels for each roof section. The final three internal variable inputs indicate the number of wind turbines from Skystream (Xzeres, 2016), Montana (National Centre for Appropriate Technology, 2016) and/or Ampyx (Ampyx Power, 2016).

At a later stage, six more internal variable inputs were added to the simulation model. These inputs did not originate from the engineers' report, but were based on Renzo Piano's ideas; he became more and more involved in the decision-making process as time went by. The first two are binary and concern a new accommodation for the restaurant facilities based on his own innovative tent-shaped design called the Piano tent, and a separate elevator for direct access to the roof. The third and fourth concern the extent to which the lower and upper roofs can be covered in a step-like planting pattern on which visitors can sit if they wish. The fifth additional input represents the presence of solar panels that can also be used as benches. The sixth concerns the instalment of Renzo Piano's innovative wind turbine design called the Piano mill. All in all, this resulted in a total of 19 internal variable inputs.

Making use of the different internal variable inputs, it was decided to work out the implications of six decision maker's options. The first option was to simply do nothing. The second was to only repair the roof. The third, fourth and fifth options consisted of repairing and insulating the roof along with a new layout focused on the garden, on wind and solar energy, and on a combination of both in accordance with the options described in the engineers' report. The sixth option was the relatively capital-intensive option of implementing Renzo Piano's ideas. For each non-trivial option, the number of square meters for each zone of the roof was input into the Responsible Business Simulator. Table 9.2 shows an overview of the internal variable inputs mapped onto the six decision maker's options.

Drawing up scenarios

Next to inputs that can be controlled by the decision maker, external variable inputs were formulated to account for exogenous uncertainties. This enabled us to draw up scenarios. We initially considered four sources of uncertainty that we wanted to monitor for their influence on the key outputs. The first external variable input was the energy price, which was used to translate the value of energy generated by the solar panels and wind turbines, and the energy saved by additional insulation, into monetary terms. The second was the factor translating the increase in customer satisfaction into additional visitors. The third was the equivalent of the second, but in terms of an increase in landmark value. The final uncertainty was the extent to which the suppliers of the wind turbines, solar panels and PowerPlanes might be willing to sponsor the purchase, considering that the placement of these systems would be an advertisement for their products.

Later on, a fifth external variable input was added to determine the relative effect that the direct elevator to the roof would have on restaurant revenues. This concerned a factor by which we could multiply our initial

Table 9.2 Specification of decision maker's options for NEMO case

Internal variable input	Decision maker's options					
	Do nothing	Just repair	Gardening	Energy	Mix	Renzo Piano
Piano tent						1 @ bar roof
Gardening			1150 m² @ upper roof 1000 m² @ lower roof		505 m² @ upper roof 500 m² @ lower roof	
Planter steps						1130 m² @ upper roof 600 m² @ lower roof
Visitor path			Yes	Yes	Yes	
PV field (solar panel)				1110 m² @ upper roof 300 m² @ bar roof 1000 m² @ lower roof	505 m² @ upper roof 300 m² @ bar roof 500 m² @ lower roof	
PV steps						1670 m² @ lower roof
Montana windmills				2 @ upper roof	2 @ upper roof	
SkyStream windmills				2 @ upper roof	2 @ upper roof	
Ampyx power planes				1 @ upper roof	1 @ upper roof	
Piano mills						2 @ upper roof
Roof repair		1 @ upper roof 1 @ lower roof		1 @ upper roof 1 @ lower roof	1 @ upper roof 1 @ lower roof	1 @ upper roof 1 @ lower roof
Extra insulation			1 @ upper roof 1 @ lower roof	1 @ upper roof 1 @ lower roof	1 @ upper roof 1 @ lower roof	1 @ upper roof 1 @ lower roof
External elevator						1 @ bar roof

estimate of this effect in order to do justice to the inherent uncertainty that surrounds the revenues of such an unusual elevator-accessed restaurant. Another reason for this separate assessment was that this revenue is not connected to additional restaurant revenues from users paying to visit the science museum, since the elevator enables direct access to the restaurant without visiting the museum.

Besides a base-case scenario, both an optimistic scenario and a pessimistic scenario were defined. Table 9.3 illustrates how the uncertainty of the external variable inputs finds expression in wide variations in the figures across the scenarios.

Constructing simulation model

The information collected so far was inserted into the Responsible Business Simulator. However, for the simulation model to provide accurate and clear insights to the decision maker, quite an amount of additional information was required. In collaboration with the stakeholders, we collected this additional information via desk research from several sources and completed the model. We distinguish fixed inputs, intermediates and dependencies, which we will now look at.

Table 9.3 Specification of external variable inputs for NEMO case

External variable input	Unit	Scenarios		
		Pessimistic	**Base case**	**Optimistic**
Price	€/kWh	€0.05	€0.06	€0.07
Increase in annual number of visitors per unit increase in customer satisfaction measured on a scale 0-10	# / year	125	150	500
Increase in annual number of visitors per unit increase in landmark value measured on a scale 0-10	# / year	100	250	400
Share of CAPEX covered by sponsoring (only for innovative energy-saving investments)	.	60%	75%	100%
Influence of elevator on restaurant revenues	.	0%	20%	60%

Fixed inputs are inputs that – in principle – are not modified during the decision-making process. Most of these are straightforward and will not be mentioned here. However, to illustrate the use of fixed inputs, here are some examples:

- costs of repairing the roof sections and fitting extra insulation;
- costs of purchase and maintenance for the three types of layouts for the roof;
- footprint of the wind turbines, PowerPlanes and Piano mills;
- average restaurant revenue and admission revenue per additional visitor;
- expected costs to remedy damage resulting from the roof not being repaired;
- expected energy savings in kWh per type of investment;
- effects of investments on customer satisfaction and landmark value.

The first four fixed inputs can be determined relatively accurately as they are predictable and more or less in control. The fifth and sixth are beyond the direct control of management, but were not deemed influential enough to be promoted to external variable inputs. Assessing the effects of investments on customer satisfaction and landmark value was a challenging task. We made these assessments by consulting NEMO on the variation in customer satisfaction as determined in surveys carried out during earlier exhibitions, and by thoroughly examining previous surveys on brand awareness. Instead of listing values of all fixed inputs, we only cite their sources. All technical data concerning repairs, insulation, purchase costs and maintenance costs of energy-saving measures – gardening, wind turbines and solar panels – was taken from the engineers' report. This report also gives expected energy savings for each wind turbine, each square metre of solar panels and each square meter of garden. For the layout of the garden, a distinction is made between extensive and intensive gardening. We have simply assumed that when a part of the roof is used as a garden, 70 per cent of its area will be extensive gardening and 30 per cent intensive gardening. The costs and expected energy yield of the PowerPlanes and the footprint needed for the investments in wind energy were looked up via desk research. The expected costs to repair damage resulting from not repairing the roof and the average revenues per visitor were easily determined on the basis of historical data held by NEMO.

To keep the calculations of key outputs based on the internal variable inputs, external variable inputs and fixed inputs easy and transparent, these have been broken down into several steps. Intermediates store the results of these steps; they are based on inputs and potentially on other intermediates as well. Formulating intermediates helps to pinpoint the influence each investment has on CAPEX, OPEX, customer satisfaction and landmark value, and how those influences in turn result in more visitors and more revenues. The intermediates formulated for NEMO depend on roof application, time or both.

Next, the way in which inputs, intermediates and outputs are mutually dependent is defined. Most of these relationships are straightforward due to the breakdown of the calculations in small steps via the introduction of intermediates. These dependencies have been fed into the Responsible Business Simulator in the form of a matrix as described in Chapter 7. We will not discuss this whole process, but restrict ourselves to some examples. The expected incremental effects on customer satisfaction and landmark value for each unit of investment in wind turbines, PowerPlanes, Piano mills, visitors' walkway, roof garden and solar panels have been modelled as linear elasticity; for each additional unit of investment, the key outputs will increase to an extent that is dependent on the kind of investment and the current level of investment. Another part of the model consists of a number of validation rules or safety measures to prevent assigning impossible combinations of values to internal variable inputs. For example, this prevents defining decision maker's options that would create a layout for the roof that is too cramped and full. The financial part of the simulation model closely resembles a traditional discounted cash flow model, with the time horizon set to 10 years and the discount rate set to 10 per cent.

After setting up these fixed inputs, intermediates and dependencies, the simulation model is ready to calculate the values of the key output per decision maker's option per scenario. This results in 8 × 6 × 3 (# key outputs × # decision maker's options × # scenarios) = 144 key output values, supplemented by values of intermediates. In order to validate the feasibility of these outcomes, we studied the graphs and tables containing various representations of this data set extensively. We also analysed the sensitivity of the outcomes for variations in the inputs, especially for those inputs that had no unequivocal source. This demonstrated that the decision maker's option to do nothing was burdened significantly by the increase in OPEX because of repairing water damage. This stage of interpretation also helped to formulate the five other options, as well as draw up the three scenarios shown in Table 9.3. These interpretations also showed that the visitors' walkway was not very profitable because of the relatively high costs associated with the additional constructional features required for the upper roof. The wind turbines were relatively unprofitable as well, due to the number of square meters required for safety margins in proportion to visitors' appreciation; moreover, the roof is not high enough for relatively small, cheap wind turbines to suffice. The model did, however, make a relatively high estimation for the additional restaurant revenues attributable to providing direct access to the roof. This estimation was further justified as it lowers the threshold for visiting the science museum after one has already visited the roof free of charge by means of a direct elevator to a spectacular restaurant. This analysis is an example of how the model was refined iteratively, because the correlation between elevator and restaurant revenues was originally not included in the set of external variable inputs.

Evaluating options by assessing strategic priorities

Having inserted all required inputs, outputs and information from desk and field research into the Responsible Business Simulator, the decision maker could easily evaluate which option is the 'best' by assigning strategic priorities to the key outputs. As in this case the key outputs were condensed into themes, NEMO's board could decide upon a 'best strategy' by assigning strategic priority to the three different themes. Table 9.1 gives a clear overview of how the key outputs are mapped onto the themes.

Figure 9.2 shows the contribution of all themes to the total appreciation of the decision maker's option for the base-case scenario. Let us first look at the lower two parts of the bars, meaning that we only focus on profit aspects. When determining the best option we see that it is a close call between the option to do nothing and the option to just repair the roof. In the first option there is no CAPEX but there are periodic repair costs. The latter option has CAPEX but performs better on OPEX, due to lower periodic repair costs and a lower energy bill. The other options perform worse because they require even more CAPEX and also some additional OPEX to maintain the additional facilities built on top of the roof, which is apparently not compensated yet by additional revenues from these facilities.

However, if we also take into account the upper parts of the bars in Figure 9.2, meaning that we give equal weight to all four themes, then we conclude that the mixed option outperforms the other option, closely followed by the Renzo Piano option. We also see that Gardening is a cheaper option than Energy, Mix and Renzo Piano, but also has less impact on People and Planet.

Evaluating options by assessing risk appetite

Up until now we have not accounted for the uncertainties that go hand in hand with the modelling process. In order to include the uncertainties in

Figure 9.2 Comparison of decision maker's options when all themes have equal weights in the base-case scenario for NEMO case

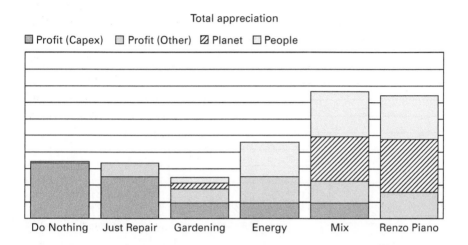

Total appreciation

☐ Profit (Capex) ☐ Profit (Other) ▨ Planet ☐ People

Do Nothing   Just Repair   Gardening   Energy   Mix   Renzo Piano

our evaluation to determine which decision maker's option is the 'best', we need to indicate a risk appetite as well as assigning strategic priorities to the themes. For example, if only the Profit themes are prioritized, the combination mix and the Renzo Piano option outperform the other decision maker's options in the optimistic scenario, since in that scenario we have an optimistic view on additional revenues from both the restaurant and admission tickets by attracting more visitors.

Figure 9.3 illustrates the performance of the various decision maker's options for the pessimistic, base-case and optimistic scenarios when all profit-related key outputs are deemed equally important. We see that the mixed option is the preferred option in the pessimistic scenario. In the base-case and optimistic scenarios the 'Renzo Piano' option is not only the best option from a profit-only perspective but also from a triple bottom line perspective.

Therefore, it transpired that the formulated decision maker's options differed considerably in their contributions and that all these contributions were also heavily dependent on the risk appetite of the decision maker.

Based on these evaluations, NEMO decided to build a restaurant on the roof that can host 300 visitors, and which can be accessed with the elevator from the main hall without it being necessary to enter the science centre itself. Initially it was thought that a new elevator had to be built to make it possible to enter the restaurant without entering the science centre, but in fact it could be achieved by turning the elevator around 180 degrees. Since

Figure 9.3 Comparison of decision maker's options when weight is assigned only to theme 'Profit' for all scenarios for NEMO case

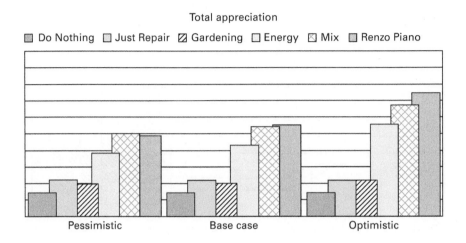

Total appreciation

☐ Do Nothing ☐ Just Repair ☑ Gardening ☐ Energy ☒ Mix ☐ Renzo Piano

the opening of the restaurant, revenues per visitor from hospitality have tripled. Furthermore, green roofing (or, as it is called further in this chapter, a garden) has been arranged in a way that keeps the restaurant cooler. Special roof insulation will soon be installed to further regulate temperatures inside the building. Next to bigger implementations, small adjustments such as automatic light switches in the toilets also work towards substantial energy savings.

Reflections

As we facilitated a series of sessions on strategic decision making, we were able to observe the process closely. During the first session, when the Responsible Business Simulator represented little more than a very high-level prototype simulation model, it was noticeable that participants were still really keen to start expanding on this model. They seemed to feel that this was possible, right from the start. Participants already knew that a great deal of data was available in the domains of finance, marketing and accommodation, and that this data had never been interlinked to support integrated decision making.

The longlist of key outputs from the initial examination proved to be very extensive indeed. This was mainly because NEMO is a socially-committed organization, and there are many stakeholders whose perspectives all have to be taken into account. The first session involved a group of participants from a wide variety of disciplines, and this proved beneficial when apprais-ing the interests of all those stakeholders. Unfortunately, the task of reducing the longlist to a shortlist and operationalizing the remaining key outputs could not be undertaken as a plenary process, but had to be split up into smaller working parties because the time allotted for the workshop simply flew by.

The variety of disciplines represented at the first sessions unlocked a treasure trove of information in the form of reports, system printouts and personal experiences that were very useful when refining the prototype model into the first 'real' version. This did much to underpin the credibility of the figures presented during the second workshop with members of the board. There was, admittedly, still some uncertainty about various crucial external variable inputs and fixed inputs, but the figures that were presented were thoroughly substantiated. The integrated approach of taking all three P aspects together also forestalled any tendency to take a 'penny wise pound foolish' approach. It was quickly obvious that there was little added value to be gained from deliberating over the enormous pile of data about wind speeds at heights of 80 metres in Amsterdam to make an estimation of the power that could be generated if wind turbines were to be located on the roof, because – although a thorough study still had to be carried out – it was already clear that scenic value would probably have a greater positive effect on visitor numbers.

The facilitator of the workshop found it simple enough to ensure that each participant could contribute, as long as he could be sure he knew which discipline that participant represented. It is easy enough, for instance, to query the validity and accuracy of an estimate for an external variable input or fixed input in the domain of expertise and so re-engage with a participant who looks ready to pull out. It might then be possible to convert the sceptic who seems to have little faith in the approach by inviting them to add extra stress scenarios or by giving them some influence in the decision-making process in another way. Last but not least, it proved to be easy to expand the simulation model when Renzo Piano suggested alternatives for the options that had been described in the engineers' report.

The added value of this new way of conducting the decision-making process does not lie solely in the fact that NEMO can now make a detailed calculation of the value of each key output score for each alternative strat-egy. More importantly, strategic decision making demonstrated that an issue that seemed to be the responsibility of the technical department – because it concerned a leaking roof – turned out to have far wider implications; it soon expanded to encompass the strategic decision-making process about a substantial expansion of the public function of the centre. In addition, it may also give rise to new revenue models, as the roof will be accessible and usable even outside NEMO's normal opening hours. A restaurant on the roof that can be accessed via an elevator has been incorporated into the plans and, at the time of writing, already has been built.

It was not, of course, possible to carry out all of those plans straightaway, but NEMO took the opportunity in the summer of 2013 to increase the green value of the roof and it is very clear that the ambitious suggestions for further 'greening' supplied by the infectiously enthusiastic Renzo Piano have excited the imagination. By 2016, almost all plans had already been executed and the restaurant is a great success. It is open to the public without the need to buy a museum ticket, and creates a new free space with a fantastic view for Amsterdam's citizens and visitors. To date, the restaurant on the green roof has created substantial increase in revenue from hospitality. Interestingly, the NEMO team's proposal convinced both the board of directors and the supervisory board that investment in the roof would have an added value, and they gave approval for a further elaboration of the architect's plans. These successes speak volumes. All in all, they demonstrate that it is certainly possible and worthwhile, in the interests of sustainable decision making, to quantify the impact that uncertain effects can have on combinations of the various aspects of People, Planet and Profit.

References

Ampyx Power (2016) Energy of the future. Retrieved from http://www.ampyxpower.com/

Hommersen, M and Kasteel, R (2010) Business case 'roof' [Business case dak], commissioned by the NEMO Green working party

National Centre for Appropriate Technology (2016) Wind power. Retrieved from http://www.montanagreenpower.com/wind/

Xzeres (2016) Skystream. Retrieved from http://www.windenergy.com/products/skystream

Choosing between various waste collection systems

10

This chapter illustrates the application of strategic decision making at Rimetaal, a Dutch metalworking company. We will introduce this company in the context of making strategic decisions to benefit people, the planet and profits.

About Rimetaal

Rimetaal B.V. was, until the end of 2014, a private limited company incorporated under Dutch law. At the end of 2014 it was taken over by Kliko, the number one specialist in waste systems and logistics in the Netherlands, where it maintains a special position as a leader in sustainable, high-end technology for smart waste systems. Rimetaal started life as a family firm and has specialized in the development, production, sale and maintenance of high-quality metal products since 1994. Their range includes underground waste collection systems and sound-insulating generator housings. The theme of sustainability is a continuous thread throughout Rimetaal's policies, aimed at sustainable products, sustainable production methods as well as social sustainability. Hence incorporating circular principles and taking social responsibility runs in the blood of both the organization and its employees. Rimetaal was one of the first partners in De Groene Zaak (Green Business), an entrepreneurial employers' organization established in 2010 and known as a collective of frontrunners in terms of sustainability. The company's annual turnover at the time of the research was approximately €5 million, and it had around 35 employees.

About sourcing waste collection systems

The market for Rimetaal's waste collection systems consists primarily of local and regional government bodies. Major investments have been made in sustainable and socially responsible production methods in recent years, and product development is a proactive response to the social demands for sustainability. In order to continue to be able to compete on price, Rimetaal has also made investments designed to cut costs, such as reducing the throughput time of the production processes, lean working, more focus on pre- and post-costing, better collaboration between internal departments, training, a higher level of mechanization of the production machinery, and stock reduction. All in all, this has led to a reduction of the production cycle from 6 to 3.5 weeks.

In producing its waste collection systems, Rimetaal already embraces People and Planet aspects in various ways. The People aspect is considered from the perspective of both employees and customers. For the employees, welding robots reduce accidents during the welding process. By providing a learning environment for students from technical colleges, and employment for rehabilitated 'problem' youngsters and people at a distance from the labour market, Rimetaal is helping specific groups to gain access to meaningful work. For customers, robust hooks for the waste systems prevent accidents during emptying. The Planet aspect becomes evident in the relatively long life cycle of the reinforced product and in low CO_2 emissions during the production process. This has been achieved thanks to the involvement of a research consultancy to help clean up the production process.

Some of Rimetaal's principal customers, local and national governments, aspire to be frontrunners in the domain of sustainable procurement. Various targets have been set so that 100 per cent sustainable procurement could be achieved in 2015. RVO, the governmental agency for stimulating entrepreneurship in the Netherlands, has drawn up a set of criteria, but they are not very stringent. On top of that, in practice, it is all too often the case that suppliers are selected more on the basis of price (ie lowest) than on the basis of sustainability. Despite the fact that 'sustainability' is cited as an essential selection criterion and suppliers can certainly supply sustainable products that work out cheaper over the entire life cycle than non-sustainable products, tenders are still being published with highly detailed technical specifications, sometimes even with photographs of the desired products and their suppliers. Consequently, manifestly more sustainable products seem to be excluded. The biggest challenge facing Rimetaal is therefore to let potential customers experience for themselves how their purchasing practices, sustainable or not, are affecting their strategic policies.

The strategic decision-making process

The decision-making process at Rimetaal has taken place in the form of multiple workshops with the executive board and content experts. When describing the process we will follow the steps as set out in Chapter 2.

Determining scope of the decision

Rimetaal has been making a loss over recent years because competitors from low-wage countries are offering comparable products, even though there are manifest quality differences, such as weaker materials and less attention given to social aspects during the production process. It has been found that potential customers – despite giving sustainability high strategic priority – ultimately choose the lowest purchase price; the municipal procurement officers clearly water down the sustainability criteria when it comes to the crunch.

Therefore, in an interactive setting, we formulated the purpose of strategic decision making at Rimetaal as follows: to offer the municipal procurement officers insight into what – for them – would be the best procurement decision.

Defining key outputs

The key outputs have been defined from the perspective of the municipal officer who needs to decide what waste systems their municipality should purchase. It is this procurement officer who actually holds the key to acquiring a sustainable product, but he must be able to compare alternative waste systems on the basis of key outputs that should be important to his decision.

In order to support the municipal procurement officer in achieving the formulated goal, together with the stakeholders, we defined key outputs such that relevant insights can be given. When defining the key outputs, it turned out that when making a decision regarding the sourcing of waste collection systems, it was important for the procurement officer to get insight into the pricing structure of a product as well as into how procurement contributes to making the organization sustainable. To get insight into this pricing structure, it should be realized that the costs are more than just the purchase price (ie the invoiced price), because they also involve administration and operational costs (ie process costs). The concept of Total Cost of Ownership (TCO), otherwise known as the life cycle concept, includes all these costs and is therefore a suitable key output.

Given that more and more purchasing is being put out to tender, procurement is the key to success in terms of making an organization sustainable. Products or services that fail to fulfil measurable and appraisable sustainability criteria will not be purchased: a 'knock-out' criterion. Determining these criteria calls for commercial, entrepreneurial and procurement competences. If the purchasing department applies the criteria in full, it will be able to make the contribution to sustainability visible. Basically, there is a need to express the effect of a decision in the same quantities or terms as those that the organization uses in its reporting. These could, for instance, be the same key outputs as are used to report on sustainability in annual reports.

Table 10.1 shows the chosen key outputs for each of the three Ps. The outputs were suggested by Agentschap NL from the side of the government (Rijksdienst voor Ondernemend Nederland, 2016) and by De Groene Zaak, an organization working to accelerate 'sustainabilization' through sustainable purchasing (De Groene Zaak, 2016). The key outputs were further elaborated and made specific for Rimetaal in consultation with Rimetaal's executive board.

Defining decision maker's options

As mentioned in Chapter 2, the internal variable inputs need to be defined for the decision maker to be able to formulate their options. From the perspective of the municipal procurement officer, they can opt for a waste system from Rimetaal or from one of Rimetaal's competitors. If they opt for Rimetaal, they can then consider leasing the waste system instead of purchasing it outright. They can also opt to take out an all-inclusive maintenance contract. Such a contract would mean that Rimetaal would bear the risk of the maintenance needed, for example, because of vandalism. Note that Rimetaal uses the access-over-ownership model by offering the option to lease. The internal variable outputs and their meaning as formulated for the municipal purchasing officer are summarized in Table 10.2.

Based on these inputs, we have formulated five options available to the decision maker. 'Traditional' describes the traditional type of decision based on price: purchase waste systems which, while cheap to buy, will be less durable. 'TradLease' describes the purchase of the same traditional systems, but within the framework of a lease construction. The options 'Rimetaal', 'RimLease' and 'RimServLease' all describe the purchase of Rimetaal systems, varying from outright purchase to lease to lease-plus-service.

Table 10.3 displays the operationalization within the Responsible Business Simulator, showing how the internal variable input relates to the different options the decision maker has.

Table 10.1   Key output definitions for Rimetaal case

Key output	Theme	Meaning
CAPEX	Profit	Capital expenditure: the one-off investment in waste systems in the event of purchase (as opposed to lease).
Total Cost of Ownership (TCO)	Profit	Total Cost of Ownership (TCO) of the waste systems. Two minor adjustments have been made to the standard definition of TCO in order to make it possible to compare the costs of leasing and buying waste systems with varying lengths of useful life:
		1 In the case of outright purchase, the loss of interest is accounted as an expense; capital to the value of the purchase price is tied up in the waste systems and therefore no longer available for investment. This capital burden declines in a linear fashion to zero, because it can be assumed that the waste systems will be fully depreciated and will have no residual value at the end of their useful life.
		2 The TCO is here expressed as average cost per annum during the useful life of the waste systems. Future cash flows are therefore not converted into cash terms on the basis of a discount rate.
CO_2 Reduction	Planet	The reduction of CO_2 emissions during the production of Rimetaal's waste systems compared with the reduction of CO_2 emissions during the production of traditional waste systems.
Rehabilitation	People	Number of jobs that can be created for the rehabilitation of problem youngsters if waste systems are ordered from Rimetaal. It is assumed that Rimetaal's competitors offer no such opportunities.
Study Tracks	People	Number of work experience placements for students that are created as a result of ordering waste systems from Rimetaal. It is assumed that Rimetaal's competitors offer no such placements.
Health and Safety Incidents	People	Number of safety incidents that occur during the production of the waste systems ordered and the number of incidents that occur during actual use by the end user.

Table 10.2   Internal variable input definitions for Rimetaal case

Internal variable input	Meaning
Share Rimetaal Systems	Percentage of inhabitants that would be served by Rimetaal's waste systems: 0% if no system is ordered from Rimetaal, 100% if only Rimetaal systems are ordered.
Lease Instead Of Buy	1 if the municipality leases the waste systems; 0 if the municipality buys the waste systems.
Service Included	1 if a service contract is taken out with Rimetaal; 0 if not (a service contract can only be taken out in combination with a lease contract).

Table 10.3   Specification of decision maker's options for Rimetaal case.

Internal variable input	Traditional	TradLease	Rimetaal	RimLease	RimServLease
Share Rimetaal Systems	0	0	1	1	1
Lease Instead Of Buy	0	1	0	1	1
Service Included	0	0	0	0	1

Drawing up scenarios

External variable input is input which the decision maker cannot control, but it plays a role when making a decision. The occurrence of breakdowns, the variability in the length of the useful life of waste collection systems, and the interest rate for calculating the capital charges are all seen as the principal uncertainties from the operational environment that have impact on the outcome of the procurement decision. Table 10.4 describes the operationalization of these three uncertainties in the form of external input.

Additionally, three scenarios have been formulated: a pessimistic, an optimistic and a base-case or neutral scenario. This enables us to account for uncertainty regarding the external variable inputs. The values will be filled out outside of the boardroom, making use of simulation.

Table 10.4 External variable input definitions for Rimetaal case

External variable input	Meaning
Breakdowns	Expected number of breakdowns per waste system per year. Breakdowns can be caused by vandalism, unexpected wear or by injudicious use.
Life Span Variability	Spread in the useful life of a waste system due to wear and tear.
Interest Rate	Interest rate for calculating the capital charges for the purchase option; in the case of lease, a margin, payable by the user (lessee), is added to this interest rate in favour of the owner (lessor).

The number of breakdowns, the number of safety incidents and the length of the useful life of the waste systems have been determined on the basis of Monte Carlo simulation techniques. As explained in more detail in Chapter 7, this technique uses random numbers to generate a large number of potential values for each of these parameters. The simulation model then computes the result for each of these values. In this way, we effectively create extra uncertainty about the input within any scenario. This makes the simulation model a stochastic model. Probability distributions suggest the likelihood of the possible values. The probability distribution for the occurrence of breakdowns is the Poisson distribution based on the number of waste systems times the external variable input 'Breakdowns'. The Poisson distribution has also been chosen for the number of safety incidents, with the number of waste systems to be produced times the expected number of safety incidents per system now as parameter. A triangular distribution has been chosen for the useful life of the waste systems, with the average useful life at the apex (this depends on the type of waste system) and with the external variable Life Span Variability as standard deviation. The resulting uncertainties are displayed in Table 10.5.

Constructing simulation model

Up until now all information collected in the group process has been completed and inserted into the Responsible Business Simulator. However, for the simulation model to provide clear insights to the decision maker, some additional information is required. Separate from the stakeholder dialogue in

Table 10.5 Specification of scenarios for Rimetaal case

	Scenarios		
External variable input	**Pessimistic**	**Base case**	**Optimistic**
Breakdowns	0.12	0.08	0.04
Life Span Variability	4	3	2
Interest Rate	0.09	0.08	0.07

steps 1–4, but in consultation with the stakeholders, we have collected this information from several sources to complete the model. The information takes the form of values of fixed inputs, definitions of intermediates, and dependencies that specify how outputs are calculated from intermediates and fixed and variable inputs.

Fixed inputs

Additional to the internal and external variable inputs, fixed inputs are inserted into the simulation model. Fixed inputs are inputs of which the values are kept constant during the decision-making process. The Rimetaal case requires a relatively large number of extra fixed inputs to be able to complete the calculation of the key outputs from the internal and external variable inputs. These extra fixed inputs were not promoted to variable inputs because possible variations were not deemed to be interesting enough to study in great detail. These inputs are both controllable (ie the decision maker can determine or set their value) and non-controllable (when the decision maker has no control over them). The fixed inputs that we have identified for Rimetaal are listed in Table 10.6.

The values given for CO_2 production are based on a report that Rimetaal commissioned from Tüv Nord in order to ascertain the sustainability of its production methods (Tüv Nord, 2010) and on the certificate issued by the Climate Neutral Group (Climate Neutral Group, 2010). Other data is drawn from Rimetaal's internal HR documentation (especially the parameters needed to calculate the People-related key outputs) and from Rimetaal's own analysis of its competitive position.

Intermediates

As set out in Chapter 7, intermediates store the results of sub-steps in the calculations that convert inputs to the simulation model to outputs of the simulation model. Intermediates are used to make calculations easy and transparent. Intermediates are based on inputs and/or other intermediates.

Table 10.6 Specification of fixed inputs for Rimetaal case

Fixed input	Value	Meaning
Number of Citizens	80,000	Number of inhabitants needed in the suburb where a new waste system is being considered.
Number of Citizens per Rimetaal System	500	Number of inhabitants that can make use of a single Rimetaal waste system.
Number of Citizens per Traditional System	500	Number of inhabitants that can make use of a single traditional waste system.
Number of Rimetaal Systems per Worker	32	Number of systems that a Rimetaal employee produces per year.
Share Rehabilitations in Workforce	15%	Percentage of employees in Rimetaal's workforce that are part of the reintegration programme.
Share Study Tracks in Workforce	25%	Percentage of work experience placements in Rimetaal's workforce.
Price per Rimetaal System	€4,000	Purchase price of a single Rimetaal waste system.
Interest Rate Leasing Surcharge	1%	Margin on the interest rate for the lease company.
Service Surcharge	2.5%	Margin added to the expected damage through vandalism to buy off the risk that the actual damage is greater than expected.
Number of Runs	50,000	Number of times that the future situation is simulated.
Confidence Level	95%	Used for aggregating the frequency distributions calculated by Monte Carlo simulation into key outputs.
CO_2 Reduction per Rimetaal System	500 kg	CO_2 reduction during production of a Rimetaal waste system in comparison with a traditional system.
Average Life Span Rimetaal System	15 years	Average useful life of a Rimetaal waste system.
Average Life Span Traditional System	13 years	Average useful life of a traditional waste system.
A Priori Probability Breakdowns	5%	A priori probability that a waste system will be affected by vandalism (per year per system).

(*continued*)

Table 10.6   (*Continued*)

Fixed input	Value	Meaning
Cost per Vandalistic Attack Rimetaal System	€1,000	Average cost of a vandalism incident to a Rimetaal waste system.
Cost per Vandalistic Attack Traditional System	€2,000	Average cost of a vandalism incident to a traditional waste system.
Health and Safety Incidents Production Rimetaal System	1%	Expected percentage of safety incidents per Rimetaal waste system.
Health and Safety Incidents Production Traditional System	2%	Expected percentage of safety incidents per traditional waste system.
Relative Surcharge Rimetaal	40%	Percentage difference between the prices of a Rimetaal and a traditional waste system.

Table 10.7 shows which intermediates must be calculated first to keep the formulas simple and to be able to display the breakdown of calculations in small steps to the user.

Dependencies

When constructing a simulation model, the user specifies via dependencies how key outputs are calculated from intermediates and fixed and variable inputs. Most of these specifications are straightforward since they follow directly from elementary business logic in combination with the names of the key outputs, intermediates and various inputs. Therefore, these are not specified here. However, it is worthwhile spending a few words on how breakdowns and the system life span have been modelled, since these are of stochastic nature. This makes the cash flow stochastic, and hence also the profit-related key outputs as well as the health and safety incidents. It is only when Rimetaal systems are chosen and procured by means of a lease-plus-service contract that the cash flows can be regarded as deterministic. The number of safety incidents remains stochastic in all cases. All stochastic outputs are calculated once for each of 50,000 simulation rounds. In each simulation round a random number generator is used to draw from a statistical distribution. To finally achieve a single score per key output

Table 10.7   Definitions of intermediates for Rimetaal case

Intermediate	Unit	Meaning
Number of Systems	#	Number of waste systems needed in the suburb for which new waste systems are considered.
Price Per System	€	Price per waste system. This corresponds to Price Rimetaal System if the Rimetaal system is chosen. If a traditional system is chosen, this price should be divided by 1+Relative Surcharge Rimetaal.
Life Span of System	year	The useful life of each waste system according to the Monte Carlo simulation.
Number of Breakdowns	#	The total number of vandalism incidents per year, calculated on the basis of Monte Carlo simulation.
Costs of Breakdowns	€	Total costs of vandalism per simulation round per year.
Service Costs	€	Service costs per year if a service contract is taken out, taking account of the margin added for transferring the risk of breakdown to Rimetaal.
Annuity	€	Debt servicing charges per simulation round per year if systems are purchased outright. The CAPEX is seen as a loan to be repaid by instalments over the useful life of the system (by conservative estimate): annual depreciation is such that repayment plus interest remains constant each year.
Interest Rate Leasing	%	Interest rate, taking the lease company's margin into account.
Lease Payment	€	Lease payments per year. These are calculated as follows: the purchase price is furnished as a loan to be repaid in instalments over the useful life of the systems: instalments are such that repayment plus interest remains constant each year.
Cash Flow	€	Cash flow for the municipality per year.

per decision maker's option and per scenario, these 50,000 values are condensed into the percentile defined by the fixed input Confidence Level. The setting of 95 per cent refers to the rather conservative case that the key outputs return the values for which the model expects that there is a 5 per cent risk that in reality the key output will score worse.

Assessing strategic priorities

For the decision maker it is crucial to account for the strategic priority ranking of the theme 'sustainability' in relation to other policy priorities. Experience and research alike corroborate that sustainability is cited as essential in nearly all policy documents. Without wishing to detract from the more successful examples, it is often quite a different matter to put sustainability into practice. If sustainability is to be given any priority, that priority must be thoroughly entrenched at executive, management and operational levels. Directors and managers must also continuously monitor the actual substance of the agreed sustainability objectives. In short, the Responsible Business Simulator must be able to quantify the degree to which non-financial objectives will be achieved and take those values into consideration. Now that all information has been inserted into the simulation model, the decision maker can indicate their strategic priorities: to what key outputs do they assign the most weight?

First the situation that only CAPEX is important to the decision maker is considered. The outcome is hardly surprising: the traditional system wins because it is cheaper to buy. All the various lease options score even better, of course, simply because there is no CAPEX. The post-purchase maintenance costs do not fall under CAPEX and can therefore be disregarded on the basis of 'let tomorrow take care of itself'. Nonetheless, this simplistic reasoning is often the reason why Rimetaal often fails to be selected as the best option in public tender skirmishes. As soon as the Total Cost of Ownership is considered, instead of only the cost of purchase, the picture changes significantly, as can be seen in Figure 10.1.

Figure 10.1   Comparison of decision maker's options when weight is assigned only to key output 'TCO' in the base case scenario for Rimetaal case

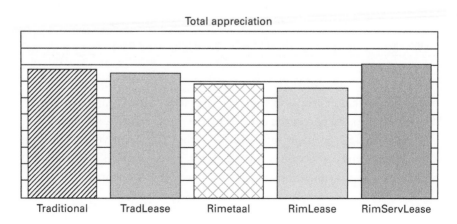

Total appreciation

Traditional   TradLease   Rimetaal   RimLease   RimServLease

Figure 10.2   Comparison of decision make''s options when all key outputs have equal weights in the base case scenario for Rimetaal case

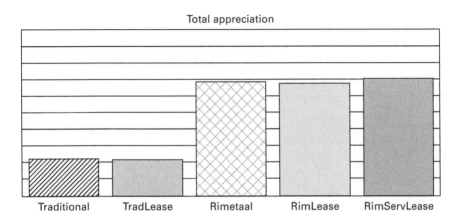

The traditional choice has to give way to the strategy to lease Rimetaal systems with a service contract.

It must be borne in mind, however, that all these considerations are based on the 'Profit only' selection criterion. That just goes to show that, in this case, sustainable decision making is aided by looking further ahead than the one-off purchase cost and considering the expenses over a longer period.

If the outputs that address the People and Planet aspects are also weighted, as in Figure 10.2, it is clear that the traditional systems soon lose ground to the more durable systems produced by Rimetaal. The question of whether it is better to lease or buy the Rimetaal systems, with or without a service contract, depends on the municipality's risk appetite, which will be discussed in the last step of the decision-making process.

Assessing risk appetite

The decision maker's risk appetite reflects how they perceive the equilibrium of its performance in terms of the risk aversion. Just like assigning weights to the key outputs, weights can be assigned to the different scenarios. In Figure 10.3 we see that the risk appetite determines which of the three options related to choosing Rimetaal systems is the preferred one. In the pessimistic case, the municipality expects more breakdowns and a shorter lifetime of the system than in the base-case and optimistic scenarios. In this pessimistic view, it is better to transfer the risk of breakdowns and shorter lifetimes to Rimetaal by choosing the lease option including service. If he is more optimistic, it becomes favourable not to pay the premium price for de-ownership and service.

Figure 10.3   Comparison of decision maker's options when all key outputs
have equal weights for all scenarios for Rimetaal case

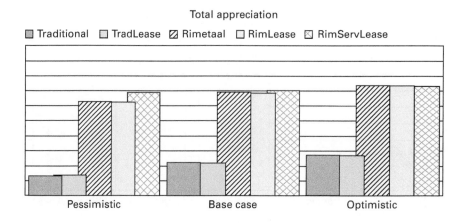

Figure 10.4   Comparison of decision maker's options when weight is assigned
only to key output 'TCO' for all scenarios for Rimetaal case

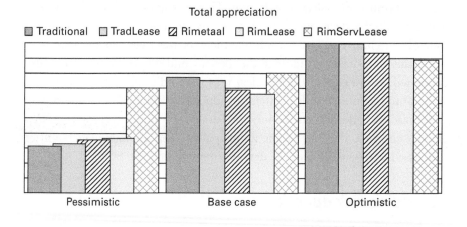

If we take a step back and again focus on TCO only, then Figure 10.4 shows
that – unlike in Figure 10.3 – in the optimistic case the outright purchase
of a traditional system is the preferred option. It is only in the optimistic
scenario that the traditional systems win, because that scenario is based on
optimistic estimates of useful life and costs due to vandalism. As soon as
those estimates are toned down to the level of the base-case scenario, the
traditional choice has to give way to the strategy to lease Rimetaal systems
with a service contract. Furthermore, we see that the more pessimistic the
view and the lower the risk appetite, the sooner thoughts turn to leasing

and a service contract, because then the interest rate risk and the risks of breakdowns and shortfalls in useful life are borne by third parties. If the scenarios are compressed by giving equal weight to each scenario, leasing the Rimetaal systems in combination with a service contract will be the first preference, followed by the purchase of traditional systems.

Reflections

If tender specifications are already full of details and descriptions of what is required, this can forestall suggestions from suppliers for innovative solutions. Detailed specifications of this nature are usually based on historic insight, knowledge and experience of products, and do not therefore stimulate innovation. Within the criteria for procurement there must be some leeway to encourage innovation. Suppliers must be able to distinguish themselves by virtue of their inventiveness, but bureaucracy stifles innovation. Experience has shown that this is precisely where the tension lies: governmental organizations and local municipalities want to maintain control over the quotation and procurement process and, because of their anxiousness to avoid legal or liability problems, do not want to be surprised by issues that have not been part of their calculations from the offset. Innovation, on the other hand, is precisely a matter of managing uncertain and unknown quantities, with a view to finding a timely solution to the problem. This perspective is far from new, even in government circles, as Rijkswaterstaat (The Dutch Department of Transport, Public Works and Water Management) has been promoting innovative tendering (Ministerie van Verkeer en Waterstaat, 2007) since 1992. In short, there is no need to produce specifications for the waste system itself, but it must be clear how the procurement of such a system contributes to the objectives of the organization that purchases it.

Since Rimetaal wants to let potential customers experience for themselves how their purchasing practices, sustainable or not, are affecting their strategic policies, it is crucial to provide insight into the uncertainty of outcomes. The procurement of waste collection systems is a long-term decision and it is impossible to accurately and reliably forecast the effect that the decision will have. The simulation model therefore needs to provide insight into the reliability of the forecasts of those effects. This is accounted for when completing the simulation model.

Setting the strategic priorities and assessing the risk appetite makes it possible to select the best strategy for the municipal procurement officer.

This selection depends on the weights that have been allocated to the key outputs and to the scenarios.

Recall from the previous section of this chapter that a comparison of the computation on the basis of CAPEX alone with the computation on the basis of TCO alone produces a very interesting observation. Only the Profit aspects were taken into account. Since the TCO evaluation would automatically lead to a sustainable choice, and this choice is not being made, there are clearly other factors to be taken into account that persuade the decision maker to give less credence to TCO.

We organized a round-table meeting and invited senior procurement officers from various municipalities to take part. We outlined the problem and explained our strategic decision-making approach. We discovered that the principle of procurement on the basis of TCO had not yet taken root in the public sector. Even though there had been reports on this subject, and there was a verbal commitment to sustainable purchasing from those in charge, the policies were not yet being put into practice. With the exception of the two largest cities, Amsterdam and Rotterdam, it seemed that procurement policies were based primarily on price. Three main reasons were pinpointed: the short time horizon of municipal appointees (four-year tenure and the need to be seen to realize objectives within that period); the separation of responsibility between investment (purchasing) and operations; and the fact that finances were often segregated by district within the cities. Another reason proved to be the vast number of policy targets and the lack of any clearly communicated priority ranking.

On the basis of the decision-making process, we concluded that it is difficult, in practice, to persuade procurement officers to allocate sufficient weight to the non-financial key outputs during their selection of suppliers. The added value of the research into this decision-making process lies in the fact that it has resulted in three options for an improvement of the procurement process:

- Require that the selection process is conducted using the principles of circularity with the aid of the Responsible Business Simulator, including the allocation of minimum weights to People- and Planet-related key outputs.

- Require that a sustainable product must fulfil a number of explicitly defined knock-out criteria in terms of sustainability. Subsequently, select the cheapest tender from the range of suppliers that fulfil these criteria. In terms of the Responsible Business Simulator, this means that the key output scores on People, Planet and Profit aspects are not aggregated when scoring the purchasing options, but are each scored separately.

- Require that a lease construction is chosen, so as to spread the cost over time. This will compel municipalities to consider TCO, because it will automatically exclude CAPEX-based reasoning. The sustainable option would then be likely to come out on top, even without allocating any explicit weights to People and Planet aspects, because we noted that some People- and Planet-related key outputs are already incorporated into the TCO concept.

After writing the first version of this case in 2014, we learned that Rimetaal went bankrupt later that year. Rimetaal paid the price for being a frontrunner in terms of dedication to high-technology, long-lasting materials and sustainable working practices. However, the metal industry was keen to keep Rimetaal precisely for these qualities, and it was not difficult to find a buyer for the company. As we were writing the update of this case, the current owner, Kliko, confirmed that it had been very important for them as waste systems company at the lower end of the technological spectrum to take over Rimetaal, which has now given them a high-end asset. Rimetaal is up to speed in production and is able to deliver much more advanced services to local municipalities and companies by teaming up with Kliko.

Investments have been made in cleaning systems for waste bins underground, and lease contracts have also been developed. In that sense the embedment of Rimetaal in the bigger Kliko company has mutual advantages. Kliko has respected the role Rimetaal plays in this industry and, although financially now part of the Kliko company, Rimetaal has retained a high level of independence in terms of management. It has kept its special character as niche player and is still true to the values of People, Planet and Profit.

References

Climate Neutral Group (2010) *Certificaat Rimetaal*, Climate Neutral Group

De Groene Zaak (2016) Creëert de economie van morgen vandaag. Retrieved from http://degroenezaak.com/

Ministerie van Verkeer en Waterstaat (2007) *Handreiking Systeemgerichte Contractbeheersing*, Rijkswaterstaat, Den Haag

Rijksdienst voor Ondernemend Nederland (2016) Rijksdienst voor Ondernemend Nederland. Retrieved from http://www.rvo.nl/

Tüv Nord (2010) *Rimetaal Green Check*, Tüv Nord, Hanover

Creating a healthy and productive working environment 11

Creating a working environment that stimulates healthy living is key to attracting talent, retaining employees who deliver better quality, and preventing sick leave. Particularly in organizations with a high stress factor, such as in healthcare, it is a challenge to shape conditions for a sustainable workplace. The IZZ Foundation (IZZ for short) is dedicated to the strategic goal of creating a better working environment and reducing the costs of health- and stress-related absenteeism. This chapter illustrates the application of strategic decision making at the IZZ Foundation. IZZ had already been investing in healthy employees for years, but never knew what the impact and effect of these investments were. Using the Responsible Business Simulator we were able to indicate very precisely where to invest and what the impact would be. Unique about the IZZ Foundation is that they embedded the strategic decision-making process in all their conversations with the boardroom members of health institutions. We will start by introducing the Foundation and its background in the context of making strategic decisions to benefit people, the planet and profits.

About IZZ

The IZZ Foundation is a non-profit organization in the Netherlands that has been promoting the interests of healthcare workers (in hospitals, nursing and care homes, home care, handicapped care, mental health and youth care) since its establishment in 1977. On the basis of its focus on People and wide knowledge of and commitment to the healthcare sector, IZZ provides healthcare insurance on a non-profit basis for almost half a million Dutch healthcare employees and their families. That insurance is tailored to the needs of this special group and takes full account of the specific health risks involved in working in the sector. IZZ is the market leader in the healthcare sector, and what makes it unique is the input and influence that employers and employees in the healthcare sector together have on improving health and healthy working conditions for healthcare professionals. On one hand there is the collective IZZ insurance, which is an important employee benefit and is therefore incorporated into many collective labour agreements, and on the other hand there is the extensive programme for improving healthy working conditions and organizational climate. The Responsible Business Simulator is part of this programme.

About sustaining employees

Currently, besides a growing demand for care personnel, the effective supply of labour is declining in the Netherlands (Raad voor de Volksgezondheid en Zorg, 2006) because of an increasing outflow of personnel as well as a traditionally high level of absenteeism due to illness in the sector (van der Velden, Francke and Batenburg, 2011). Although the overall frequency of absenteeism in this sector has remained stable over the last years, the number of long-term sickness absences (92 to 720 days) has increased (Skipr, 2015). The probability that someone will change jobs in the healthcare sector is linked to employee satisfaction. The Dutch national healthcare monitor showed that in 2011 no less than 54 per cent of the employees in the healthcare sector had considered looking for another job outside the sector (ADV Market Research, 2011). For 93 per cent of this group, the most important reason was poor employee benefits. Other reasons given were high levels of pressure, low salary and too much bureaucracy. Contact with clients was the single most positive aspect of a job in healthcare (according to 81 per cent), even though strict scheduling often means that staff don't have time for a chat with clients. These developments were to IZZ a call to action.

With a purely financial approach there is a risk of becoming embroiled in a downward spiral. Costs must be reduced, and this means it is no longer possible to invest in staff. This leads to less committed personnel, which in turn leads to greater staff turnover and more absenteeism. The consequence is an increase in personnel costs, which necessitates further reductions. Once a downward step has been taken, it is very difficult for organizations to extricate themselves from the spiral.

In an integrated approach, the starting point is different and the spiral need never develop. Sustainable measures must be taken to ensure the deployability of personnel, so that future clients of healthcare institutions can be cared for at an acceptable price. Investing in staff leads to greater employee commitment and satisfaction, as a result of which staff turnover and absenteeism decrease. The knock-on effect is an overall reduction of costs. Both the Profit and the People objectives are achieved if this eventual cost reduction is greater than the investment made in the staff.

This knowledge, along with innovation and renewal, plays an important role in IZZ's strategy to maintain optimal deployability for employees in this sector. Some examples are programmes to reduce absenteeism among care-sector employees and to improve their productivity and employability. Such programmes could prove invaluable, given the current shortages in the health-care sector labour market. IZZ's specific knowledge of and involvement in this market puts it in a unique position to create added value for healthcare institutions. As part of its strategy for innovation and renewal, IZZ applied the concept of strategic decision making using the Responsible Business Simulator.

The aim of strategic decision making at IZZ is to satisfy the need to sustain employees in the healthcare sector by quantifying the effects of various interventions. In other words, translate 'gut feelings' into statistics, so that a healthcare institution can take well-founded action.

The strategic decision-making process

The strategic decision-making process at IZZ has taken place in the form of multiple workshops with the executive board and in close collaboration with content experts from IZZ and several healthcare institutions. When describing the process we will follow the steps as set out in Chapter 2.

Describing strategic challenge that requires a decision

IZZ's rationale is that if the image of the healthcare sector is to be improved and the severe staff shortages are to be resolved, it is important that sustainable ways are found to make the profession more attractive. This will not only help the people who work in the sector, but will also help the patients and ultimately society as a whole.

As the introduction makes clear, there is a serious need for measures that will help achieve a balance between supply and demand in the healthcare sector while taking the welfare of personnel into account. This means that it will need to be determined, from the perspective of a healthcare institution, what measures will help make healthcare a more pleasant, efficient and attractive working environment.

The hypothesis is that by investing in People aspects, positive effects will also occur on the Profit side. The purpose of using the Responsible Business Simulator has been formulated as follows: enable the IZZ Foundation to offer healthcare institutions objective insight into what – for them – is the optimal decision regarding the sustainability of their employees.

Defining key outputs involving stakeholders

The objective for IZZ in this case is to contribute to the People and Profit aspects by supporting healthcare institutions with their decision making. Goals that fall within this remit are: healthy, committed and motivated healthcare workers; sustainable deployment of personnel in the healthcare sector; access to top-quality care; keeping sector-specific health problems at manageable levels; low staff turnover costs; low costs of absenteeism; and conditions of employment that have a specific added value for the healthcare sector.

The key outputs are those by which the organization seeks to achieve its goal. With the above-mentioned goals in mind, the key outputs are defined not only from the perspective of the decision maker within the healthcare organization, but also from the perspective of its employees and customers. This decision maker can be a board member in the organization, but can also be an HR officer. In order to give insight to the decision maker in whether it pays off to invest in employees, key outputs addressing People aspects are formulated next to key outputs addressing Profit aspects. The process of defining and refining the key outputs initially took place in close collaboration with the board and content experts from IZZ. Next, in an explorative dialogue, stakeholders and experts occupying various functions within several healthcare institutions were asked for their feedback on first drafts of sets of key outputs. This resulted in Table 1.1, which lists all the key outputs, to which theme they relate, and their description.

Note that the key outputs are all expressed in terms of changes to current levels. To determine these changes, we calculate the difference in value between the original situation and the final situation after the interventions have been applied. As such, the key output Total Investment also relates to a change in investments in employees compared to current levels of investments.

It should be realized that the simulation model primarily assumes that the production volume remains constant. This implies that when productivity increases, the same work can be performed by fewer people and wage costs decrease. However, one could also conclude that increased productivity releases capacity that can be deployed elsewhere. Wage costs would

Table 11.1 Key output definitions for IZZ case

Key output	Theme	Description
Decrease in staff turnover costs	Profit	Reflects the decrease in staff turnover costs caused by the internal variable inputs that affect staff turnover costs.
Decrease in absenteeism costs	Profit	Reflects the decrease in absenteeism costs caused by the internal variable inputs that affect absenteeism costs.
Decrease in wage costs	Profit	Reflects the decrease in wage costs caused by the internal variable inputs that affect wage costs. An 'effect on wage costs' can only occur in the simulation model if productivity changes; the effect that absenteeism and staff turnover have on wage costs is therefore not included in this key output.
Increase in production capacity	Profit	If productivity increases, more production capacity becomes available.
Total investment	Profit	Sum of all types of investment in all employees.
Decrease in staff turnover %	People	Reflects the decrease in turnover percentage caused by the internal variable inputs that affect turnover percentage.
Decrease in absenteeism %	People	Reflects the decrease in absenteeism percentage caused by the internal variable inputs that affect absenteeism percentage.
Increase in employee satisfaction	People	Reflects the increase in employee satisfaction caused by the internal variable inputs that affect employee satisfaction.
Increase in customer satisfaction	People	Reflects the increase in customer satisfaction caused by an increase in employee satisfaction.

then remain constant but more revenues could be generated. Since we want to refrain from modelling the revenue side as well, for the financial business case we focus on the decrease in wage costs. However, the increase in production capacity is also reported as a key output. In Step 6 of the decision-making process, we will see that we make a choice between focusing on reducing costs or increasing capacity by setting weight on either Decrease in wage costs or Increase in production capacity.

Determining decision maker's options

This stage in the process concerns the defining of the internal variable inputs, the inputs which can be controlled by the decision maker. In this case, these take the form of several types of investments (also referred to as measures or interventions) in employees of healthcare institutions aimed at improving their working conditions. Measures suggested by nurses and care workers that would make the healthcare profession more attractive are: better opportunities for personal growth and development; measures to reduce the pressure of work; involvement in policy and decision making; appreciation from co-workers; independence to carry out their work; and a more socio-emotional style of leadership (as opposed to a more instrumental style) (Maurits et al 2014). Further research has shown that healthcare professionals feel that there is room for improvement in the conditions under which they work. Almost half of the nurses' and care workers' absenteeism is caused by physical burden (Ministerie van Sociale Zaken en Werkgelegenheid, 2012) and nearly three quarters (71 per cent) of them feel they have to work under pressure (de Vries and Vroonhof, 2011). Around a quarter find it difficult to achieve a good work-life balance (Eurofound, 2012) and more than a quarter (26 per cent) feel that there are insufficient opportunities for training and/or development (Maurits et al, 2014). Finally, over half (65 per cent) are dissatisfied with their salaries (ADV Market Research, 2011).

On the basis of this research and IZZ's own experience, nine internal variable inputs were chosen; these have an impact on the working conditions of staff in the care sector and thus have an impact on the key outputs. We divided the nine internal variable inputs into the categories of psychological, physical and other, as seen in Table 11.2. These internal variable inputs are inserted into the simulation model in terms of 'euros per employee' and refer to a collective term for the type of investment indicated by the name of the internal variable input. The exact details of these type of investments were deemed to be less important. The idea behind this philosophy is that, given the strategic priorities of a healthcare institution, there will be many market parties that have the expertise needed to put the budget available for each type of investment to optimum use. For example, in determining the investment for training and education, the simulation model makes no recommendations for specific courses; this could be looked at as a follow-up with the aid of a specialized training agency.

Now that the internal variable inputs have been determined, it is time to attach numbers to these inputs, thus specifying the decision maker's options. For reasons of confidentiality, we will do so on the basis of an imaginary

Table 11.2 Internal variable input definitions for IZZ case

Internal variable input	Category	Description
Psycho-social stress reduction	Psychological	Investments to counter or prevent pressure of work, aggression and violence on the work floor: the relief of psycho-social stress has a positive effect on staff turnover, absenteeism and productivity.
Work-life balance	Psychological	Investments to improve the balance between the individual, his or her private life and the working environment: an improved work-life balance has a positive effect on staff turnover and employee satisfaction.
Physical strain reduction	Physical	Investments to counter or prevent physical strain caused by work and job-related movements: reducing physical strain has a positive effect on staff turnover, absenteeism and employee satisfaction.
Physical exercise	Physical	Investments to encourage physical activity that has no relationship to the employee's tasks: getting enough physical exercise has a positive effect on productivity and absenteeism.
Smoking reduction	Physical	Investments to reduce or avoid the time that people spend smoking: prevention of smoking has a positive effect on productivity and absenteeism.
Healthy eating	Physical	Investments to encourage employees to eat more vegetables and fruit: consuming sufficient vegetables and fruit has a positive effect on absenteeism.
Training and development	Other	Investments to improve the individual skills of employees: opportunities for training and personal development have a positive effect on staff turnover and employee satisfaction.
Salary increase	Other	Investments in the gross salary of an employee: a good salary has a positive effect on staff turnover and employee satisfaction (as long as this is combined with other appropriate investments).
Leadership development	Other	Investments to improve the management qualities of and the relationships between employees: good leadership has a positive effect on staff turnover and employee satisfaction.

geriatric care institution named Golden Years. In the remainder of this chapter, we illustrate the application of the Responsible Business Simulator to Golden Years. However, values shown here are representative of those used by many health institutions that followed this decision-making process.

Golden Years is aware that its employees work under great pressure and are struggling to maintain a good work-life balance. It considered three options for the decision maker, each with an investment price tag of €100 per employee but with different focus areas:

- *Physical.* An investment of €50 in physiotherapy sessions, €20 in a company fitness scheme, €20 in an anti-smoking programme and €10 to make fruit available in the workplace.

- *Social.* An investment of €35 in a session with a psychologist, €25 in a programme to improve work-life balance, €25 in competence training, €5 in increased salaries and €10 in a leadership course for the line managers.

- *Mix.* An investment of €11 in each of the interventions, with €1 extra for psycho-social stress.

Drawing up scenarios

Now that the decision maker's options are defined, we arrive at the stage of the strategic decision-making process in which we define the external variable inputs, ie exogenous factors related to the business environment in which the organization operates.

We distinguish between direct and indirect effects: the direct effects indicate a change in intermediates or key outputs that are directly affected by a change in the internal variable inputs; the indirect effects indicate a change in intermediates or key outputs due to changes in other intermediates and key outputs as a result of direct effects. These two types of effects form the basis for the scenarios. This way, the Responsible Business Simulator allows us to investigate how sensitive key outputs and intermediates are to any change in internal variable input. Here, we defined six external variable inputs for these effects.

Additionally, we decided on a pessimistic, a neutral and an optimistic scenario. For example, let's say, in the pessimistic scenario, that the value of the external variable input that relates to the effect of employee satisfaction on productivity is 0.9. The effect of employee satisfaction on productivity that was initially estimated on the basis of literature sources and/or expert opinions is multiplied by 90 per cent.

Table 11.3 Specification of scenarios for IZZ case

External variable input	Scenarios		
	Pessimistic	Neutral	Optimistic
Direct effect on productivity	0.9	1	1.1
Indirect effect on productivity	0.5	1	1.3
Direct effect on absenteeism %	0.9	1	1.1
Direct effect on staff turnover %	0.9	1	1.1
Direct effect on employee satisfaction	0.5	1	1.1
Indirect effect on customer satisfaction	0.7	1	1.3

Table 11.3 displays the external variable inputs and the value with which they will be multiplied. The values, depending on the scenario, have been determined with the consultation of experts in the healthcare sector and are often kept the same when applied to different institutions.

Constructing the simulation model

Up till now all information has been collected in the explorative dialogue with stakeholders and experts. However, for the Responsible Business Simulator to provide clear insights to the decision maker, additional information is required. Outside of the boardroom, but in collaboration with the stakeholders, desk and field research has been performed to complete the model. This section discusses this additional information and its origins. Subsequently, the information specific to the health organization at hand, additional characteristics of the nine types of investments in employees, and types of dependencies between the outputs and inputs are discussed. Finally, the conversion from input to output is described.

Input related to health organization

Table 11.4 specifies some characteristics of Golden Years. Obviously, these are needed to calculate the key outputs.

Input related to impact of investments

Table 11.5 displays four characteristics of the investments that are taken into account when modelling the impact of the investments on the key outputs.

The first three inputs in Table 11.5 only relate to the type of investment. Their values and – if available – references to their sources are listed in Table 11.6. The probability of success and the saturation points were mostly determined by experts.

Table 11.4 Specification of fixed inputs for imaginary elderly healthcare institution Golden Years for IZZ case

Fixed input	Value	Description
Current number of employees	1200	Current headcount.
Average number of workable days per year per employee	175	Number of days in the year minus weekends, holiday leave and compulsory training days, multiplied by the average part-time factor.
Average wage cost per employee per annum, excluding absenteeism	€40,000	Total annual wage cost divided by the total number of employees.
Current productivity level	70%	Average percentage of the workable day that an employee is engaged in carrying out his or her assigned tasks, excluding absenteeism.
Average cost of a day lost through absenteeism	€500	Average wage cost per day multiplied by the loss of productivity around the days of absenteeism (Burdorf and Elders, 2010).
Current absenteeism %	6.4%	Total number of days of absenteeism in the past year divided by the current total number of employees, multiplied by the number of workable days per year.
Average cost of staff turnover	€3,000	All costs that are incurred when an employee leaves and is replaced by a new employee, eg the costs of the interview and recruitment procedure, and the cost of training up a new employee.
Current turnover %	8.6%	Relative number of employees that have left the organization in the past year as a percentage of the total number of employees.
Current employee satisfaction	6.0	Average of the scores that employees gave their employer during the most recent employee satisfaction survey on a scale of 1 to 10.
Current customer satisfaction	6.5	Average of the scores that customers gave the organization during the most recent customer satisfaction survey on a scale of 1 to 10.

Table 11.5 Fixed inputs definitions for direct effect calculations for IZZ case

Fixed input	Description
Accessible population	Percentage of the population on which the investment will have an effect. The statistics are based primarily on literature research.
Probability of success	Likelihood that the investment will prove successful. These statistics are based on expert knowledge.
Saturation point	Maximum effective investment, or the ceiling above which further investment has no further effect on productivity, absenteeism, staff turnover and employee satisfaction. Here, too, the statistics are based on expert knowledge.
Maximum possible effect	Maximum proportion of lost productivity, absenteeism, staff turnover and lack of employee satisfaction that can be eliminated with an optimal intervention. These statistics are also based primarily on literature research.

Table 11.6 Specification of fixed inputs for IZZ case

Type of investment	Accessible population	Probability of success	Saturation point
Psycho-social stress reduction	71% (ADV Market Research, 2011)	20%	€180
Work-life balance	24% (Eurofound, 2012)	40%	€270
Physical strain reduction	19% (CBS Statline, 2013)	50%	€200
Physical exercise	50% (van der Lucht and Polder, 2010)	25%	€125
Smoking reduction	23.2% (CBS Statline, 2016)	13.7% (Halpern et al, 2015)	€390
Healthy eating	92% (van der Lucht and Polder, 2010)	80%	€100
Training and development	57% (Maurits et al, 2014)	80%	€2,000
Salary increase	65% (ADV Market Research, 2011)	70%	€3,600
Leadership development	73% (Maurits et al, 2014)	70%	€1,500

The maximum possible effects do not only depend on the type of investment, but also on what is affected: absenteeism, staff turnover, employee satisfaction or productivity. Their values are listed in Table 11.7, again including – if applicable – their reference. In case a cell contains no value, it

Table 11.7 Specification of maximum effects for IZZ case

Type of investment	Absenteeism	Staff turnover	Employee satisfaction	Productivity
Psycho-social stress reduction	33% (ArboNed, 2015)	–	–	7% (van Wormer et al, 2011)
Work-life balance	38% (Antai et al, 2015)	95.8% (Saeed et al, 2013)	64% (Mercer, 2011)	–
Physical strain reduction	30% (AZW, 2015)	50% (Veer et al, 2007)	57% (Mercer, 2011)	–
Physical exercise	4% (van der Lucht and Polder, 2010)	–	–	10% (Robroek et al, 2011)
Smoking reduction	21% (Weng, Ali and Leonardi-Bee, 2013)			25% (Robroek et al, 2011)
Healthy eating	2% (van Rossum et al, 2011)	–	–	–
Training and development	–	19% (Anis et al, 2011)	39% (Concrete Training, 2013)	–
Salary increase	–	33% (Veer et al, 2007)	10% (Glassdoor, 2015)	–
Leadership development		0% (Sellgren, 2007; Long et al, 2012)	22% (Saleem, 2015)	–

means that no relevant literature or expert opinion could be found and we assume, implicitly, that there is no correlation.

A result of the literature research that may look surprising is the zero maximum effect of leadership development on staff turnover. Although it may seem logical that this effect would exist, various researchers that investigated it came to the conclusion that there is no relation between leadership style and staff turnover. By default, we copy this scientific result, but of course, during the dialogue stakeholders may argue that a certain leadership development programme may have an effect on staff turnover within Golden Years. If so, this stakeholder is asked to what extent they think this may cut down staff turnover and the resulting value is imported into the model as expert opinion. The added value of using the Responsible Business Simulator lies in the ease of assessing the sensitivity of the key outputs for changes in this expert opinion. Depending on this sensitivity one may decide to put further effort in investigating the effectiveness of leadership development for staff turnover reduction.

Combining the information from Tables 11.6 and 11.7 with the investment amounts, the direct effect of each investment can be calculated. The direct effect of an investment i on j, where j is either absenteeism, staff turnover, employee satisfaction or productivity is calculated by means of the following formula:

$$\text{Direct effect}_{ij} = \text{Accessible population}_i * \text{Probability of success}_i$$
$$* \frac{min(\text{Investment amount}_i, \text{Saturation Point}_i)}{\text{Saturation Point}_i}$$
$$* \text{Maximum possible effect}_{ij}$$

In this constellation, we assume that the effect of the investment increases in a linear fashion up to the saturation point and that investments larger than this saturation point do not result in any additional effect. This holds for all investments, except for the investment in salary. For an investment in salary, we also take into account the so-called extinction effect: if increases in salary are not accompanied by a sufficient volume of other investments, the effect of the salary increase will be short-lived. This is reflected in the model by assuming the saturation point for salary decreases to zero when the investment in salary amounts to more than half of the total investments.

On the side of caution, we assume that no investment will have any further effect after one year. In reality, an employee can experience a positive effect from an internal variable input for a far longer period; take, for example, a training course for helping to deal with stress in the workplace. But limiting the shelf life of internal variable input to just one year reduces the risk of over-estimating the effective period.

By way of illustration, let us consider an investment to encourage healthy eating, specifically providing two pieces of fruit for each employee every day. It is estimated that this is going to cost €100 per employee per annum. Let's suppose that we want to know what direct effect this investment has on absenteeism. From the literature we know that 92 per cent of the Dutch population (ie the accessible population) eats too little fruit and that 2 per cent of absenteeism through illness (the maximum possible effect) is caused by not eating enough fruit. Experts have determined that this intervention has an 80 per cent probability of success, and that those two pieces of fruit represent the saturation point. The direct effect of this investment in fruit on absenteeism is a reduction of absenteeism through illness of 92% × 2% × 80% = 1.5%. This means that the new level of absenteeism can be expected to be 100% − 1.5% = 98.5% of the current level, simply by providing the fruit. Let's assume now that an institution is not willing or not able to spend €100 per employee on the purchase of fruit, but only €75. The direct result is then $1.5\% \times \left(\dfrac{75}{100} \right) = 1.1\%$. The institution could therefore reduce absenteeism by 1.1 per cent by investing €75 per employee in the healthy eating option.

We also modelled two indirect effects, which are the effects of a change in employee satisfaction on customer satisfaction and productivity. Both are drawn straight from the literature. Harter, Schmidt and Hayes (2002) concluded that an increase in employee satisfaction automatically led to greater productivity. The measure of the relative productivity increase as a result of greater employee satisfaction proves to be approximately 23 per cent. A similar correlation has been proven to exist between customer satisfaction and employee satisfaction. Research carried out by the Corporate Leadership Council (2003) in fact showed that when employee satisfaction increases, customer satisfaction increases as well. For any given increase in employee satisfaction, customer satisfaction will rise by approximately 26 per cent of that increase. Just as the saturation point ensures that unrealistically large direct effects are pared down, a similar mechanism has been incorporated to achieve the same result for indirect effects. A comprehensive description of such technical details can be found in Chapter 7.

Conversion of inputs to outputs

The conversion of inputs to outputs is effected in four steps. First we calculate the direct effects of the investments in terms of productivity, absenteeism and staff turnover, and employee satisfaction as illustrated above. Recall from Chapter 2 that in order to provide transparency, the results of sub-steps in the calculations that convert inputs to outputs are stored in intermediates.

These, amongst others, concern the new number of employees, new productivity level, new cost of absenteeism, new turnover percentage and new level of employee satisfaction. As the effect on employee satisfaction has a knock-on effect on productivity and customer satisfaction, these indirect effects are calculated in the second step. In the third step we make use of the external variable inputs to quantify the key outputs' sensitivity to fluctuations in the estimations of effects. In the final step we express the effects on productivity, absenteeism and staff turnover in monetary terms as well as in percentages, so that we can appraise the People- and Profit-related key outputs. At this stage we also incorporate extra management information in the form of additional outputs. In this case the additional outputs include both the absolute and relative return on investment as well as the new customer satisfaction.

By way of illustration, let us consider how the key output 'Decrease in absenteeism costs' comes about. First we calculate the current cost of absenteeism on the basis of organization-specific input:

current cost of absenteeism

> = Average cost of a day lost through absenteesim
> * Current absenteeism % * Average number of workable
> days per year employee * Current number of employees

The new cost of absenteeism is then calculated – by analogy – after the necessary adjustments have been made. The 'decrease in absenteeism cost' is then the difference between the new and the current cost of absenteeism.

Using all of the above, the Responsible Business Simulator calculates all key outputs for all combinations of the decision maker's options and scenarios. This amounts to the calculation of 81 key output scores (9 key outputs × 3 decision maker's options × 3 scenarios).

Evaluating options by assessing strategic priorities

To be able to create the best possible mix of internal variable inputs, the key output scores will need to be weighted against each other. Before this can be done, the key outputs have to be made mutually comparable by means of appreciation functions. In this case, we rely on the Responsible Business Simulator's automatic calculation of these function. For a comprehensive description of how these appreciation functions are calculated and applied we refer to Chapter 7.

Returning to our example case and using the mixed intervention and the neutral scenario as a basis, we illustrate how the key outputs can be interpreted. Table 11.8 sets out the relevant nine key output values for Golden Years.

Table 11.8   Key output values calculated for mixed intervention in neutral scenario for IZZ case

Key output	Value
Total investment	€120,000
Decrease in staff turnover costs	€3,650.61
Decrease in absenteeism costs	€99,200.92
Decrease in wage costs	€217,428.93
Increase in production capacity	764 days
Decrease in staff turnover %	0.06%
Decrease in absenteeism %	0.05%
Increase in employee satisfaction	4.45%
Increase in customer satisfaction	1.16%

We see that the mixed intervention calls for an investment of €100 for each employee, leading indeed to a total of €120,000. Golden Years can easily recoup this investment, primarily through the positive effect on absenteeism costs and, in case the production capacity remains at the same level, wage costs. If we express the increase in productivity of employees in being able to perform more work with the same number of employees, we see that the investment leads to an extra production capacity amounting to approximately 764 days or five employees.

Figure 11.1 illustrates how the different decision maker's options are evaluated when the key outputs are made mutually comparable via appreciation functions. To avoid information overload, the data has been aggregated to theme level (People or Profit). When all key outputs are equally weighted, the Physical option proves to be best. The natural question is whether the settings of this option, which were defined in Step 3, can be improved. More precisely, is there a better way to divide the €100 per employee between the various investment types than the way defined by the Physical option, given that all key outputs are deemed equally important? To answer this question, we employ the optimization algorithm within the Responsible Business Simulator. The results are also shown in Figure 11.1, from which it is clear that the Physical option can be 'beaten'. The optimal decision turns out to be to invest in a mix of one physical and one social intervention, highly skewed to the physical intervention: €90.96 per employee should be spent on physical strain reduction and €9.04 on psycho-social stress reduction. Of course, this decision is only optimal if the exogenous factors behave as described in the neutral scenario, if all key outputs are deemed to be equally important, if all organization-specific data has been put in correctly, and – last but not least – if one is willing to

Figure 11.1 Comparison of decision maker's options when all key outputs have equal weights in neutral scenario for IZZ case

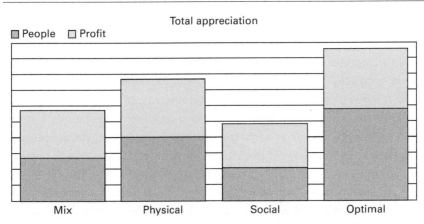

accept all expert opinions and all results and assumptions in the literature employed in this case.

To illustrate the effect of adjustments in strategic priorities, let's now look at which decision maker's option scores best if we only put – equal – weight on staff turnover and absenteeism reduction. Figure 11.2 illustrates that for this setting of strategic priorities, the Social option now scores better than the Physical option. Again, the optimization engine is able to outperform that option, in which case the advice is to spend €74.67 on psycho-social stress reduction and the remaining €25.33 on work-life balance.

Figure 11.2 Comparison of decision maker's options when equal weights are assigned to absenteeism and staff turnover only in neutral scenario for IZZ case

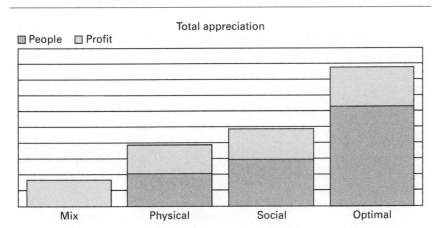

Evaluating options by assessing risk appetite

In the last step of the seven-step decision-making process, we investigate the impact risk appetite has on decisions. For this case, it turns out that the afore-mentioned optimal decisions are robust in the sense that they outperform the other options in optimistic, neutral and pessimistic scenarios. However, this is not always the case. Let's suppose that the decision maker could only choose between investing €100 per employee in physical strain reduction and investing €100 per employee in psycho-social stress reduction. For this situation, Figure 11.3 shows that the investment in physical strain reduction outperforms the investment in psycho-social stress reduction in the neutral and optimistic scenarios. In the pessimistic scenario, it is the other way around. If all three scenarios are weighted equally, then the decision maker should choose physical strain reduction, because the positive differences in the optimistic and neutral scenarios outweigh the negative difference in the pessimistic scenario. If the decision maker has a very low risk appetite, more weight could be assigned to the pessimistic scenario and the investment in psycho-social stress reduction would eventually win. It turns out that this happens as soon as the weight of the pessimistic scenario is at least 4.5 times higher than the (equal) weights of the other two scenarios. Figure 11.3 also shows that when comparing scenarios, physical strain reduction behaves in a more volatile way than psycho-social stress reduction. So if the decision maker prefers certainty about the outcome over the attractiveness of the outcome, then psycho-social stress reduction is also the option of choice. This illustrates how this last step can facilitate a dialogue on risk appetite.

Figure 11.3   Score per scenario for two specific decision maker's options when all key outputs have equal weights for IZZ case

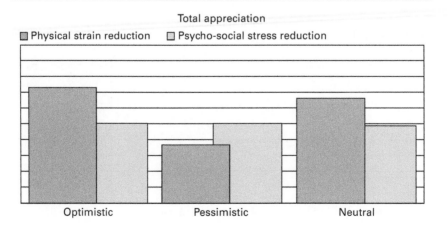

Reflections

The IZZ Foundation played an important role – from the very beginning – by helping to ensure that the decision-making instrument really reflected the world in which a healthcare institution operates. Modelling has been an interactive process, involving various participants from the IZZ Foundation as well as decision makers from other healthcare institutions. A number of sessions were held which were not only aimed at ensuring that the simulation model worked as it should, but also that it accurately reflected the decision-making process. In determining the interventions, there was constant attention paid to the issues and the occupational hazards that are inherent to the healthcare sector. The IZZ Foundation was able to incorporate its first-hand knowledge of the sector into the model and provide relevant literature.

Steps 6 and 7 of the decision-making process confirmed once more that the best strategy for any healthcare institution depends on both its strategic priorities (the weighting of the key outputs) and its risk appetite (the weighting of the scenarios). Irrespective of how advanced the construction of the simulation model is, it will not provide these weights; they can only be provided through strategic dialogue.

In this case, the Responsible Business Simulator comprises organization-specific input, literature research and expert opinions, and as a result it can be used to determine what the best intervention would be for any particular healthcare institution. This application of strategic decision making actually evolved into a ready-to-use application known as 'Simulatiemodel Gezond werken in de zorg' (Simulation model for sustainable healthcare work). This model is being made available to healthcare institutions so that they – with assistance from IZZ – have an instrument with which to steer their own strategic healthcare policies.

From the beginning of this exercise, the perspective of the healthcare institution has taken centre stage in the decision-making process surrounding the decision maker's options and scenarios, the pivotal question being: in which way (with which options) can a healthcare institution improve itself in the People domain?

Getting a healthcare institution involved right from the beginning of the decision-making process has some distinct advantages. Besides the actual modelling, it provokes other and new discussions that lead to further improvement and possible adaptations or adjustments for the future. According to Dominique Vijverberg, CEO at the IZZ Foundation, IZZ distinguishes three strategic themes (Vijverberg, 2012):

1 Prevention and demand for care: how can we do more in terms of prevention so that the demand for care decreases?

2 Innovation and working methods: how can we work in a modern and innovative way so that we work more efficiently and effectively?

3 Give direction, steering: how can the targeted changes best be implemented?

One question that the model provoked was: how do you go about putting the investments into practice? Despite its popularity in other sectors, the trend towards more flexible working in terms of both hours and location (known in Dutch as 'the new way of working') has not really found its way into the healthcare sector, probably because everyone feels that it would be impossible to implement it. After all, care workers need to be physically present to provide good care. Nonetheless, there are other ways in which more flexible working practices could be implemented in the healthcare sector. Giving employees the opportunity to determine their own working schedules, more flexibility in working times, more employee responsibility and less control are all matters that are central to this new way of working and that could also be introduced into healthcare.

Another possibility is the use of social media and e-health (ten Arve, 2012), whereby care worker and client have remote (ie non-physical) contact with each other. This makes it easier for the healthcare worker to decide where his or her help is most urgently needed, without needing to make the usual rounds first. That would be beneficial to the client and to the employee as well.

For the client it is reassuring to know that a care worker is available whenever it suits the client best. For the care worker it means better oversight, more autonomy and a less monotonous routine. It would be interesting to see what benefits a relatively small investment in a course on the effective use of social media would ultimately have for the employee (in terms of self-development, sense of well-being) and for the client (in terms of customer satisfaction).

The simulation model is a dynamic instrument for strategic decision making which can be adapted at any time in the future to reflect the changing needs of healthcare institutions. The issue of flexible working could be incorporated, for example, as could other issues such as 'inspiration' and 'presenteeism' (mental absenteeism). All these are subjects which, because of its modular design, could be added to the Responsible Business Simulator.

In 2016, the model 'Simulatiemodel Gezond werken' has been successfully applied in the negotiations between Dutch employers' associations ActiZ and BTN on the one hand and labour unions CNV Zorg en Welzijn and NU '91 on the other (ActiZ; BTN; CNV Zorg en Welzijn; NU '91, 2016).

References

ActiZ, BTN, CNV Zorg en Welzijn and NU ´91 (2016) Onderhandelaarsakkoord CAO voor de verpleeg en -verzorgingshuizen en thuiszorg en jeugdgezondheidszorg 2016–2018. Retrieved from https://www.mijnvakbond.nl/Documenten%20 MijnVakbond.nl/Zorg/onderhandelaarsakkoord%20VVT%202016.pdf

ADV Market Research (2011, last accessed 2013) Zorgbarometer. Retrieved from www.werknemersindezorg.nl/overzicht-inhoud/arbeidsomstandigheden/ zorgbarometer

Anis, A et al (2011) Employee retention relationship to training and development: a compensation perspective, *African Journal of Business Management*, 5 (7), pp. 2679–85

Antai, D et al (2015) A 'balanced' life: work-life balance and sickness absence in four Nordic countries, *International Journal of Occupational & Environmental Medicine*, 6 (4), pp. 205–22

ArboNed (2015) Ziekteverzuim naar oorzaak en geslacht. Retrieved from https:// www.volksgezondheidenzorg.info/onderwerp/ziekteverzuim

AZW (2015) *Arbeid in Zorg en Welzijn 2014*. Retrieved from https://www. rijksoverheid.nl/documenten/rapporten/2014/05/27/arbeid-in-zorg-en-welzijn-2014

Burdorf, L and Elders, L (2010) *Werkvermogen en Productiviteit: Feiten en fabels*, Erasmus Medisch Centrum, Rotterdam

CBS Statline (2013) Arbeidsomstandigheden werknemers; geslacht en leeftijd 2005–2013. Retrieved from http://statline.cbs.nl/StatWeb/publication/default. aspx?VW=T&DM=SLNL&PA=71204NED&D1=a&D2=1-2&D3=0&D4=a&HD=110413-1433&HDR=G2%2cG1%2cG3&STB=T

CBS Statline (2016) Leefstijl, preventief onderzoek; persoonskenmerken; 2010–2013. Retrieved from http://statline.cbs.nl/StatWeb/publication/?VW=T&DM= SLNL&PA=81177NED&D1=0-1%2c4-5%2c8-12&D2=0-2%2c5-13%2c34-38&D3=0&D4=l&HD=110905-0957&HDR=G3%2cG2%2cT&STB=G1

Concrete Training (2013, last accessed 1 September 2013) Opleiden verhoogt medewerkerstevredenheid. Retrieved from http://www.concretetraining.nl/ nw-24886-7-3489281/nieuws/opleiden_verhoogt_medewerkerstevredenheid.html

Corporate Leadership Council (2003) Linking Employee Satisfaction with Productivity, Performance, and Customer Satisfaction, Corporate Executive Board, Arlington County, Virginia

de Vries, H and Vroonhof, P (2011) *Onderzoeksprogramma Arbeidsmarkt Zorg en Welzijn*, Panteia, Zoetermeer

Eurofound (2012) Human health sector: working conditions and job quality. Retrieved from http://www.eurofound.europa.eu/publications/information-sheet/2014/working-conditions/human-health-sector-working-conditions-and-job-quality

Glassdoor (2015, 18 June) Does money buy happiness? The link between salary and employee satisfaction. Retrieved from https://www.glassdoor.com/research/does-money-buy-happiness-the-link-between-salary-and-employee-satisfaction/

Halpern, S D et al (2015) Randomized trial of four financial-incentive programs for smoking cessation, *The New England Journal of Medicine*, **372**, pp. 2108–17

Harter, J K, Schmidt, F L and Hayes, T L (2002) Business unit-level relationship between employee satisfaction, employee engagement, and business outcomes: a meta-analysis, *Journal of Applied Psychology*, **87** (2), pp. 268–79

Long, C S et al (2012) Leadership styles and employees' turnover intention, *World Applied Sciences Journal*, **19** (4), pp. 575–81

Maurits, E E M et al (2014) *De Aantrekkelijkheid van Werken in de Zorg 2013*, Nivel, Utrecht

Mercer (2011) What's working. Retrieved from www.mercer.nl/press-releases/minderheid_nederlanders_tevreden_over_salaris

Ministerie van Sociale Zaken en Werkgelegenheid (2012) *De Juiste Hulpmiddelen Verlichten het Werk en Verminderen de Arbeidsrisico's*, Rijksoverheid, Den Haag

Raad voor de Volksgezondheid en Zorg (2006) *Arbeidsmarkt en Zorgvraag*, Raad voor de Volksgezondheid en Zorg, Den Haag

Robroek, S J W et al (2011). The role of obesity and lifestyle behaviours in a productive workforce, *Journal of Occupational & Environmental Medicine*, **68** (10), pp. 134–39

Saeed, R et al (2013) Work-life balance and stress with the turnover rate of the employees. *World Applied Sciences Journal*, **26** (6), pp. 834–39

Saleem, H (2015) The impact of leadership styles on job satisfaction and mediating role of perceived organizational politics, *Procedia - Social and Behavioral Sciences*, **172**, pp. 563–69

Sellgren, S F (2007) *Leadership and Staff Turnover*, Karolinska Institutet, Stockholm

Skipr (2015) Ziekteverzuim in zorg gelijk gebleven. Retrieved from http://www.skipr.nl/actueel/id21493-ziekteverzuim-in-zorg-gelijk-gebleven.html

ten Arve, A (2012, 12 April) *Sustainable Business Modelling*, interview with Jacques de Swart

van der Lucht, F and Polder, J J (2010) *Towards Better Health: Main report on the public health status and forecasts 2010*, National Institute for Public Health, Bilthoven

van der Velden, L F J, Francke, A L and Batenburg, R S (2011) *Vraag-en Aanbodontwikkelingen in de Verpleging en Verzorging in Nederland*, Nivel, Utrecht

van Rossum, C et al (2011) *Dutch National Food Consumption Survey 2007–2010: Diet of children and adults aged 7 to 69 years*, National Institute for Public Health, Bilthoven van Wormer, J J et al (2011) Stress and workplace productivity loss in the Heart of New Ulm project, *Journal of Occupational and Environmental Medicine,* 53 (10), pp. 1106–09

Veer, A J E et al (2007) *De Aantrekkelijkheid van het Beroep: Een peiling onder het panel verpleegkundigen en verzorgenden,* Nivel, Utrecht

Vijverberg, D (2012, 12 April) *Sustainable Business Modelling,* interview with Jacques de Swart

Weng, S F, Ali, S and Leonardi-Bee, J (2013) Smoking and absence from work: systematic review and meta-analysis of occupational studies, *Addiction,* 108 (2), pp. 307–19

Quantifying the contribution of sports 12

This chapter illustrates the application of the Responsible Business Simulator in the case of the Koninklijke Nederlandse Voetbalbond (KNVB), the Royal Dutch Football Association. This chapter is an adaptation of their full report on the contribution of football, published by KNVB and PwC in 2015 (PwC, 2015). We will start by introducing the Dutch Football Association in the context of strategic decision making.

About KNVB

KNVB is the Netherlands' largest sports association, with 1.2 million members and over 500 employees. KNVB considers sports as the perfect way to include and unite people as well as to inspire them to get in motion, with football in particular seen as the glue for a stronger and tighter society. As football is the number one national sport in the Netherlands, it receives a lot of positive as well as negative media attention. On the one hand, football is promoted because it contributes to better physical as well as mental health (Bernaards, Hildebrandt and Stubbe, 2013; de Graaf, ten Have and Monshouwer, 2009). On the other hand, football is vituperated as it can have associations with aggression and violence (Centraal Informatiepunt Voetbalvandalisme, 2013). KNVB aims to make football attractive, accessible and fun for as many people as possible and at the same time turn around negative trends like aggression and violence. KNVB's mission is uniting people to enjoy football for a lifetime, for each other, for the game and for the future (KNVB, 2015).

About quantifying the value of sports

Just like in the corporate world, the attention on and importance given to sustainability and social responsibility has increased in the world of sports (Dijk & van Eekeren, 2013; van Eekeren, Dijk and Brinkhof, 2012). Various research has been executed around the social and economic role of sports in general and football in particular. ECORYS, a Dutch research and consulting institute has, at the request of KNVB, calculated the economic value of football as the sum of society-related expenses and has evaluated the utility of these expenses (Briene, Koopman and Goessen, 2005). WESP (2015), a collaboration between Dutch academies, universities and research institutes, continuously evaluates the economic impact that sport events have on society via primary research. Commissioned by the Dutch Ministry of Health, Welfare and Sport, the Central Bureau of Statistics (2012) investigated the contribution of sports to the Dutch economy. In collaboration with Sportbank, the Verwey Jonker Instituut has undertaken an extensive literature review that confirms, based on national and international research, that it pays off to invest in sports (Boonstra and Hermens, 2011).

Even though previously performed research on the impact of sports is quite extensive, it is either focused on the financial or on non-financial impact of sports, or football in particular. KNVB wants to go one step further by considering the contribution of football as a combination of financial and non-financial aspects.

This chapter describes how KNVB joined forces with Stichting Meer dan Voetbal (More than Football Foundation), Eredivisie CV (Premier League LP), Coöperatie Eerste Divisie (First League Cooperative) and Universiteit Utrecht to provide integrated insights into the financial as well as non-financial value of football. All parties find it crucial to objectify the aforementioned positive and negative sentiments regarding football. The application of the Responsible Business Simulator has enabled them to not only quantify the current contribution of football to society, but also to provide insights into how the contribution of football can be increased. Note that football is the focus of this case study, but this approach can easily be used with other sports.

The strategic decision-making process

For the development of the strategic decision-making process, we worked in a diverse team with members of the Dutch Football Association, the More than Football Foundation, Premier League LP, First League Cooperative and

Universiteit Utrecht. This way, the team members' knowledge covered a range of aspects and interests within the football world, and resulted in meaningful dialogues. The team's broad knowledge made the data collection process easier. In order to include even more points of view, during the explorative dialogue phase interviews took place with the boards of the professional Dutch football organizations Feyenoord, Heracles Almelo, FC Eindhoven and SC Telstar.

Describing strategic challenge that requires a decision

The brainstorm with experts resulted in the formulation of the following strategic challenge: how to increase the contribution of football. To face this challenge, the first step was to determine the current value that football adds to society. For the calculation of the current financial and non-financial contribution of football to society, a broad definition of football was applied. Professional and non-professional football clubs as well as the national team and international matches on Dutch soil were included as factors that add value.

Defining key outputs involving stakeholders

Before formulating relevant key outputs, the main stakeholders essential for determining how the value of football can be increased were identified. Table 12.1 lists and describes these stakeholders.

With these stakeholders in mind a distinction was made between the financial and non-financial contributions of football. Financial contribution is defined and measured as the contribution to the Gross Domestic Product (GDP). Non-financial value refers to the intrinsic values that football has by nature: football may contribute to a healthier lifestyle, it can create cohesion between people and may contribute to the nurturing of youth as well as adults. Based on this distinction four themes were formulated: Economy, Cohesion, Health and Nurture. These themes represent the most important areas where football can be influential. As a result of translating the high-level theme descriptions into measurable quantities, key outputs were formulated per theme.

The Economy theme can be mapped one to one onto financial contribution, which is defined and measured as the contribution to GDP. In order to determine which cash flows generated by football contribute to the GDP and which do not we used the expenditure approach as defined by the International Monetary Fund (Callen, 2012): 'The *expenditure approach* adds up the value of purchases made by final users – for example, the

Table 12.1   Overview of stakeholders for KNVB case

Stakeholder	Definition
KNVB	Dutch national football association including employees and the national teams.
Professional football organizations	Football clubs in the Premier League and First League including their employees.
Non-professional football organizations	Non-professional football clubs including their employees.
Advocates of football	People that have a positive attitude towards football.
Opponents of football	People that do not have a positive attitude towards football.
Business partners	Organizations that have a sponsorship with professional or non-professional football organizations.
Suppliers	Retail, cable operators, electronics suppliers, hotels, gambling organizations, transport providers and health insurers.
Media	TV, radio and printed press.
Dutch national police	Dutch national police.
Government	Central and regional governments excluding the Dutch national police.

consumption of food, televisions, and medical services by households; the investments in machinery by companies; and the purchases of goods and services by the government and foreigners'.

Please note that the cash flow of a company paying salaries or providing income to its employees is not considered to be part of the expenditure approach. Including this would introduce double counting as it would also be part of the income approach. The same holds for taxes and subsidies, as there is no purchase made by a final user.

Figure 12.1 displays all cash flows that have been identified for the case of KNVB. Please observe that cash flows 3 and 6 concern taxes and subsidies and cash flow 7 concerns primary income and therefore, according the expenditure approach defined above, are not considered to be part of the GDP. Also, a dotted arrow can be observed in cash flows 1 and 8, which implies an 'incomplete' flow. In both cash flows services are purchased by a final user, but only a share of their money is traded for services; the other part of the money concerns sponsoring or contribution.

Figure 12.1   Cash flows for KNVB case. * refers to both professional and non-professional football clubs

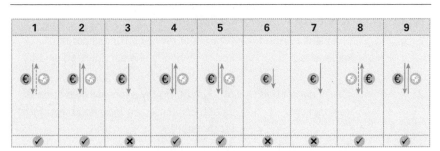

For a more concrete example, suppose that a football canteen sells a cup of coffee for €1.50. The football canteen's expenses were €0.50. According to the IMF definition, only the amount that the consumer spends in the football canteen (€1.50) is counted as contributing to the GDP as this is the final user.

The key outputs that have been formulated for Economy theme are displayed in Table 12.2. The first column lists the type of cash flow (as explained in Figure 12.1) that corresponds to a key output.

In the Netherlands, the total business partner expenses for professional football clubs that can be summed up as a contribution to the Dutch GDP in 2014 was €156,177,000. As the total number of key outputs exceeds 40, when describing the remaining themes we will highlight a selection per theme.

Cohesion refers to connecting members, volunteers, fans and business partners inside and outside the stadium. Having football as a common denominator of interest, both players, fans, volunteers and business partners connect on the grandstands, on the field, in locker rooms, around the coffee machine at work and so on. Key outputs formulated for this theme are for example the number of fans, the number of incidents football-related violence or aggression, and the time in hours spent by volunteers. In the Netherlands, for example, non-professional football clubs counted almost 400,000 volunteers in 2013 (Sportlink, 2014).

Exercise or workouts contribute to physical as well as mental health. Regular practising of sports reduces absenteeism as well as the possibility of several diseases (Bernaards, Hildebrandt and Stubbe, 2013; de Graaf, ten Have and Monshouwer, 2009). Conversely, injuries caused by sports have a negative effect on physical health. Key outputs formulated for the Health theme include the number of injuries and the absenteeism percentage. We learned that in the Netherlands there were 764,000 injuries caused by (non-professional) football at football clubs in 2011 (Bernaards, Hildebrandt and Stubbe, 2013).

Table 12.2   Key output definitions for Economy theme for KNVB case

Cash flow type	Key output	Definition
1	Business partner expenses	Amount of money business partners spend on goods and services, eg skybox tickets or seats.
2	Club's contribution to suppliers	Amount of money a football club spends as end consumer, eg food and beverages for the staff.
4	Safety-related expenses	Amount of money the government spends on the National Police in order to maintain safety.
5	Consumer spending on football club	Amount of money consumers spend on a football club, eg match tickets, food and beverages.
5	Consumer spending on media	Amount of money consumers spend on media, eg sports magazine or a football channel contract.
8	Club's payments to KNVB	Amount of money a football club spends on the education of trainers. Non-professional football clubs also pay dues for communication and participation in the football competition.
9	Club's payments to media	Amount of money a football club spends on marketing and advertisements.

For active practitioners of football, there is also a nurturing effect: participation in a football match teaches individuals to cope with hierarchy, winning and losing, and to collaborate, to have respect and to take responsibility. The number of certified trainers (in FTE) that are contracted by a football club and the number of football players that receive education from a football club are among the key outputs formulated for the Nurturing theme. For the Netherlands, the total investment that professional football clubs made in youth education was €26,786,000 in the season of 2011/2012 (KNVB Expertise, 2012).

Note that Economy is the only theme that links to financial contribution, whereas the other themes refer to the non-financial contribution.

Determining decision maker's options

Recall from Chapter 2 that in order to formulate the decision maker's options, internal variable inputs are formulated first. In this case we also refer to these as types of interventions. The internal variable inputs selected to improve the contribution of football together with a short explanation and the themes that they affect are listed in Table 12.3.

The unit of all internal variable inputs is euro (€). Even though all types of interventions are applicable to professional as well as non-professional football clubs, for illustrational purposes the focus in this case will be on executives of N.E.C. Nijmegen (in short N.E.C.) as decision makers. N.E.C. is a Dutch professional football association that was founded in 1910. Together with their foundation, named 'N.E.C. Doelbewust', which roughly means 'N.E.C. aware of goals'. N.E.C. wants to stimulate cohesion in the neighbourhoods of Nijmegen as well as offer tomorrow's generation the opportunity to develop themselves (N.E.C. Doelbewust, nd).

In the evaluation of the decision maker's options, we assume that N.E.C. invests a total amount of €100,000, as is demonstrated in Table 12.4. This

Table 12.3 Internal variable input definitions for KNVB case

Internal variable input	Explanation	Theme affected
Invest in stadium capacity	An increase of the stadium capacity means more seats and potentially more visitors who spend money and may bond.	Economy, Cohesion
Invest in health programmes	Implementation of health programmes that stimulate exercise improves the health of the participants.	Health
Invest in participation programmes	Implementation of participation programmes that stimulate cohesion increases the social cohesion.	Cohesion
Invest in education of youth players	More education of youth players means more young people that exercise and learn about norms and values.	Health, Nurture
Invest in education of trainers	More education of trainers results in an increase of trainers and/or an improvement of the quality of trainers. This in turn increases the capacity to train and to educate (youth) players.	Nurture, Health
Invest in relations with business partners	Having more business partners means more money spent on the football club.	Economy

Table 12.4 Specification of decision maker's options for KNVB case

Internal variable input	Decision maker's options			
	Option 1	Option 2	Option 3	Option 4
Invest in stadium capacity	€100,000			
Invest in health programmes				€20,000
Invest in participation programmes		€50,000	€30,000	€15,000
Invest in education of youth players		€25,000	€25,000	€30,000
Invest in education of trainers		€25,000	€25,000	€30,000
Invest in relations with business partners			€20,000	€5,000

Table 12.5 Specification of baseline key output values for N.E.C. for KNVB case

Baseline key output values	Value	Source
Economic value	€35,973,514	Allocation principle.
Number of spectators	10,887	(KNVB Expertise, 2014a)
Number of active fans	24,932	Allocation principle.
Number of passive fans	116,631	Allocation principle.
Number of volunteers	310	(Goessens, 2016)
Time spent by volunteers in hours	34,359	Allocation principle.
Number of football players (in training)	102	Allocation principle.
Number of participants in health programmes	2,433	(Goessens, 2016)
Number of participants in participation projects	1,382	Uniform share.
Number of certified trainers	10	N.E.C. Annual report 2014/2015.
Number of partners	356	(Benchmark Betaald Voetbal, 2014)

amount is invested in one internal variable input only (Option 1) or spread over various internal variable inputs (Options 2, 3, 4). Implicitly, we assume that the interventions that are investments in programmes by default concern investments in the best possible programmes that are available on the market.

Drawing up scenarios

Complementary to inputs that are controlled by the decision maker, external variable inputs were formulated in order to account for possible uncertainties in the decision-making process. This enabled us to draw up scenarios. The uncertainties that were formulated can be summarized as the impact that internal variable inputs have on the key outputs: in a pessimistic scenario, the effect on an investment is lower than in a base-case scenario, whereas the effect of an optimistic scenario enlarges the effect that is defined in the base-case scenario. These enlarging and diminishing effects are operationalized in the form of factors by which the initially calculated (base-case) effects are multiplied. For the pessimistic scenario these factors are between 0.5 and 1; in the optimistic scenario between 1 and 1.5.

For example, according to literature, sports can cause a maximum decrease in absenteeism of 7 per cent (TNO, 2003). However, a decision maker might have a more positive effect in mind and can increase this number by indicating that they want to evaluate the different key outputs using an optimistic scenario. In that case, the maximum decrease would become $1.1 \times 7\% = 7.7\%$. If the reverse is the case, namely when the decision maker expects a more negative effect, then evaluating the key outputs in a pessimistic scenario would yield a maximum effect of $0.9 \times 7\% = 6.3\%$.

Constructing simulation model

The information collected so far was inserted into the Responsible Business Simulator. As explained earlier in this chapter, before the strategic challenge for KNVB as well as for an individual football club could be addressed, it was necessary to complete the model with additional data. This concerned information on the current contribution of football (ie without doing any additional investment), but also on the several dependencies that follow from literature research.

Current contribution of football

The process of feeding the simulation model with additional data was operationalized in two stages. First, all the information was collected on a national level, incorporating all parties that add financial as well as non-financial contributions to society via football. National data and football club-specific data was subtracted from several sources (KNVB, 2014; KNVB Expertise, 2014a; KNVB Expertise, 2014b; Sportlink, 2014; Benchmark Betaald Voetbal, 2014; Stichting Kijkonderzoek, 2014). This enabled us to calculate the national contribution of football. Combining all the information subtracted from previously listed sources provided several key insights into the contribution of football in the Netherlands in 2014:

- professional football clubs mainly contribute to the financial impact of football whereas amateur clubs are the main contributors to the non-financial impact;

- the financial contribution of football in the Netherlands was €2.18 billion in 2014, which is 0.34 per cent of the entire GDP.

Having calculated the current national contribution of sports, the values of previously defined key outputs are allocated proportionally to the individual football clubs. The concept of drivers is used to determine the proportion of a club with respect to all professional football clubs. Knowing the proportion, drivers are then used to approximate the key outputs.

An example in which a driver is used to approximate the value of a key output is the calculation of the number of passive fans. Passive fans are those people that are advocates of football but are not directly involved with football-related activities. As the number of passive fans is difficult for a club to disclose, calculating a club's proportion as part of the total of the football clubs is the best estimator. We use the assumption that the estimate of the number of passive fans is driven by the number of spectators. Hence the number of spectators serves as a driver. Since only the national number of passive fans is known, the number of passive fans for a club is calculated by dividing the number of spectators a club has by the national number of spectators and multiplying this proportion by the national number of passive fans. We translated this allocation principle for the calculation of all key outputs j with drivers i into the following formula:

$$Club\,Key\,Output_j = \frac{Club\,Value\,Driver_{i(j)}}{National\,Value\,Driver_{i(j)}} * National\,Key\,Output_j$$

The formula completed for calculation of the number of passive fans of N.E.C., which has 10,887 spectators (KNVB Expertise, 2014a), would look as follows:

$$
\begin{aligned}
Number\,of\,passive\,fans_{N.E.C.} &= \frac{Number\,of\,spectators_{NEC}}{Number\,of\,spectators_{National}} \\
&\quad * Number\,of\,passive\,fans_{National} \\
&= \frac{10,887}{407,538} * 4,345,000 = 116,631
\end{aligned}
$$

Once the proportion of each football club for each key output is determined, we know the baseline contributions of the key outputs. For some key outputs we do not use the allocation principle, but we just distribute the national *contribution* uniformly over the clubs. This, for example, is the case with the number of participants in health programmes. Naturally, a club's decision maker has the opportunity to overrule these numbers with more recent data from their annual report or own research. Table 12.5 specifies the baseline key output values for N.E.C., their description and whether or not they are calculated.

Dependencies

Now that the baseline values are known, we continue with the calculation of the impact that the interventions have on intermediates and key outputs. For this calculation we again use an allocation principle. However, this principle is different from the one explained in the previous section since the national value does not play a role. We will restrict ourselves here to one example and refer to the full report on the contribution of football for more details.

Suppose for example that a club's decision maker invests in stadium capacity. They expect that an increase in stadium capacity will cause an increase in the number of spectators. The increase in spectators in turn potentially increases amongst other things the number of active fans, the number of volunteers and the consumer expenses. For example, the increase of active fans of N.E.C. after an investment in stadium capacity would be calculated as follows. First, we determine the current proportion of active fans per number of spectators, which is $24,932/10,887 = 2.29$. Second, we calculate the number of spectators per chair, which is 0.878 (KNVB Expertise, 2014a). This way we can calculate that for each additional chair that N.E.C. buys, the number of fans increases by $0.878 \times 2.29 = 2.01$.

Evaluating options by assessing strategic priorities

Now that the Responsible Business Simulator has been completed with all model elements and data from desk and field research, the decision maker can easily evaluate which option is 'best', given their strategic priorities. The key outputs can be evaluated individually as well as aggregated per theme.

Using the decision maker's options as formulated above and assuming that N.E.C's board deems all themes equally important, it follows from Figure 12.2 that the optimal strategy would be Option 4, to spread the investment over all internal variable inputs except for stadium capacity. If the board prefers the themes Economy or Cohesion over the other themes, Option 1, only investing in stadium capacity, will be preferred. Even though Economy is a necessity for self-preservation, we learned that N.E.C. values the themes Cohesion and Nurture the most. Inserting these preferences into the Responsible Business Simulator by assigning less weight to Economy and Health, would lead to Option 3 as the preferred option. In Option 3 the investment budget is spread over the same internal variable inputs as in Option 2 but a different

Figure 12.2 Comparison of decision maker's options when all themes have equal weights in base case scenario for KNVB case

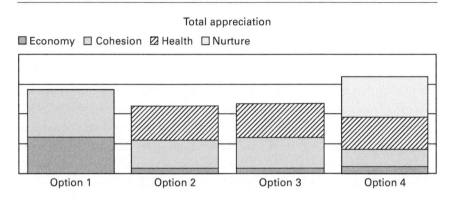

Total appreciation

☑ Economy ☐ Cohesion ☒ Health ☐ Nurture

distribution is used and additionally a part of the investment is done with business partners. Based on gut feeling, one might have expected that Option 2 would be recommended. However, then one would be neglecting the fact that investing in business partners contributes to Cohesion as well.

Evaluating options by assessing risk appetite

Next we take into account the decision maker's risk appetite. Figure 12.3 shows that – when all themes are still deemed equally important – Option 4 is beaten by Option 1 in the optimistic scenario. So an optimist only putting weight on this scenario may prefer Option 1. However, a decision maker looking for a decision that is robust under all scenarios by assigning equal weight to all three scenarios should still choose Option 4.

Figure 12.3 Score per decision maker's option when all key outputs have equal weights for all scenarios for KNVB case

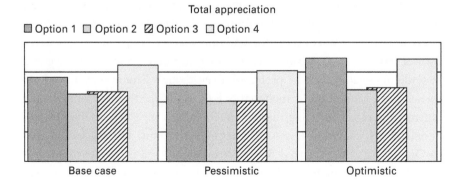

Total appreciation

☑ Option 1 ☐ Option 2 ☒ Option 3 ☐ Option 4

Reflections

The KNVB Foundation played an important role – from the very beginning – by helping to ensure that the decision-making instrument truly reflected the football world. The modelling process has been an interactive one, involving various stakeholders and decision makers. The boards of professional organizations provided their input such that the simulation model not only worked as it should, but also accurately reflected the decision-making process. The strategic dialogue phase was executed with more than 10 professional football clubs, including Feyenoord, PSV Eindhoven, FC Eindhoven, N.E.C. and VVV Venlo. In addition, the Responsible Business Simulator was used in discussions with municipalities and in a round-table session during the annual Dutch national football conference of 2015. The simulation model provided the various participants insights into the effects of potential investments on the different themes. Besides valuing these insights, the clubs also indicated that they greatly valued the explorative dialogue. This new way of approaching a business case and thinking about stakeholders was considered at least as important as knowing the precise effects of potential decisions.

The strategic dialogue has inspired N.E.C. to use an innovative approach to providing insights to potential funders of their stadium, namely by pointing out the financial as well as the non-financial added value of the stadium.

A session at the Dutch Ministry of Health, Welfare and Sports indicated that an adaptation of the simulation model regarding other sports, for example hockey, could easily be made. At the same time, it should be clear that the existing simulation model offers room for extension: from the different sessions with various football clubs we learned the desire to evaluate additional elements such as gender, ethnic and age diversity.

References

Benchmark Betaald Voetbal (2014) *Tabellenboek Benchmark BVOs*, KNVB Expertise, Zeist

Bernaards, C M, Hildebrandt, V H and Stubbe, J H (2013) *Trendrapport Bewegen en Gezondheid 2010/2011*, TNO, Leiden

Boonstra, N and Hermens, N (2011) *De Maatschappelijke Waarde van Sport*, Verwey-Jonker Instituut, Den Haag

Briene, M, Koopman, A and Goessen, F (2005) *De Waarde van Voetbal: Maatschappelijke en economische betekenis van voetbal in Nederland, eindrapport*, ECORYS Nederland B.V., Rotterdam

Callen, T (2012) Gross domestic product: an economy's all, *Finance and development*. Retrieved from http://www.imf.org/external/pubs/ft/fandd/basics/gdp.htm

Centraal Bureau voor de Statistiek & Hogeschool van Arnhem en Nijmegen (2012) *De Bijdrage van Sport aan de Nederlandse Economie*, Centraal Bureau voor de Statistiek, Den Haag

Centraal Informatiepunt Voetbalvandalisme (2013) *Jaaroverzicht 2012/2013: Veiligheid en openbare ordebeheersing rondom het Nederlands betaald voetbal*, CIV, Utrecht

de Graaf, R, ten Have, M and Monshouwer, K (2009) *Sporten en Psychische Gezondheid (Netherlands Mental Health Survey and Incidence Study)*, TRIMBOS Instituut, Utrecht

Dijk, B and van Eekeren, F (2013) *Rendement van Maatschappelijk Verantwoord Ondernemen door BVOs, Seizoen 2011-2012*, Universiteit Utrecht, Utrecht

Goessens, J (2016) NEC club details, interview with Myrthe van der Plas

KNVB (2014) *Jaarverslag 2012/2013*, KNVB, Zeist

KNVB (2015) Missie en visie. Retrieved from http://www.knvb.nl/over-ons/over-de-knvb/missie-en-visie

KNVB Expertise (2012) *Benchmark Betaal Voetbal*, KNVB Expertise, Zeist

KNVB Expertise (2014a) *Eredivisie Fan Onderzoek 2013/2014*, KNVB Expertise, Zeist

KNVB Expertise (2014b) *Jupiler Leage fan Onderzoek 2013/2014*, KNVB Expertise, Zeist:

N.E.C. Doelbewust (nd, retrieved 10 July 2016) Visie en missie. Retrieved from http://www.necdoelbewust.nl/visie-en-missie/

PwC (2015) *De Kracht van Voetbal: Sturen op de maatschappelijke impact van voetbal*. Retrieved from http://www.knvb.nl/downloads/bestand/4608/rapport-de-kracht-van-voetbal

Sportlink (2014) *Geaggregeerde Data 2012/2013*, Sportlink, Zeist

Stichting Kijkonderzoek (2014) *Jaarrapport 2013*. Retrieved from https://kijkonderzoek.nl/images/SKO_Jaarrapport/SKO_jaarrapport_2013.pdf

TNO (2003) *TNO Arbeid Rapport*. Retrieved from https://www.10000stappen.nl/uploaded/TNO%20Arbeid%20rapport.pdf

van Eekeren, F, Dijk, B and Brinkhof, S (2012) *Rendement en Kritische Succesfactoren van Maatschappelijk Verantwoord Ondernemen door BVO's, Seizoen 2010/2011*, Universiteit Utrecht, Utrecht

Werkgroep Evaluatie Sportevenementen (2015) WESP studies. Retrieved from http://www.evenementenevaluatie.nl

WorldBank (2014) Data – Netherlands – GDP at market prices, *Data Worldbank*. Retrieved from http://data.worldbank.org/country/netherlands

Responding to the refugee influx in Europe

13

The massive influx of refugees and economic migrants in Europe during the summer of 2015 caused much debate. According to international law, countries have obligations towards refugees. The enduring war in Syria and the unstable and unsafe situations in other countries in the Middle East and Central Asia have caused many casualties. With ongoing threats, dozens of cities demolished and overpopulated refugee camps in neighbouring countries, many people have fled these countries, resulting in a rush of more than a million people from different nations, nationalities and cultures seeking sanctuary in Europe. It is not the first time in recent history that this kind of movement of people has taken place. During the late 1990s, Europe had an influx of refugees fleeing civil war in former Yugoslavia. Nevertheless, the first months of recent refugee influx were rather complex as many people were shifted between temporary refugee camps throughout the corridor stretching from Greece through the Balkan states to Hungary, Austria, Germany (which was the main destination), Sweden and the Netherlands.

In this chapter we focus on strategic decision making at the level of municipalities in the case of the refugee influx. In this sphere, politicians, civil servants, authorities, refugee organizations, employers and volunteers are the actors who have to handle the influx, integration and perspective on a new future for the newcomers. Taking into account what has been learned from other refugee streams, what could and should be done better this time? And what opportunities are created by the refugee influx? Since Europe in 2016 is not the same as Europe 20 years ago, this must be done by taking into account the economic crisis which is still present in parts of Europe; many economic reforms are underway, causing unrest and instability. Nowadays, populist parties are part of the political system in many democratic countries in Europe and sometimes part of the government. In this situation, xenophobia and stigmatization of foreigners can become much more acceptable. Frequently heard complaints are that criminality and unemployment increase and economic growth decreases with the arrival of refugees (Noack, 2015; BBC News, 2015; Robins-Early, 2015). However, taking a closer look at the increased crime rate it turns out that if one controls for age, gender, marital status and whether or not someone receives social benefits, then an increase in crime cannot be ascribed to ethnic background (Engbertsen et al, 2015). In this highly complex arena, we see Europe struggling between the humanist side wanting to offer a helping hand and shelter, and political opportunism blaming 'foreigners' and newcomers for problems in society.

It is not easy to come to a consensus at a European or local level. Tensions are present and the debate around the European refugee influx is sometimes based on emotion instead of on facts (Kurtz, 2015; The Telegraph View, 2015). What can the Responsible Business Simulator do and how can it add value to the strategic decision-making process? By giving all stakeholders a voice in the debate and translating these voices into numbers, we were able to facilitate politics based on facts. Creating a level playing field by pinpointing the facts based on the justified data we researched, we opened the floor for more and better choices at municipality level to allocate budgets for the integration of refugees with a residence permit (status holders). We simulated different options for spending the budget in relation to shaping the best chances for prospective employment; the outcome was different to what had so far been done by the national authorities.

About the refugee influx

The International Organization for Migration (2016) counted 1,011,712 migrants and refugees crossing the southern border of the European Union in 2015. If we look at the total amount of asylum requests for Europe in 2008 it was 225,000; the total amount in 2015 was 1,321,600. The influx of refugees and economic migrants in their slipstream had been increasing since 2008, but it doubled from 2014 to 2015 and is still very large. The distribution of requests for asylum is unevenly spread over Europe. With 476,500 requests for asylum in 2015, Germany was leading by far, followed by Hungary with 162,500, Sweden with 162,500, Austria with 88,200, Italy with 84,100, France with 75,800, the Netherlands with 45,000 requests, Belgium with almost the same amount at 44,700, Switzerland with 39,400, and the United Kingdom with 38,800. The Nordic countries take a fair share of the refugees, which is less the case for the Baltics, the majority of the Eastern European countries (with the exception of Bulgaria and Hungary), the Balkan countries and the Iberian Peninsula (CBS Statline,

2016). For 2016, the Dutch Central Bureau of Statistics (2015) expected more than 70,000 asylum requests in the Netherlands. A (temporary) residence permit that grants asylum is only awarded to refugees, not to economic migrants who come from countries that are regarded as safe and not at war. This chapter will focus on those refugees who receive a residence permit, referred to as refugee status holders or just refugees. Overall, we can see that in the past few years the number of refugees with a permit increased to levels not seen before.

Due to the high number of refugees and the uncertainty about the true motivation of the immigrants asking for asylum, the Dublin Regulation and the Schengen accord as well as country-specific asylum regulations are currently under pressure (Barker and Brunsden, 2015). The public debate around the European refugee influx is often based on emotion, fed by populist parties instead of on facts. Newspapers and media report emotional encounters in town council meetings and community centres (Voorn, 2016) and protests in general against refugees (Reuters, 2016). Notwithstanding the negative sentiments, there are at the same time countless volunteers, people from NGOs and companies who are at pains to help and support refugees to integrate in their new countries of residence.

Matching refugees with host municipalities

According to the Dutch Knowledge Platform Integration and Society, in which over 200 municipalities are represented, 60 per cent of the refugees are only able to work after following an educational programme or by doing voluntary work. Thirty per cent of the refugees are seen as impossible to guide to (paid) work. Since the burden of social costs lies particularly with municipalities, it is in their interest to know more about the background of refugees in order to guide them through integration processes that will have a more positive impact. Currently only 16 per cent of the municipalities say they know enough about the background of the accepted and licensed refugees to guide them to work (Razenberg and De Gruijter, 2016). The more refugees are active in work, the better it is for the refugees, municipalities and society at large (Economist, 2015).

In the Netherlands a working group set up by the Ministry of Social Affairs, 'Working and Integration', came with the advice to start with early screenings and assessments of work experience, educational qualifications and skills while refugees are still in asylum accommodation. The goal is to make matches with municipalities that have specific industries and needs for skilled labour. A city like Eindhoven would be a better place for refugees with ICT work experience than for those with a farming background. The early screening can also lead to quicker guidance towards education and work in those places where refugees have the best potential to integrate into the society. The advantage of early screening and assessment is that municipalities get a much better idea of what kind of refugees they will have to find housing for and what kind of jobs could be searched for. This adds value to the waiting time between arrival in the asylum centres and departure to municipalities for a longer stay. In the meantime, more focused activities can be organized in terms of acquiring general knowledge about the new country, participating in voluntary work, learning the language, or preparing for education and internships to get more work experience. Since mid-2016, screening and assessment have been taking place in one of the asylum centres and it is foreseen that this approach will be expanded to many more places. These types of policies will ultimately increase the effectiveness of the measures taken at the municipality level which will be discussed in this chapter.

Special attention for young refugees

There has not been much research so far on the position of young asylum seekers and their integration via education and work. The Verwey-Jonker Institute undertook exploratory research commissioned by Movisie about young refugees in the Netherlands (Stavenuiter et al, 2016). The main conclusions are that young asylum seekers in the age group 13–23 years old who have a license to stay, form a pool of under-utilized talent. Due to limitations in language fluency, many young refugees are placed at education levels lower than their capabilities. This can lead to frustrations, particularly among those that have higher intellectual capabilities. Additional language programmes provided by educational institutions are highly regarded, because fine-tuning of the language is an important ticket to the labour market. Peer coaching during education offers additional support for youngsters. Providing access to networks that can be useful for internships, temporary work experience, or professional work is an important asset for integration. Getting to know local people and having contacts is necessary to take the first steps towards work; lack of it is an obstacle to integration. The resulting waste of these young refugees' talent stresses the need for a more fact-based dialogue concerning the integration of refugees.

About allocating budget for integration of refugees

Since municipalities in particular are called to take action in these situations where emotions play a role, it is crucial for decision makers to motivate their actions with fact-based information. A quantification of the effects of their actions facilitates a constructive dialogue, where opinions are traded for facts and figures, and resistance for mutual understanding. In this complex setting, a decision maker needs to obey the law and at the same time address citizens' concerns and the opinions of differently minded politicians. It should not be surprising that these concerns and opinions are not always aligned and can cause conflicts of interest.

Several municipalities are trying out a mix of activities consisting of language programmes, voluntary work, learning activities and helping with the daily routines of the temporary asylum centres, such as cleaning, cooking, and playing with the children. The recommendation is to keep refugees busy in a meaningful way, lowering the risk of frustration and increasing the sense of safety in the community. Notwithstanding the many positive initiatives at the municipal level, it remains very difficult to decide what to do and when. What has the highest impact? Since municipalities are the main governmental actors in accommodating and integrating refugees, we approached several municipalities to try out the Responsible Business Simulator techniques for making strategic decisions on the refugee issue.

The simulation model discussed in this chapter has been developed for policy makers at the municipal level. The application of the Responsible Business Simulator in this context has the purpose of supporting policy makers in their decision-making process regarding their response to the refugee crisis and the dialogue around it. In the simulation model, effects that have already been researched are disclosed and combined such that policy makers are provided with quantitative insights that make the decision-making process easier and enable a fact-based dialogue.

The strategic decision-making process

For the development of the strategic decision-making process, we worked with a team of different experts from academia, charity organizations, and local and national governments. The expertise comprised real estate, municipalities, refugees, strategy, data analytics and communication. Experts from central and local government were consulted throughout different stages of the process. In various workshops the inputs for and the outputs of the strategic decision-making process were validated.

Describing strategic challenge that requires a decision

As mentioned in the introduction, policy makers have a lot of stakeholders with different interests to account for when deciding upon what actions regarding the refugee influx are best for their region. The strategic challenge for a decision maker is therefore formulated as how to accommodate refugees in their region. In the remainder of this case a region is considered to be a municipality, in which the decision maker typically is a mayor, alderman or specially appointed officer.

Defining key outputs involving stakeholders

In order to address the strategic challenge of refugees who are allocated to a municipality, the municipality's inhabitants, local entrepreneurs and employers are identified as key stakeholders. Inhabitants' political preferences, reflected in their opinions towards the arrival of the refugees and their actions regarding the refugees, go in various directions. Refugees, in turn, are affected by the sentiments and attitudes of their neighbours and the actions that a municipality takes. Arguments raised for and against the shelter of refugees can be considered aspects that policy makers should take into account when deciding upon an action. These arguments concern the quality of life, criminality, unemployment and economic growth. Based on these topics and the experience of policy makers from different municipalities, we formulated and validated six key outputs. These key outputs can be allocated to two themes: Economy and Society. Table 13.1 gives an overview of these key outputs, to which theme they relate and a brief description.

To measure quality of life we use the definition as formulated by the Dutch Central Bureau of Statistics (Beuningen and Kloosterman, 2011). According to their definition, quality of life depends on eight factors, namely material living conditions, economic risks, health, education and occupation, social participation and trust, social relations, safety, and the (living) environment.

Determining decision maker's options

The arrival of refugees may have both positive and negative effects on key outputs. Municipalities or local decision makers want to mitigate or

Table 13.1 Key output definitions for Refugees case

Key output	Unit	Theme	Description
Unemployment rate reduction refugees	%	Society	Decrease in unemployment rate of refugees due to policy maker's actions.
Unemployment rate reduction inhabitants	%	Society	Decrease in unemployment rate of inhabitants due to policy maker's actions.
Economic impact	€	Economy	Economic growth due to policy maker's actions.
Crime rate reduction refugees	%	Society	Decrease in crime rate of refugees due to policy maker's actions.
Quality of life improvement refugees	.	Society	Increase in quality of life of refugees due to policy maker's actions.
Quality of life improvement inhabitants	.	Society	Increase in quality of life of inhabitants due to policy maker's actions.

neutralize the negative effects as much as possible and exploit the positive effects as much as they can. Based on the discussions with refugee experts from several municipalities, six possible actions or internal variable inputs have been formulated. These are displayed in Table 13.2

Since in this case all internal variable inputs are formulated in terms of investments, in the remainder they may be referred to as such. To illustrate the practical application of the simulation model, we will use the Dutch municipality of Eindhoven. We expect this municipality to invest €2,370 per refugee, which equals the amount that Dutch municipalities receive for each refugee from the Dutch state. Eindhoven formulated four decision maker's options:

- Do nothing: the received amount per refugee is not spend at all.
- Mix: the budget per refugee is spread equally over all six internal variable inputs (€395 per input).
- Employment, language and integration: the budget per refugee is divided equally over the internal variable inputs Employment (€1,185) and Language and integration courses (€1,185).
- Language and integration only: the entire budget per refugee is invested in language and integration courses.

Table 13.2   Internal variable input definitions for Refugees case

Internal variable input	Description
Higher education	An investment in one year of tertiary education with the purpose to increase refugees' chances in the labour market.
Neighbourhood diversity	An investment in residential brokerage to spread refugees over town, instead of allocating them all together.
Sports and associations	An investment in membership of sports clubs or sports associations to improve the well-being of refugees as well as their integration into the community.
Language and integration course	An investment in language and integration courses to ease up the integration process, to improve the social cohesion and increase chances in the labour market.
Buddy support	An investment in a coach, buddy or group therapy to improve the mental well-being of refugees. Treatment of serious mental health issues like Post Traumatic Stress Disorder (PTSD) are assumed to be reimbursed by health insurance and are therefore not considered as part of buddy support.
Employment	An investment in coaching regarding job finding and the application process with the purpose to decrease unemployment amongst refugees.

Drawing up scenarios

Besides inputs that are controlled by the decision maker, external variable inputs have been formulated in order to account for exogenous uncertainties. This enables us to draw up scenarios. We consider seven sources of uncertainty that we want to monitor for their influence on key outputs. From Table 13.3 it can be deduced that six of them refer to the monthly salary that an inhabitant earns if jobs are created because of investments in one of the internal variable inputs. If a decision maker decides to invest in one or more of the options to accommodate refugees as listed in Table 13.2, these options need to be facilitated and this creates jobs for the inhabitants. The remaining external variable input concerns the minimum investment in language and integration that is necessary for a full employment effect to be realized for a refugee. The assumption is that successful language and integration courses are crucial for the refugees in their job-search process. If the investment in language and integration courses is too small, then a significantly lower effect is expected from the investment in employment. We will elaborate on this so-called interaction phenomenon further on in this chapter. As we have used expert opinion to determine the minimum investment, we offer the decision maker the opportunity to assess the impact of variations in this value.

We have formulated three scenarios. Since all external variable inputs refer to labour (although it is important to stress that the first six relate to labour for inhabitants and the latter relates to labour for refugees), we have named these scenarios labour optimistic, base case and labour pessimistic. In a labour optimistic scenario the decision maker expects lower salaries for inhabitants, thus increasing the return of a given investment. At the same time, the minimum investment needed in language and integration to create the full employment effect for refugees is expected to be smaller in the labour optimistic scenario. The opposite is the case in the labour pessimistic scenario. The exact definitions of the scenarios are in Table 13.3.

Constructing the simulation model

The information collected so far has been inserted into the Responsible Business Simulator. However, for the simulation model to provide accurate and clear insights to the decision maker, quite an amount of additional information is required. Via comprehensive desk research and in collaboration with the stakeholders we have collected the missing information and

Table 13.3 Specification of scenarios for Refugees case

External variable input	Scenarios			Source base case
	Labour optimistic	Base case	Labour pessimistic	
Salary higher education	€3,098	€3,323	€3,481	(Loonwijzer.nl, nd)
Salary neighbourhood diversity	€2,644	€2,748	€2,821	(Loonwijzer.nl, nd)
Salary sports and associations	€2,153	€2,318	€2,433	(Loonwijzer.nl, nd)
Salary language and integration course	€2,879	€3,076	€3,215	(Loonwijzer.nl, nd)
Salary buddy support	€2,588	€2,740	€2,846	(Loonwijzer.nl, nd)
Salary employment	€2,306	€2,438	€2,530	(Loonwijzer.nl, nd)
Minimum investment in language and integration for full employment effect	€500	€500	€1,300	Expert opinion

completed the simulation model. This information can be broken down into inputs related to a municipality, direct effects and indirect effects.

Input related to a municipality

For each municipality, characteristics that distinguish them in this context from other municipalities are needed in the calculation of the key outputs. Table 13.4 specifies the two most important characteristics for the municipality of Eindhoven. These inputs are necessary for the calculation of the inhabitants' unemployment rate reduction, their quality of life, and the economic impact.

Input related to direct effects

The effects that investments have on key outputs are modelled in various steps. In the first step, the direct effect is calculated. Typically, this first step does not yet model the impact of an investment on a key output. A good example is Quality of Life, which consists of eight factors. In the first step, we model the effect that investments may have on these factors.

Table 13.5 displays four characteristics of the investments that are taken into account when modelling the direct effects of the investments.

Table 13.4 Specification of fixed inputs for municipality Eindhoven for Refugees case

Fixed input	Value	Description
Number of inhabitants	218,433	Current number of inhabitants.
Number of refugees	9,081	Current number of refugee status holders.

Table 13.5 Definitions of fixed inputs related to direct effects for Refugees case

Fixed input	Description
Accessible population	Percentage of the population on which the investment will have an effect. The statistics are primarily based on literature research.
Probability of success	Likelihood that the investment will prove to be successful. These statistics are partially based on expert knowledge.
Saturation point	Maximum effective investment, or the ceiling above which further investment has no further effect. Here, the statistics are also primarily based on literature research.
Maximum possible effect	Maximum effect obtained when investing an amount greater or equal than the saturation point. Since an investment may have more than one direct effect, for each investment, various maximum possible effects need to be specified. These statistics are also primarily based on literature research.

The first three inputs in Table 13.5 only relate to the type of investment. Their values and – if available – references to their sources are listed in Table 13.6. If no source is listed, experts have been consulted. As described earlier, the decision maker has the possibility to add an uncertainty to these expert opinions via the use of scenarios.

As explained in Table 13.5, the maximum possible effects of investments do not only depend on the type of investment, but also on what they impact. These can be key outputs and intermediates, where intermediates refer to variables that are calculated to break down the modelling process in several steps. Here, the only key output that is directly impacted by investments is the unemployment rate reduction of refugees. The intermediates are most of the components that are used in the calculation of quality of life improvement. Another intermediate directly impacted by investments is the percentage of refugees that act as volunteers. In the next section we will see that this percentage affects feelings of unsafety and crime rates. The values of the maximum possible effects are listed in Table 13.7, again including – if applicable – their reference. If a cell contains no value, this means that no relevant literature or expert opinion could be found and we assume, conservatively, that there is no effect.

Combining the information from Tables 13.6 and 13.7 with the invested amounts, the direct effect of each investment can be calculated. The direct effect of an investment i on intermediate or key output j, where i and j refer to the rows and columns of Table 13.7, respectively, is calculated by means of the following formula:

$$\text{Direct Effect}_{ij} = \text{Accessible Population}_i \times \text{Probability Of Success}_i$$
$$\times \frac{min(\text{Investment Amount}_i, \text{Saturation Point}_i)}{\text{Saturation Point}_i}$$
$$\times \text{Maximum Possible Effect}_{ij}$$

In this constellation, we assume that the effect of all investments increases in a linear fashion up to the saturation point and that investments larger than this saturation point do not result in any additional effect. Additionally, for the investment in employment we take into account a so-called interaction effect: if an investment in employment is not accompanied by a minimum investment in language and integration courses, then the effect of an investment in employment is only one-fifth of the maximum effect. This is reflected in the model by assuming that the maximum effect for employment is reduced by 80 per cent when the investment is not accompanied by a minimum investment of €500 in language and integration courses.

Table 13.6 Values of fixed inputs related to direct effects for Refugees case

Internal variable input	Accessible population	Probability of success	Saturation point
Higher education	21% (Central Intelligence Agency, nd; Unicef, nd)	71% (Central Bureau of Statistics, 2007)	€12,674 (OECD, 2014)
Neighbourhood diversity	100%	100%	€750 (Gemiddeldgezien.nl, nd) (Woonbemiddeling Nederland, nd)
Sports and associations	63% (Central Intelligence Agency, nd)	70%	€500 (Bremmer, 2008)
Language and integration course	100%	70% (Maastricht University, 2014)	€1,395 (Suitcase talen, nd)
Buddy support	61% (Gojer and Ellis, 2014)	40%	€3,177
Employment	63% (Central Intelligence Agency, nd; Engbertsen et al, 2015)	60%	€2,500 (SEO Economisch Onderzoek, 2010)

Table 13.7 Specification of maximum direct effects for Refugees case. * means that the maximum effect only applies to inhabitants. Otherwise the effects are only applicable to refugees

Internal variable input	Affected intermediates or key outputs							
	Social cohesion	Social participation refugees	Social trust	Health score refugees	Average household income	Education level	% volunteers	Unemployment reduction refugees
Higher education					70% (OECD, 2014)	100%	6.2% (Campbell, 2006)	10% (OECD, 2014)
Neighbour-hood diversity*	-18.8%* (Lancee and Dronkers, 2008)		-2.7%* (Lancee and Dronkers, 2008)					
Language and integration course	3.8% (Stone and Hulse, 2007)		1.8% (Stone and Hulse, 2007)		17% (Hanushek and Zhang, 2009)	100%	8% (Choi and DiNitto, 2012)	2.2% (Groot and Maassen van den Brink, 2006)
Sports and associations	12% (Toepoel, 2013)	100%		37.51% (Lawlor and Hopker, 2001)			165% (Choi and DiNitto, 2012)	
Buddy support								0.5% (Frijters, Johnston, and Shields, 2010)
Employment								30% (Weber and Hofer, 2004)

To illustrate this mechanism, let us consider a decision maker who wants to invest in higher education. Suppose we want to know the direct effect that this investment has on the unemployment rate reduction amongst refugees. From literature we have learned that 21 per cent of the refugees have an educational basis that enables them to enter higher education (ie the accessible population = 21 per cent), that an increase of education level can reduce unemployment by 10 per cent (ie the maximum possible effect = 10 per cent) and that investing in higher education has a desired effect on 71 out of 100 participants (ie probability of success = 71 per cent). The direct effect of this investment on unemployment is therefore a reduction of at most 21% * 10% * 71% = 1.49%.

This is the case if a decision maker invests the maximum effective amount or the saturation point. From literature we have learned that the saturation point for investing in higher education is €12,674. Let us assume now that the decision maker has an available study budget of €500, which is considerably lower than the saturation point. The direct result would then be: $1.49\% * \left(\dfrac{500}{12,674} \right) = 0.06\%$. By investing €500 per refugee in higher education, a municipality could therefore reduce the unemployment rate of the refugees by 0.06 per cent.

Figure 13.1 illustrates the rationale described above. On the horizontal axis the amount invested in higher education is displayed, and the vertical axis shows the attainable reduction in the unemployment rate of the refugees. The bending line indicates the sensitivity of the unemployment rate reduction to changes in higher education (with a maximum of 1.49 per cent), the straight line is at the intersection of the investment of €500 with the sensitivity. This intersection indicates a reduction of 0.06 per cent which is in line with the calculation above.

Input related to indirect effects

From Table 13.7 we know that except for the reduction in refugee unemployment, key outputs are not directly affected by any one of the internal variable inputs. The internal variable inputs have an effect on several variables that in turn affect the key outputs, the so-called intermediates. Both the effects that intermediates have on other intermediates and key outputs, and the effects key outputs have on each other are called indirect effects. Their maximum values are displayed in Table 13.8. The '*' earmark refers to effects that are applicable to both inhabitants and refugees. Otherwise the effect is only applicable to refugees.

Figure 13.1 Sensitivity of 'Unemployment rate reduction refugees' to changes in 'Higher education' for Refugees case

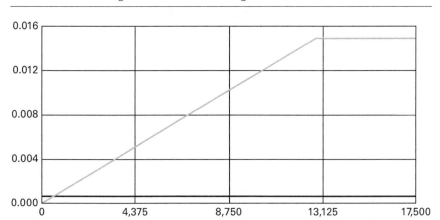

Effects on economic impact are excluded from Table 13.8. This is because the value of this key output is calculated based on the changed income of refugees and inhabitants due to a change in the unemployment rates caused by (a combination of) the investments.

On the side of caution we assume that effects of investments are limited to one year. In reality, a refugee or inhabitant can experience positive effects of investments for a far longer period. Limiting the shelf life of internal variable inputs to just one year reduces the risk of overestimating the effective period.

Evaluating options by assessing strategic priorities

Having inserted all required information into the Responsible Business Simulator, the decision maker can easily evaluate which of the four decision maker's options defined earlier is the 'best' by setting strategic priorities via assigning weights to key outputs. By default, all key outputs are assigned equal weights.

Before proceeding to assigning weights to the key outputs, let us first take a look at how each key output performs for two of the four defined decision maker's options. This is displayed in the spider plot in Figure 13.2. Recall from Chapter 7 that the further an option is plotted away from the origin, the better the score of the corresponding key output. Using this reasoning we see that refugees' quality of life improvement and crime rate reduction have the highest value when the decision maker's Mix option is chosen, while economic impact and unemployment rate reduction for both inhabitants and refugees, and quality of life improvement for inhabitants attain their highest

Table 13.8 Specification of maximum indirect effects for Refugees case

Intermediate or key output	Intermediate or key output			
	Unsafety feelings	Social trust	Crime reduction refugees	Quality of life
Social trust				20.9%* (Beuningen and Kloosterman, 2011)
Unsafe feelings				-22.9%* (Beuningen and Kloosterman, 2011)
Social cohesion			26% (Beuningen et al, 2013)	36.3%* (Beuningen and Kloosterman, 2011)
Education level				-6.8% (Beuningen and Kloosterman, 2011)
Health score				112% (Beuningen and Kloosterman, 2011)
Social participation				39.1% (Beuningen and Kloosterman, 2011)
Average household income			26% (Beuningen et al, 2013)	
% volunteers			25% (Beuningen et al, 2013)	
Unemployment reduction		1% (Stone and Hulse, 2007)		26.6%* (Beuningen and Kloosterman, 2011)
Crime reduction refugees	-29%* (Boers, Steden and Boutellier, 2008)			

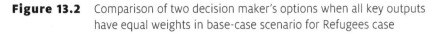

Figure 13.2   Comparison of two decision maker's options when all key outputs have equal weights in base-case scenario for Refugees case

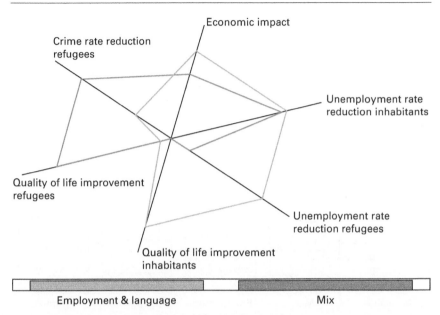

values when the Employment and Language option is selected. Therefore, which of these two options is best depends on the weights of the key outputs.

We will now compare the four decision maker's options under the assumption that the municipality of Eindhoven deems all key outputs equally important. Figure 13.3 illustrates how each option performs under this assumption, and we deduce that the overall recommended strategy is to invest in 'Employment and Language'. Also, we see that 'No action' outperforms 'Mix' with respect to the key output of quality of life improvement for the refugees. This might seem counterintuitive but it can be supported by our literature research results: when people receive higher education, which is part of the investment for the 'Mix' option, their education level goes up. From Table 13.8 we learned that – according to research conduct by Beuningen and Kloosterman (2011) – a higher education level can diminish quality of life as education level is negatively correlated with quality of life. Of course, highly educated people may have a higher quality of life than poorly educated people because of other aspects contributing to quality of life, such as material living conditions, but impact on material living conditions is not expected to happen within one year.

Considering all key outputs to be equally important could for instance be a strategic priority for a municipality with divergent opinions and preferences within their town council. To evaluate other perspectives as well, we

Figure 13.3 Comparison of decision maker's options when all key outputs have equal weights in base-case scenario for municipality Eindhoven for Refugees case

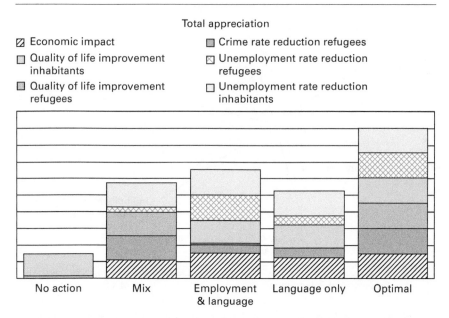

Total appreciation

☑ Economic impact   ▦ Crime rate reduction refugees
☐ Quality of life improvement   ▨ Unemployment rate reduction
   inhabitants   refugees
☐ Quality of life improvement   ☐ Unemployment rate reduction
   refugees   inhabitants

No action   Mix   Employment   Language only   Optimal
                    & language

inserted a political preference that only focused on the well-being of the refugee status holders. This manifested itself in assigning weight only to refugees' quality of life and unemployment. Given these strategic priorities, 'Mix' would be the recommended option.

Additionally, we used the optimization mechanism within the Responsible Business Simulator; details of the workings of this optimization are described in Chapter 7. Optimizing the decision maker's options, given that all key outputs are deemed equally important, shows that the four options considered so far are suboptimal. Spending a budget of €2,370 and considering Eindhoven's desire to perform well on all key outputs, the optimization engine recommends investing €483 in sports and associations, €500 in language and integration courses and €1,387 in employment.

Evaluating options by assessing risk appetite

Up until now we have not accounted for the uncertainties that go hand in hand with the modelling process. However, we earlier distinguished three scenarios – base case, labour optimistic, and labour pessimistic. In terms of risk appetite, the risk-averse person would pay more attention to the risk of high salaries for staff needed to execute the interventions. Therefore, this person would put

Figure 13.4 Four decision maker's options evaluated under three scenarios and compared to optimization for municipality Eindhoven for Refugees case

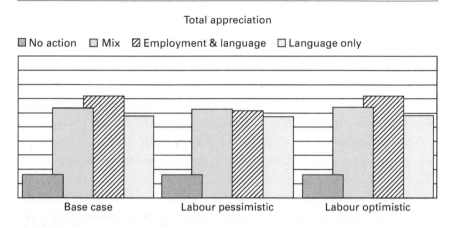

Total appreciation

☐ No action ☐ Mix ☒ Employment & language ☐ Language only

Base case   Labour pessimistic   Labour optimistic

more weight on the labour pessimistic scenario. Conversely, the person with a larger risk appetite would put more weight on the labour optimistic scenario. Figure 13.4 shows that a decision maker who puts all weight on the labour pessimistic scenario should invest in the 'Mix' option, whereas putting all weight on the labour optimistic scenario leads to 'Employment and Language' as the preferred option. Here, we again assume that all key outputs are deemed equally important. This change in preferred option upon change in risk appetite can be explained when recalling that a labour pessimistic person has set a higher minimum threshold on investing in language and integration than a labour optimistic person. When the minimum threshold is not met, which is the case for both decision maker's options for the risk-averse person, the effectiveness of investing in employment will be decreased. Therefore, the 'Mix' option outperforms the 'Employment and Language' option as it still 'scores' on other aspects, while 'Employment and Language' does not. Since the threshold of the risk-loving person is set much lower, capping on the effectiveness of investing in employment will not take place for the 'Employment and Language' option, but it will in the 'Mix' option, and this explains the difference.

Reflections

In practice we can already see that some Dutch municipalities are taking an innovative and more diversified approach to stimulating the integration process of new refugees with a permit to stay. For example, in Leiden, a renowned university town, the medical university, which is in close proximity to the asylum accommodations, has started giving special lectures for lectures to refugees with a higher level of education, like doctors, engineers and economists. These lectures cover a wide range of topics, not just the standard culture and language classes as taught to many refugees, and are also aimed at offering these educated refugees entertainment and a chance to build their networks. For example, they give lectures in the setting of museums in the city of Leiden. This brings together refugees from different backgrounds, stimulates content-rich conversations and approaches higher-educated people at a level that is stimulating and aspiring. This contributes to better well-being for refugees.

The municipality of Haarlem had to deal suddenly with accommodating large groups of refugees. Although this was initially a shock to some inhabitants and administrators, solidarity with the humanitarian aspects of the situation prevailed. In order to quickly start the integration process for a specific group of refugees, a plan was made to mix the refugees with students. Combining housing facilities with students had the advantage that the refugees were not placed in an isolated location. This helped these refugees to meet locals immediately and possibly even become motivated to start studying themselves. A sign of the attitude with which Haarlem received the refugees is that the largest problems that arose were not created by refugees, but were due to the fact that so many people wanted to go by the asylum accommodation to drop off goods for the benefit of refugees that it created traffic jams. It showed a warm welcome to the refugees, and as a positive outcome, most of the refugees that received a permanent residency permit chose to stay in Haarlem.

In the municipality of Amstelveen the mayor went against the standard policy of the national government, which is to provide sober initial accommodations for refugees that have just arrived (providing a bed, bath and bread). The mayor and her staff, however, wanted to treat the refugees from day one as if they would never leave and chose to treat them as citizens of the municipality. Instead of segregating them, they started immediately offering language courses, activities and gatherings with the locals. Also, on top of catering services, they made sure the refugees had their own kitchens and were given the opportunity to volunteer, immediately giving them a meaningful way to keep busy. Lastly, against national protocol, multiple entrepreneurs stayed with their companies in the building that housed the refugees. This mix created even more interaction between the existing and new inhabitants of Amstelveen. The engagement with the inhabitants actually resulted in a situation in which the number of volunteers helping refugees became larger than the number of refugees themselves. It shows the willingness in society to take an active part in the integration process, which is often not mentioned in the wave of negative publicity in the media.

The strategic decision-making process as developed in this context has the purpose of supporting policy makers in their decisions concerning the accommodation of refugees in their municipality as well as in the allocation of budgets available to stimulate the integration of newcomers in society. The strategic decision-making process has been introduced to a dozen municipalities of different sizes and with different strategic priorities, as well as in a round-table meeting with model experts, content experts and policy makers from different municipalities.

During the strategic dialogues we observed that the majority of the municipalities were determining the allocation of the proposed budgets from their functional departments instead of allocating it based on predicted impact for a successful integration. The Responsible Business Simulator played a crucial role in the shift from budget thinking with the sole focus on language training inside the refugee centres, towards impact thinking for integration. Listening to refugees, learning from previous refugee influxes, as well as making use of the many volunteering citizens wanting to make life for refugees more meaningful, led to the proposition of a different type of allocation. The Responsible Business Simulator shows that a mix of activities within the same budget has a better effect than focus on language only. In the mix is the natural embedding of communication, meeting people, and trying to understand each other in different situations. This is a more stimulating way to get to know the new environment for living, working and studying than staying isolated in the refugee centres. In addition, we noticed that the strategic decision-making concept as developed can also support several other policy decisions.

International discussions have indicated the need for this model as well as its international applicability for each region that wishes to accommodate refugees. The model is currently under the attention of the European Commission, the Business Refugee Action Network and is also about to be applied in Sweden and Italy.

References

Barker, A and Brunsden, J (2015) Migrant flows put EU's Schengen under pressure, *Financial Times*, 1 September

BBC News (2015) Migrant crisis: Finland's case against immigration, *BBC News Europe*. Retrieved from http://www.bbc.co.uk/news/world-europe-34185297

Beuningen, J v et al (2013) *De Samenhang Tussen Etnische Diversiteit en Criminaliteit: De rol van sociaal kapitaal*, Centraal Bureau van de Statistiek, Den Haag

Beuningen, J v and Kloosterman, R (2011) *Subjectief Welzijn: Welke factoren spelen een rol?* Centraal Bureau van de Statistiek, Den Haag/Heerlen

Boers, J, Steden, R v and Boutellier, H (2008) Het effect van positieve en negatieve factoren op veiligheidsbeleving, *Tijdschrift voor Veiligheid*, 7 (3)

Bremmer, D (2008) Kind op sport, wat kost dat? *Plus Online*, 11 August. Retrieved from http://www.geldenrecht.nl/artikel/2008-08-11/kind-op-sport-wat-kost-dat

Campbell, D (2006) What is education's impact on civic and social engagement? Paper presented at the Symposium on Social Outcomes of Learning, Copenhagen

CBS Statline (2016) Asielverzoeken Internationaal. Retrieved from http://statline.cbs.nl/StatWeb/publication/?VW=T&DM=SLnl&PA=80498NED&LA=nl

Central Bureau of Statistics (2007) Jonge vrouwen hoger opgeleid dan mannen. Retrieved from https://www.cbs.nl/nl-nl/nieuws/2007/10/jonge-vrouwen-hoger-opgeleid-dan-mannen

Central Bureau of Statistics (2015) CBS: Bijna kwart miljoen immigranten verwacht in 2016. Retrieved from http://www.cbs.nl/nl-NL/menu/themas/bevolking/publicaties/artikelen/archief/2015/bijna-kwart-miljoen-immigranten-verwacht-in-2016.htm

Central Intelligence Agency (nd, accessed 22 February 2016) Syria, *The World Factbook*. Retrieved from https://www.cia.gov/library/publications/the-world-factbook/geos/sy.html

Choi, N and DiNitto, D (2012) Predictors of time volunteering, religious giving, and secular giving: implications for nonprofit organizations, *Journal of Sociology & Social Welfare*, **XXXIX** (2)

The Economist (2015, 12 December) Getting the new arrivals to work, *The Economist*. Retrieved from http://www.economist.com/news/business/21679791-businesses-could-benefit-and-refugees-integrate-faster-if-newcomers-europe-were-able

Engbertsen et al, (2015) Geen tijd verliezen: van opvang naar integratie van asiel-migranten, WWR – Policy Brief 4. Den Haag: Wetenschappelijke Raad voor het Regeringsbeleid

Frijters, P, Johnston, D and Shields, M (2010) *Mental Health and Labour Market Participation: Evidence from IV panel data models*, IZA, Bonn

Gemiddeldgezien.nl (nd, accessed 24 February 2016) Gemiddelde huurprijs, *Gemiddeld gezien.nl*. Retrieved from http://gemiddeldgezien.nl/gemiddelde-huurprijs

Gojer, J and Ellis, A (2014) Post-traumatic stress disorder and the refugee determination process in Canada: starting the discourse, *UNHCR*. Retrieved from http://www.unhcr.org/research/working/53356b349/post-traumatic-stress-disorder-refugee-determination-process-canada-starting.html

Groot, W and Maassen van den Brink, H (2006) *Stil Vermogen: Een onderzoek naar de maatschappelijke kosten van laaggeletterdheid*, Stichting lezen en schrijven, Den Haag

Hanushek, E and Zhang, L (2009) Quality-consistent estimates of international schooling and skill gradients, *Journal of Human Capital*, pp. 107–43

International Organization for Migration (2016) Mediterranean update: migration flows europe: arrivals and fatalities, *Missing Migrants*. Retrieved from http:// missingmigrants.iom.int/sites/default/files/Mediterranean_Update_19_ February_2016_0.pdf

Kurtz, H (2015) Covering Syrian refugee debate: lots of emotion, bursts of bias, *Fox News*. Retrieved from http://www.foxnews.com/politics/2015/11/23/ covering-syrian-refugee-debate-lots-emotion-bursts-bias.html

Lancee, B and Dronkers, J (2008) Etnische diversiteit, sociaal vertrouwen in de buurt en contact van allochtonen en autochtonen met de buren, *Migrantenstudies*, **4**

Lawlor, D and Hopker, S (2001) The effectiveness of exercise as an intervention in the management of depression: systematic review and metaregression analysis of randomised controlled trials, *BMJ*, **322**

Loonwijzer.nl (nd, accessed 22 February 2016) Salaris check, *Loonwijzer.nl*. Retrieved from http://www.loonwijzer.nl/home/carriere/functie-en-salaris

Maastricht University (2014) *Feiten & Cijfers Geletterdheid*, Stichting Lezen en Schrijven, Maastricht

Noack, R (2015) This map helps explain why some European countries reject refugees, and others love them, *Washington Post*. Retrieved from https://www. washingtonpost.com/news/worldviews/wp/2015/09/08/this-map-helps-explain-why-some-european-countries-reject-refugees-and-others-love-them/

OECD (2014) *Education at a Glance 2014*. Retrieved from http://www.oecd.org/ edu/Education-at-a-Glance-2014.pdf

Razenberg, I and De Gruijter, M (2016) *Vluchtelingen aan het Werk: Enquête onder gemeenten over arbeidstoeleiding van statushouders*, Kennisplatform Integratie & Samenleving, Utrecht

Reuters (2016) German far-right protests against refugees turn violent, *Al Jazeera America*. Retrieved from http://america.aljazeera.com/articles/2016/1/9/ germanys-merkel-toughens-tone-on-refugees-amid-competing-protests1.html

Robins-Early, N (2015) 5 Major myths of Europe's refugee and migrant crisis debunked, *Huffington Post*. Retrieved from http://www.huffingtonpost.com/ entry/europe-refugee-migrant-crisis-myths_us_55f83aa7e4b09ecde1d9b4bc

SEO Economisch Onderzoek (2010) Kosten en resultaten van re-integratie. Retrieved from http://www.seo.nl/uploads/media/2010-33_Kosten_en_ resultaten_van_re-integratie.pdf

Stavenuiter, M et al (2016) Onderwijs en doorstroom naar de arbeids-markt van jonge nieuwkomers in Nederland, *Verwey-Jonker Institute*. Retrieved from http://www.verwey-jonker.nl/publicaties/2016/ onderwijs-en-doorstroom-arbeidsmarkt-nieuwkomers

Stone, W and Hulse, K (2007) *Housing and Social Cohesion: An empirical exploration*. Retrieved from https://www.ahuri.edu.au/media/documents/

research-reports/AHURI_Final_Report_No100_Housing_and_social_cohesion_
an_empirical_exploration.pdf

Suitcase talen (nd, accessed 22 February 2016) Nederlands leren. Retrieved from
http://www.suitcase.nl/nederlands-leren-groepscursus.html

The Telegraph View (2015) The refugee crisis requires a pragmatic response, not
emotion, *Telegraph*. Retrieved from http://www.telegraph.co.uk/comment/
telegraph-view/11846673/The-refugee-crisis-requires-a-pragmatic-response-not-
emotion.html

Toepoel, V (2013) Ageing, leisure, and social connectedness: how could leisure help
reduce social isolation of older people? *Social Indicators Research*, **113** (1), pp.
355–72

Unicef (nd, accessed 22 February 2016) At a glance: Syrian Arab Republic.
Retrieved from http://www.unicef.org/infobycountry/syria_statistics.html

Voorn, C (2016) De onvrede achter de rellen in Geldermalsen, *NOS*. Retrieved
from http://nos.nl/nieuwsuur/artikel/2081236-de-onvrede-achter-de-rellen-in-
geldermalsen.html

Weber, A and Hofer, H (2004) Employment effects of early interventions on job
search programs, *IZA*. Retrieved from http://ftp.iza.org/dp1076.pdf

Woonbemiddeling Nederland (nd, accessed 22 February 2016) Tarieven. Retrieved
from http://www.woonbemiddeling.nl/tarieven.html

Attracting investment at a social enterprise

14

This chapter illustrates the application of strategic decision making at Amplino, a social enterprise that develops portable malaria diagnostics. The purpose of Amplino is to contribute to the eradication of malaria by means of applying proven lab diagnostics with a portable device in low-tech areas, such as the malaria-burdened areas of Africa. Amplino claims it can bring the most advanced diagnostic method with this portable device to remote areas, meaning lower costs with fewer medical staff. With its affordable mobile malaria diagnostics it can lower the levels of incorrect diagnosis as well as the taking of preventive medication if there is no reason for it. This would contribute to a decrease in antimicrobial resistance, which is a threat to global public health, and hence will increase the sustainability of fighting malaria.

Amplino wanted to apply strategic decision making to provide potential investors insights into the advantages and disadvantages of different ways of fighting malaria. Funding was needed for further testing and development of the mobile diagnostics kit; this way the investor can decide upon an investment strategy to fight malaria that meets his preference. We will start by introducing this social enterprise in the context of making strategic decisions to benefit people, the planet and profits.

About Amplino

Amplino, founded in 2012, is a start-up company that dedicates itself to the development of portable malaria diagnostics. The diagnostics are based on real-time Polymerase Chain Reaction (PCR) technology. PCR enables researchers to produce millions of copies of a specific DNA sequence in approximately two hours and is considered one of the most advanced technologies for malaria detection (Händscheid and Grobusch, 2002). The name Amplino is a concatenation of parts of the words *amplifying*, the strengthening of a signal which is partially how the PCR methodology works, and *Arduino,* an open-source electronic element that the founders used during the initial construction of the device. The portable device currently under development is called *Amplino Scout*, where *scout* refers to Amplino's desire to test for malaria in remote, undiscovered areas. Even though the PCR methodology implemented in the diagnostics device could be applied to combat several diseases, Amplino Scout focuses on fighting malaria.

The purpose of Amplino is to contribute to the eradication of malaria by means of applying proven lab diagnostics with a portable device in low-tech areas, such as the disease-burdened areas of Africa. In these areas conventional lab-bound biotechnology is not yet accessible for several reasons such high costs, lack of mobility, lack of trained medical staff and poor reliability of electricity supply. Sub-Saharan Africa carries a disproportionately high share of the global malaria burden. In 2015, the region was home to 89 per cent of malaria cases and 91 per cent of malaria deaths (WHO, 2015b).

About malaria diagnosis

Malaria is an infectious disease caused by parasites and transferred by mosquitos onto humans and animals, causing symptoms such as fever, fatigue, vomiting and headaches. In 2015 there were 214 million cases of malaria and 438,000 deaths (WHO, 2015b). There are two ways to combat malaria: preventive and curative. Preventive refers to 'before the fact' and entails among other things the use of pesticides to kill the mosquitos, the use of mosquito nets, and the ingestion of medication without proper diagnosis. Curative refers to 'after the fact' and denotes treatment for those already diagnosed with malaria.

If no proper diagnostics are used, it is difficult to diagnose whether someone is infected with malaria. This is especially the case in less-developed countries, where it is too expensive to carry out a thorough analysis of blood. As a result, people are often diagnosed incorrectly and consequently receive an unnecessary malaria treatment, or just take medication as a matter of prevention. In 2013 this concerned about 20 per cent of the population in Africa (WHO, 2014). The worst scenario is when people die because malaria is not detected even though it is present, which concerned about 10 per cent of the population in the WHO African Region in 2013 (WHO, 2014).

Incorrect diagnosis, as well as taking preventive medication, will increase antimicrobial resistance unnecessarily. According to WHO, antimicrobial resistance is a serious threat to global public health that requires action across all government sectors and society (WHO, 2015a).

Malaria can be diagnosed in several ways, the three most frequently used methods being:

- Microscopy: identification of malaria parasites by examination of blood under a microscope (Center for Disease Control, 2016);
- Rapid Diagnostic Test (RDT): detection of evidence of antigens for malaria parasites in human blood (WHO, 2016);
- Polymerase Chain Reaction (PCR): detection of parasite nucleic acids (Center for Disease Control, 2016).

The last method is the most exact approach for malaria diagnosis. In contrast to the alternatives, PCR can test 'special groups' like pregnant woman or HIV-positive people for malaria. At the same time it is the most expensive method, for which advanced laboratory equipment, access to electricity and trained medical staff are required. So it's great on the People front, but less so for Profit objectives. Together with the high number of malaria deaths, this has been the motivation for Amplino to develop an affordable mobile diagnostics device that applies the PCR methodology and can be rolled out at locations where it is most needed, but does not depend on a laboratory, electricity or trained medical staff. Additionally, Amplino Scout has an innovative GPS functionality which can be used for the monitoring and mapping of malaria (outbreaks) via data collection. This is a first step towards the eradication of malaria. The device under construction will be compliant with World Health Organization (WHO) requirements for medical diagnostics and can increase the accessibility of healthcare diagnostics in the developing world tremendously (Bruins, 2014).

Amplino has the potential to outperform alternative malaria diagnostics tools but still lacks funding for the execution of the final tests and product developments before production can take place. The challenge Amplino faces is to find potential investors to support them. Therefore, we formulated the purpose of applying the Responsible Business Simulator at Amplino as follows: provide potential investors with insights into the advantages and disadvantages of different ways to fight malaria. This way the investor can decide upon an investment strategy to fight malaria that meets his preferences.

The strategic decision-making process

For the development of the strategic decision-making process at Amplino, various types of external expertise were merged with the knowledge of Amplino's management. The combined expertise covered the areas of finance and strategy, accounting for the investment perspective, as well as the areas of medicine and biology to address the diagnostics perspective. These various perspectives facilitated a constructive dialogue in which inputs and outputs were formulated, added, refined or deleted.

Describing strategic challenge that requires a decision

Since Amplino's main concern was to collect funding for the further testing and development of the existing prototype, a first brainstorm with the team of experts resulted in defining the decision maker's perspective as that of a potential investor in fighting malaria. The potential investor hasn't decided yet on whether to fight malaria in a preventive or a curative way, and could be a bank or an institution such as the Bill & Melinda Gates Foundation. Using the investor's perspective, it was straightforward to formulate the decision maker's strategic challenge as 'How to fight malaria'.

Defining key outputs involving stakeholders

The key outputs have been defined from the perspective of a potential investor. This potential investor wants to be able to measure the contribution that an investment in Amplino Scout makes to the eradication of malaria, but also wants to be able to compare it to the impact of its alternatives. Based on the available data and knowledge of the expert team the key outputs in Table 14.1 were defined.

Sensitivity and specificity are commonly used terms in medical science for determining the two types of correct diagnosis from a test. Table 14.2 illustrates the so-called decision matrix containing the four possible situations when testing the hypothesis that a person is infected with malaria, which are referred to as True Positives (TP), False Positives (FP), True Negatives (TN) and False Negatives (FN).

Sensitivity is calculated as the percentage of people infected with malaria and diagnosed as such: TP/(TP+FN). Specificity is calculated as the percentage of people not infected with malaria and diagnosed as such: TN/(TN+FP). In statistical hypothesis testing, the number of people infected with malaria

Table 14.1   Key output definitions for Amplino case

Key output	Theme	Description
Sensitivity	People	Probability of a positive test given that a person suffers from malaria; a positive test is a test in which the outcome reads that the tested person is infected with malaria.
Mortality reduction	People	Reduction in the number of people dying because of missing out on medication due to incorrect malaria diagnosis.
Specificity	People	Probability of a negative test given that a patient does not suffer from malaria; a negative test is a test in which the outcome reads that the tested person is not infected with malaria.
Antimicrobial resistance	People	Number of people taking medication; an increase in medication taken leads to an increase in antimicrobial resistance.
Mobility	People	Possibility of bringing malaria diagnostics into the field measured by the necessity for laboratory equipment and electricity.
Ease of use	People	Possibility of bringing malaria diagnostics into the field measured by the necessity for trained medical staff.
Clinical data mapping	People	Possibility of geographical monitoring and mapping of malaria using GPS.
Economic impact	Economy	Amount in dollars that can be added to the GDP per capita via additional income gathered by people being diagnosed correctly and cured (and hence able to work).

but diagnosed as not being infected (FN) is also referred to as Type I error or α-risk. Similarly, the number of people not infected with malaria but diagnosed as being infected (FP) is known as the Type II error or β-risk.

From the definitions in Table 14.1, it can be deduced that mortality reduction is closely related to sensitivity: a higher sensitivity means a higher number of correct diagnoses of people infected with malaria, and thus results in more people being correctly treated, thereby reducing mortality. Antimicrobial resistance relates to specificity in a similar manner: a higher specificity leads to less antimicrobial resistance. In other words, if people who are not infected with malaria receive fewer incorrect diagnoses, fewer people take medication erroneously, thereby decreasing antimicrobial resistance.

Table 14.2   Malaria diagnosis decision matrix for Amplino case

Conclusion state	True state	
	Person is infected with malaria	*Person is not infected with malaria*
Person is diagnosed with malaria (positive test)	True positive (TP) Sensitivity Confidence	False positive (FP) β-risk Type II error
Person is not diagnosed with malaria (negative test)	False negative (FN) α-risk Type I error	True negative (TN) Specificity Discriminatory power

Determining decision maker's options

In order to formulate the decision maker's options, internal variable inputs are formulated first. The decision awaiting the decision maker is whether to invest in prevention, in Amplino, or in one of Amplino's alternatives. This implies the internal variables listed in Table 14.3.

All internal variable inputs take the form of invested amounts. By assigning different values to these internal variable inputs, various decision maker's options can be obtained. An investor can decide to invest all his money in a single solution (prevention or one of the four types of malaria diagnostics

Table 14.3   Internal variable input definitions for Amplino case

Internal variable input	Description
Invest in prevention	Invest in medication without performing diagnosis.
Invest in PCR Amplino	Invest in diagnosis of malaria using a portable PCR device.
Invest in traditional PCR	Invest in diagnosis of malaria using a traditional PCR device.
Invest in RDT	Invest in diagnosis of malaria by detecting evidence of antigens for malaria parasites in human blood.
Invest in microscopy	Invest in diagnosis of malaria via microscopic examination of blood.

including treatment) or spread his money over the various alternatives. In the Responsible Business Simulator, six decision maker's options have been formulated. In each of these options an amount of €1,000,000 is invested. The first five options relate to investing solely in prevention, in PCR Amplino, in traditional PCR, in RDT or in microscopy. The sixth option refers to dividing that same amount equally over all five internal variable inputs.

Drawing up scenarios

Next to inputs that can be controlled by the decision maker, external variable inputs have been formulated in order to account for possible uncertainties in the effect of an investment on the output. This enables us to draw up scenarios. An overview of the three scenarios for the external variable inputs for the case of Amplino is presented in Table 14.4

Uncertainty factors impacting sensitivity and specificity are added for Amplino, since this diagnosis method has not been properly tested yet. In the base-case scenario, we assume that Amplino performs as well as the traditional PCR methodology, although a pessimist might want to weaken this assumption. The malaria rate indicates the percentage of malaria infections within the population. According to WHO, the malaria infection rate in sub-Saharan Africa is 33.8 per cent (WHO, 2013). The GDP per capita indicates how much income a person generates per year. According to the World Bank, the GDP in Sub-Saharan Africa was $1,480 in 2013 (World Bank, 2013). The uncertainty in these data points is modelled by decreasing or increasing their values in the non-base-case scenarios.

Note that mobility, ease of use and clinical data mapping do not depend on scenarios.

Table 14.4 Specification of scenarios for Amplino case

	Scenarios		
External variable input	**Pessimistic**	**Base case**	**Optimistic**
Sensitivity factor Amplino	79%	100%	100%
Specificity factor Amplino	90%	100%	100%
Malaria rate	36%	33.8%	33%
GDP per capita	$1300	$1480	$1600

Constructing the simulation model

Up until now all information has been collected from the explorative dialogue with stakeholders and experts. However, for the Responsible Business Simulator to provide clear and accurate insights to the decision maker, detailed characteristics of the five alternative ways to fight malaria have to be collected.

Table 14.5 displays the mobility, ease of use and possibility of clinical data mapping for each type of detection or treatment. These characteristics are all binary, meaning that they are either 'true' or 'false'. We have decided to treat these inputs simply as fixed inputs whose values were prompted by experts, which means that the Responsible Business Simulator does not examine possible deviations of those values. If such an examination is deemed necessary, the user could, of course, choose to promote these inputs to external variable inputs.

Table 14.6 lists the sensitivity, the specificity and the costs per test or treatment, including – if available – their source in literature.

Note that no references are listed for the sensitivity and the specificity of prevention. The reason for this is that we decided to model prevention as treatment after diagnosing every person as being infected with malaria. Thus, the α-risk reduces to zero at the cost of a β-risk of 100 per cent. Consequently, the sensitivity and specificity of prevention equal 100 per cent and 0 per cent respectively. The unit cost of traditional PCR was provided by an expert.

Next, some intermediate outputs are calculated to make calculations easy and transparent. Examples of intermediates are: invested amount, α-risk, β-risk, and the number of treatments and tests that can be executed per investment type.

Invested amount is simply the sum of all internal variable inputs per decision maker's option. Recall from Table 14.2 that α-risk and β-risk follow

Table 14.5 Specification of effects for Amplino case

	Key output or intermediate		
Internal variable input	**Mobility**	**Ease of use**	**Clinical data mapping**
Invest in prevention	Yes	No	No
Invest in Amplino	Yes	No	Yes
Invest in RDT	Yes	No	No
Invest in microscopy	No	Yes	No
Invest in traditional PCR	No	Yes	No

Table 14.6 Specification of maximum effects for Amplino case

Internal variable input	Key output or intermediate		
	Sensitivity	Specificity	Cost per test or treatment
Invest in prevention	100%	0%	$4.03 (White et al, 2011)
Invest in Amplino	100% (Osman et al, 2010)	100% (Osman et al, 2010)	$5.10 (Bruins, 2014)
Invest in RDT	69% (Osman et al., 2010)	84% (Osman et al, 2010)	$4.70 (Chanda, Castillo-Riquelme, and Masiye, 2009)
Invest in Microscopy	85.7% (Osman et al, 2010)	100% (Osman et al, 2010)	$8.20 (Chanda, Castillo-Riquelme, and Masiye, 2009)
Invest in traditional PCR	100% (Osman et al, 2010)	100% (Osman et al, 2010)	$9.43

straight from sensitivity and specificity. If there is a partial investment in prevention, the number of possible treatments is calculated as:

$$\text{Number Of Treatments}_{Prevention} = \text{Invested Amount}_{Prevention} / \text{Cost Per Treatment}$$

For any type of investment, the number of tests as well as the number of treatments are calculated to account for the fact that people diagnosed with malaria need to receive medication too (in case of prevention, we consider an imaginary, zero-cost test having a positive outcome all the time). Therefore, we first calculate the rate of tested people that will be diagnosed with malaria. This equals all positive test results regardless of whether they are correct or incorrect:

$$\text{Positive Test Rate}_i = \text{Sensitivity}_i * \text{Malaria Rate} + \beta\text{-risk}_i * (1 - \text{Malaria Rate})$$

where i represents the type of investment. Using this positive test rate, the number of tests can be calculated as:

$$\text{Number Of Tests}_i = \text{Invested Amount}_i / (\text{Cost Per Test}_i + \text{Cost Per Treatment} * \text{Positive Test Rate}_i)$$

After all intermediate outputs have been calculated, the key outputs follow rather easily. As an example, we will illustrate the calculation of mortality reduction and antimicrobial resistance.

Every positive outcome of a diagnostic test on a person infected with malaria followed by a treatment results in one person less dying from malaria. Translated into a formula this looks as follows:

$$\text{Mortality Reduction} = \sum_i \text{Number Of Tests}_i * \text{Sensitivity}_i * \text{Malaria Rate}$$

Antimicrobial resistance is caused by people receiving treatment after scoring positive in a test, irrespective whether they are – in reality – infected with malaria. To translate this into a formula, we exploit the positive test rate, which was computed as intermediate, as follows:

$$\text{Antimicrobial Resistance} = \sum_i \text{Number Of Tests}_i * \text{Positive Test Rate}_i$$

Evaluating options by assessing strategic priorities

Now that all the information has been processed and computed, the decision maker can use the Responsible Business Simulator to easily evaluate which option is 'best' given their strategic priorities. As mentioned in Chapter 2, strategic priorities will be accounted for by assigning weights to key outputs. Given the decision maker's options as described earlier in this chapter, it follows which option is the best strategy.

If the decision maker only assigns value to the economic impact, out of the six options, it is best to invest in prevention, as can be seen from Table 14.7.

However, if the decision maker also cares about other aspects like antimicrobial resistance, mobility and ease of use, and therefore assigns equal

Table 14.7   Comparison of decision maker's options for key output 'Economic impact' in base-case scenario for Amplino case

Decision maker's option	Economic impact
Prevention	$124,129,032.26
PCR Amplino	$77,410,888.65
PCR traditional	$46,352,252.66
RDT	$56,894,795.23
Microscopy	$45,765,931.44
Mix	$70,110,580.05

Figure 14.1 Comparison of decision maker's options when all key outputs have equal weights in base-case scenario for Amplino case

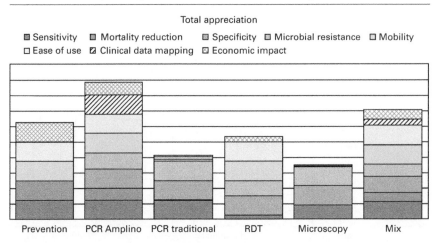

importance to all key outputs, investing in Amplino turns out to be the preferred decision maker's option, as shown in Figure 14.1, because this investment option has the ability to address every key output to an at least reasonable extent. The preference for Amplino will grow when more weight is placed on microbial resistance, and it will shrink when more weight is placed on economic impact. How to make a trade-off when choosing between these two key outputs can be discussed in the strategic dialogue during which different values for these weights are tested and the turning point is made visible.

Evaluating options by assessing risk appetite

Up until now, the uncertainty induced by scenarios has not been accounted for. In order to do this, the decision maker can evaluate their decision by indicating their risk appetite next to their strategic preferences. The best strategy then depends not only on weights assigned to key outputs but also on weights assigned to scenarios. Suppose that sensitivity, specificity and economic impact are the only key outputs the decision maker deems – equally – important. As can be seen from Figure 14.2, the best decision maker's option now depends on their risk appetite. In the base-case and optimistic scenarios, the option to invest in PCR Amplino is still the preferred option. However, in the pessimistic scenario, where the sensitivity and specificity of Amplina is no longer assumed to be 100 per cent, the mix option and the traditional PCR should have a slight preference over PCR Amplino. These options give potential investors a better foundation upon which to make their investment decision.

Figure 14.2　Comparison of decision maker's options when equal weight is put on sensitivity, specificity and economic impact only for all scenarios for Amplino case.

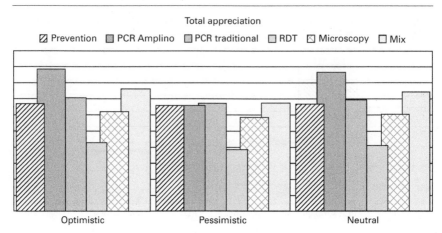

Total appreciation

☑ Prevention ■ PCR Amplino ■ PCR traditional ☐ RDT ⊠ Microscopy ☐ Mix

Optimistic　　　　　Pessimistic　　　　　Neutral

Reflections

Being a start-up, Amplino had the challenge of introducing a novel type of medical product in a relatively traditional market. They had to motivate and provide the added value of their business model as well as their contribution to the several People aspects. The process of strategic decision making supported them to formulate their strengths and weaknesses in a structured way. Via strategic decision making, Amplino were able to underpin their claims with quantitative facts. This made it possible for them to show the unique selling points of their product and the potential impact it could make. The Responsible Business Simulator projected the potential that Amplino had in the market, which in turn helped justify substantial investments to be made to ensure market introduction.

References

Bruins, W (2014) Interview with Myrthe van de Plas, Amsterdam
Center for Disease Control (2016) Malaria diagnosis. Retrieved from https://www.cdc.gov/malaria/diagnosis_treatment/diagnosis.html
Chanda, P, Castillo-Riquelme, M and Masiye, F (2009) Cost-effectiveness analysis of the available strategies for diagnosing malaria in outpatient clinics in Zambia, *Cost Effectiveness and Resource Allocation*, 7 (5)

Händscheid, T and Grobusch, M (2002) How useful is PCR in the diagnosis of malaria? *Trends in Parasitology,* **18** (9), pp. 395–98

Osman, M M M et al (2010) Informed decision-making before changing to RDT: a comparison of microscopy, rapid diagnostic test and molecular techniques for the diagnosis and identification of malaria parasites in Kassala, eastern Sudan, *Tropical Medicine & International Health,* **15** (12), pp. 1442–48

White, M T et al (2011) Costs and cost-effectiveness of malaria control interventions – a systematic review, *Malaria Journal,* 337

WHO (2013) *World Malaria Report 2013,* World Health Organization, Geneva

WHO (2014) *World Malaria Report 2014,* World Health Organization, Geneva

WHO (2015a) Antimicrobial resistance factsheet. Retrieved from http://www.who.int/mediacentre/factsheets/fs194/en/

WHO (2015b) Malaria, factsheet no 94. Retrieved from http://www.who.int/mediacentre/factsheets/fs094/en

WHO (2016) Malaria rapid diagnostic tests. Retrieved from http://www.who.int/malaria/areas/diagnosis/rapid-diagnostic-tests/en

World Bank (2013) GDP per capita: Sub-Saharan Africa. Retrieved from http://data.worldbank.org/region/SSA

Conclusions 15

Responsible Business Simulator facilitates decision making for systems change

The historic UN Paris agreement on climate change, adopted by 192 countries in December 2015, signals an age of systems change towards a sustainable and inclusive economy. The widespread acceptance by companies of the social development goals to make the world a better place give clear directions for purpose driven business strategies. Through insight and understanding of the limitations of the dominant economic and financial logic and with the help of new knowledge and disruptive technologies we are witnessing the beginning of a long-term systems change. A key element of the systems change is that sustainable practice will become the rule more than the exception. A transformation means a rethinking of business models, including the reshaping of supply chains, use and re-use of materials, modes of transportation, as well as searching for balanced ways of working and healthier living. These combined efforts can lead to a better, more sustainable balance between People, Planet and Profit objectives in the corporate world and society at large. Where in the past businesses and authorities considered sustainability as costs, more and more frontrunners in business and government institutions see the new growth potential. Creating shared value by investing in societal challenges is serious business, for here are the explorative fields for innovation led by business.

Contributing to systems change means making strategic choices and allocating investments. With this book we introduce the Responsible Business Simulator as a decision tool for decision makers, entrepreneurs, advisors, policy makers and those interested in sustainable business growth. The Responsible Business Simulator is the product of the qualitative strategic dialogue and the quantitative modelling software for simulation and visual clarification of the impact of potential decisions. Together these two elements form the Responsible Business Simulator as a powerful tool for helping decision makers reach profound decisions in the transition towards a circular economy. The strategic dialogue is based on action research and action learning and sets the interactive context in which management, employees and stakeholders can formulate strategic goals, milestones and priorities. The strategic dialogue activates the participants in the search for facts, figures, reports, and formal and informal knowledge. The results of the strategic dialogue and fact finding form the resource material for the quantitative modelling and simulation processes. The smart use of data science techniques and the complex computation modelling bring forward factual outcomes of clear potential choices based on strategic goals and priorities set in the strategic dialogue. The Responsible Business Simulator makes it possible to avoid vague discussions in the boardroom and with outside stakeholders. It enables transparency in the decision-making process by combining strategic goal setting with the robust justification of data. Choices for less or more sustainable business decisions can be clarified and explained. With the Responsible Business Simulator, decision makers can fine-tune their choices and adapt them over time, making it a dynamic learning tool on the way towards creating a circular economy integrating economic, social and environmental objectives.

Although we are approaching the tipping point through a multitude of developments, this does not mean that it is easy to implement sustainable business practices. First, the fact that the world is changing at a rapid speed forces companies to respond by making strategic decisions with more uncertainty. Second, balancing People, Planet and Profit objectives, instead of solely focusing on financial profits, only increases the problem of having highly diffuse strategic considerations. Third, in general the focus is often more on the short term to satisfy shareholders, whereas sustainable business development requires a medium- to long-term vision. The implementation of investments that change the system and its logic may not be seen in the next quarter, but in the years ahead. Not all companies and organizations can convince their shareholders and stakeholders that a bold decision for sustainability and a circular economy will pay off in the short timeframes management is often confronted with. In short, even those companies and organizations that want to go forward towards a more balanced way are seeking ways of how to do it in practice. With the organizational tools and software techniques combined in the Responsible Business Simulator we make life easier for top management when it comes to strategic decision making towards a circular economy. In all the case studies we were able to show that the strategic dialogue with employees, management and stakeholders leads to ambitions and the formulation of highly concrete key outputs to make those ambitions happen. The data science techniques offer the possibility to make big data computations for the numerous relationships between the different key outputs, scientific data and the potential amount of investment.

Standard in the academic world is the knowledge that by realizing change within a system you forego the opportunity to acquire 'pure' academic insight; change and insight are to be separated. However, within the paradigm of systems change we cannot pause change in order to gain insight. In such a shift there is a need to realize change while gaining knowledge, which can be done using action research. By creating iterative cycles of intervention, investigation and reflection, action research has the potential to realize insights and learning dynamics within a changing environment while contributing to fine-tuning the impact of a decision or investment to be made. This kind of action research is not damaging the integrity of the knowledge obtained; it is making action research more relevant. This is where the toolbox of the corporate decision maker collides with the methodology of the action researcher. Hence action research was not only used in the development of the Responsible Business Simulator; we applied it in the cases, and based on the results we now recommend it as an integral part of the Responsible Business Simulator.

Big data will become a powerful input for decision makers. This will not in itself solve any problems though. As with other technologies, big data brings its own pitfalls and can only be a powerful input when it is used correctly and effectively by professionals who know how to use it and interpret it. It is important that data science techniques are used to support decisions and decision makers, not to dictate to them. Used correctly, data science techniques enable decision makers to utilize large amounts of data in a transparent, testable and flexible manner. Hence the Responsible Business Simulator was built to facilitate strategic dialogue and bring to the forefront facts and figures to make informed and justified decisions, and not replace the importance of face-to-face communication during the strategic dialogue.

In a rapidly changing environment, decision makers cannot afford to let opportunities go to waste. This is why we recommend that interactive sessions with management, employees and external stakeholders be incorporated into the strategic decision-making process. By bringing together true cross-sections of employees, management and stakeholders, it can be guaranteed that a diversity of knowledge, experience and latest insights will be available as inputs for the decision-making process to formulate goals. Hereby it is possible to identify unsubstantiated assumptions, which can sometimes prove vital to altering the way the strategy is looked at.

The interactive strategic dialogue in an action research setting unleashes the informal and formal knowledge underlying the long-term mission of the organization and its potential to realize the goals. It makes strategic decision making a holistic method by incorporating all strategic considerations. By combing this method with data science it becomes an active exercise and not a 'black box' as would be the case when advisors are allowed to conjure statistics from Excel files like rabbits out of a top hat. This combined effort of qualitative and quantitative approaches, of data and dialogue as applied in the cases is meaningful for decision makers, especially for those who look ahead and have to meet People, Planet and Profit objectives in a society at the brink of a new paradigm, moving towards a circular economy.

Overview of cases

Following is an overview of the companies and organizations that we worked with and the resulting cases in this book. It is worth mentioning that these are all companies and organizations that were already on the path of incorporating sustainable practices and anticipating the transition towards a circular economy. In the first three cases – concerning DSM, NEMO and Rimetaal – our research focused on sustainability and Planet issues. The latter four cases – IZZ Foundation, KNVB, refugee integration and Amplino – have more focus on health and People-related issues. Within all of these cases, however, we have been able to do justice to People, Planet and Profit considerations. In order to guide the decision-making process with the Responsible Business Simulator we had multiple iterative group sessions with all stakeholders involved. We obtained consent from all these stakeholders to present the cases in this book.

DSM

Company: Royal DSM (DSM) is a global science-based company active in health, nutrition and materials. By connecting its unique competences in life sciences and materials sciences, DSM is driving economic prosperity, environmental progress and social advances to create sustainable value for all stakeholders simultaneously. DSM operates in global markets such as food and dietary supplements, personal care, feed, medical devices, automotive, paints, electrical and electronics, life protection, alternative energy and bio-based materials.

   Case: This case elaborates the decision making at DSM, who want to anticipate climate change by addressing their own environmental and carbon footprint by means of reducing greenhouse gas emissions and becoming more energy efficient. Their strategic challenge, therefore, has been formulated as how to source energy. The described strategic decision-making process at DSM was a multiple competency collaboration within the organization and triggered the already ongoing discussion of using an internal carbon price to evolve to a more strategic and fact-based dialogue.

Key insight: An internal carbon price is necessary in any organization that has a strong focus on profit-related objects, and favours energy from renewable sources over non-renewable sources.

Key impacts: There is a large price difference between grey and renewable energy, and the Responsible Business Simulator showed that the internal carbon price needs to exceed the range of \$78–\$137, depending on the risk appetite, before a decision for sustainable energy sourcing is made. The Responsible Business Simulator approach stimulated the existing internal discussion on the use of internal carbon price, but now with a more strategic and fact-based dialogue. It contributed to the process of taking externalities into account in the decision-making process for energy sourcing.

NEMO

Company: NEMO Science Museum (NEMO) in Amsterdam is the biggest and most entertaining science museum in the Netherlands and Benelux countries. The iconic building with an impressive roof designed as a city piazza is designed by Renzo Piano, and with its five floors full of interactive, interesting things to do and to discover, it is an exciting place, visited by more than 500,000 people every year who want to be introduced to science and technology in a playful manner. For the education sector, NEMO is the biggest interactive non-school-like informal learning environment and is part of many educational programmes relating to science and engineering. NEMO also organizes training programmes for teachers and has intensive exchange programmes with an international network of science museums.

Case: This case addresses NEMO's decision-making process towards solving its problems with the roof. Recurring leaks required complicated and expensive repairs and the roof also fell short of the insulation standards for this type of public building. The strategic decision-making process facilitated NEMO's expansion plans to do more than just repair a roof. In the process with the Responsible Business Simulator the importance of the public space on the roof and the iconic function of the building for the city of Amsterdam were underlined. More intensive use of the roof would also lead to more visitors to NEMO. Multi-functionality turned out to be key in the decision-making process on the investments for the roof. In close collaboration with architect Renzo Piano, multiple uses and designs of the roof were discussed. The new roof opened in Spring 2016. Nowadays the roof of the NEMO building is the highest city square in the Netherlands. It is the location of the open-air exhibition Energetica with interactive sculptures, a large terrace and a restaurant, all with beautiful views of the city of Amsterdam.

Key insights: Interactivity and acknowledging the expertise of the participants engaged all of them with the decision at hand. The integrated approach of taking all three aspects of People, Planet and Profit into account from the beginning also forestalled any tendency to take a short-term 'penny wise pound foolish' decision. Expanding the simulation model at a later stage, as was done with Renzo Piano's alternative suggestions for the design of the roof, proved to be easy to do. It did not diminish the clarity of the simulation model.

Key impact: Integration of data within the domains of finance, marketing and accommodation, which had never been linked before, unlocked a treasure trove of information. Another key impact came from a casual comment in a technical report about the possible effect of a sustainable roof on visitor numbers. The Responsible Business Simulator turned this information into quantified data. The simulation also showed that the possible power generation on the roof would be less important in terms of financial income than the revenues from visitors enjoying the scenic view of the city of Amsterdam. The simulation also demonstrated the potential of new revenue models, specifically a restaurant on the roof.

Rimetaal

Company: Rimetaal is an innovative metal construction company that focuses on the development, production, sales and maintenance of high-quality metal products, for example (underground) garbage collection systems. Sustainability is key within Rimetaal's policy, having a focus on sustainable products, sustainable production and social sustainability. The company proactively anticipates the societal necessity for sustainability, as well as considering government policy and competitive advantages. Furthermore, Rimetaal is a partner of 'De Groene Zaak', a Dutch employers' organization founded in 2010 and known as a protagonist for sustainability. Rimetaal B.V. was until the end of 2014 a private limited company incorporated under Dutch law, but is now part of Kliko, the number one specialist in waste systems and logistics in the Netherlands.

Case: This case explains how Rimetaal demonstrates how its principal customers, local municipalities and national government, do not practice what they preach. The criteria set by RVO, the governmental agency for stimulating entrepreneurship in the Netherlands, are not stringent enough when it comes to the purchasing of sustainable products by governmental institutions. Rimetaal's track record showed that too often municipalities and other governmental organizations said they wanted to have sustainable products but in the end selected suppliers more on the basis of price (ie lowest) than on the basis of sustainability. This occurred time and again, despite the fact that 'sustainability' is cited as an essential selection crite-rion in the purchasing process.

Key insights: Suppliers can certainly supply sustainable products that work out cheaper over the entire life cycle than non-sustainable products. Rimetaal, as one these sustainable suppliers, therefore took action and used strategic decision making to show that investing in sustainable systems pays off in the long term. Another insight the Responsible Business Simulator confirmed was the assumption that leasing a Rimetaal system in combina-tion with a service contract for maintenance would be the best choice for customers and for the company. It would lead to sustainable solutions and contribute to a circular economy. Lease takes into account the time factor and this is not the case in total cost of ownership.

Key impact: Purchasing officers from municipalities realized that selecting the cheapest tender while asking for products that comply with strict criteria in terms of sustainability is not fair. They also saw that leasing contracts spread the costs over time. Sustainable solutions, which may cost more, but last longer and need less maintenance, are more favourable from a circular economy point of view. However, it requires more collaboration between different parts of the (local) bureaucracy.

IZZ

Company: The IZZ Foundation (IZZ) is a non-profit organization in the Netherlands that has been promoting the interests of healthcare workers (in hospitals, nursing and care homes, home care, handicapped care, mental health and youth care) since its establishment in 1977. On the basis of its wide knowledge of and commitment to the care sector, IZZ provides healthcare insurance on a non-profit basis for almost half a million Dutch healthcare employees and their families. That insurance is tailored to the needs of this special group, and takes full account of the specific health risks involved in working in the sector. Being a market leader, what makes IZZ unique is the input and influence that employers and employees in the healthcare sector together have on the terms and conditions of their health insurance.

Case: This chapter describes how IZZ offers healthcare institutions objective insights into what – for them – is the optimal strategy with regard to the People pillar, mainly focusing on the employability of their employees. There is a serious need for measures that will help achieve a balance between supply and demand in the healthcare sector but also account for the welfare of personnel. IZZ uses the strategic decision-making process to support many healthcare institutions in finding out what measures will help make healthcare a more pleasant, efficient and attractive working environment.

Key insight: If there is a higher risk appetite, an intervention focussing on the physical well-being of employees should be the preferred intervention, while with a lower risk appetite a social intervention is preferred. The Responsible Business Simulator showed what options work best under different circumstances.

Key impact: The first-hand knowledge and experience of the IZZ Foundation has become available in a model for the entire healthcare sector. Participation in the Responsible Business Simulator project led to the creation of a simulation model on healthy working in healthcare, a ready-to-use application for healthcare institutions to steer strategic decision making with assistance from IZZ.

KNVB

Company: Koninklijke Nederlandse Voetbalbond (KNVB) is the Royal Dutch Football Association. KNVB is the Netherlands' largest sports association, with 1.2 million members and over 500 employees. It considers sports as the perfect means to include and unite people as well as to inspire them to get in motion and be healthy. KNVB sees football as the glue for a stronger and tighter society, stimulating social cohesion and inclusion.

Case: This chapter describes how the contribution of football to economy and society is quantified. As football is the number one national sport in the Netherlands, it receives a lot of positive as well as negative media attention. On the one hand football is promoted because it contributes to better physical as well as mental health; on the other hand, it is vituperated as it comes with associations with aggression and violence. KNVB aims to make football attractive, accessible and fun for as many people as possible while at the same time turning around negative trends like aggression and violence. The strategic decision-making process provided integrated insights into the added financial as well as non-financial value of football, objectifying positive and negative sentiments regarding football.

Key insights: The stakeholders of KNVB, especially the clubs, considered the outcome of the business case approach using the Responsible Business Simulator very relevant and applicable to other sports. Football clubs expressed the desire to evaluate additional non-financial factors such as gender, ethnicity and age diversity. It broadened their scope and showed the importance of sports for societal values.

Key impact: The Responsible Business Simulator provided understanding of the effects of potential investments on broader themes, such as economic development, cohesion, health and nutrition. As a side effect, the project provided a professional football club with an innovative approach to pointing out the financial as well as the non-financial added value of their stadium.

Refugees

Situation: The International Organization for Migration (2016) counted 1,011,712 migrants and refugees crossing the southern border of the European Union in 2015, which some have dubbed a 'refugee crisis'. A distinction can be made between refugees and economic migrants. Economic migrants are, contrary to refugees, not forced to leave their country because of war or another humanitarian crisis, but move to a new country in order to find work or have a better standard of living. Europe currently has to cope with both. A (temporary) residence permit that grants asylum is generally only awarded to refugees. This permit is a ticket for integration into society, for work and education.

Case: This chapter discussed how strategic decision making was used in the debate around the European refugee influx in the Netherlands and the distribution over municipalities. This debate is sometimes based on emotion instead of on facts, but by giving all stakeholders a voice in the debate and translating these voices into numbers, we facilitated policies in several municipalities based on facts and figures.

Key insight: The Responsible Business Simulator showed how the limited amount of money per refugee with a permit (status holder) could be allocated best. Instead of putting almost all the budget on learning the language, a mix of activities showed better results in preparing refugees to integrate into the society. The best-performing investment portfolio was a mix of sports, voluntary work, learning the language, integration, and employment.

Key impact: Showcasing the usefulness of integrated decision making with the Responsible Business Simulator brought it to the attention of the European Commission, the Business Refugee Action Network (BRAN) and the Swedish and Italian governments.

Amplino

Company: Amplino, founded in 2012, is a start-up company that dedicates itself to the development of portable malaria diagnostics. The diagnostics are based on real-time Polymerase Chain Reaction (PCR) technology. The purpose of Amplino is to contribute to the eradication of malaria by means of applying proven lab diagnostics with a portable device in low-tech areas, such as the disease-burdened areas of Africa. In these areas conventional lab-bound biotechnology is not yet accessible for several reasons such as high costs, lack of mobility, lack of trained medical staff and poor reliability of electricity supply.

Case: This case focuses on the issue that social enterprise Amplino, which has the potential to outperform alternative malaria diagnostics, lacks funding for the execution of the final tests and product development before final production can take place. The challenge Amplino face is to find potential investors to support them using insights into the advantages and disadvantages of different ways to fight malaria. The strategic decision-making process was used to facilitate Amplino to motivate and prove the added value of their business model as well as their contribution to several societal concerns. In conversations with potential investors the Responsible Business Simulator was used to underpin possible investment decisions with quantitative facts and to formulate the strengths and weaknesses of possible choices in a structured way.

Key insight: Since there are a multitude of ways to fight malaria, the number one killer of humankind in the world. It is difficult for investors to forecast the effectiveness of investing in companies that come up with new approaches.

Key impact: The Responsible Business Simulator was applied to support Amplino in formulating their strengths and weaknesses in a structured way. Ultimately it enabled Amplino to underpin their claims with quantitative facts. It made it possible for Amplino to showcase the unique selling points of their mobile lab product and the potential impact it could make for possible investors. The Responsible Business Simulator helped justify substantial investments to ensure market introduction.

Reflection and looking forward

Combining qualitative action research methodology in the process of the strategic dialogue with data science techniques applied in the above-mentioned cases shows that there is added value in applying the Responsible Business Simulator in strategic decision-making processes to reach a balance between People, Planet and Profit objectives. The cases consider very different types of companies and organizations. The reason for this was to test out the Responsible Business Simulator in different contexts, from a profit-oriented international corporation to a startup social enterprise looking for investors and from a sustainability-conscious metal company to a human-centred healthcare insurance foundation and a science museum. This diversity was not a hindrance in applying the Responsible Business Simulator. However, we did see that the more employees, managers and external stakeholders were actively involved in the process of dialogues, visioning and gathering of documentation, the better the formulation of the key outputs, and the more accurate the interpretation of the visualization of the facts and figures. The quality of the action research process with iterative cycles is critical for gaining access to data to justify and validate key outputs. Moreover, this process can guarantee a larger understanding within the group of the technical steps we take in the strategic decision-making process. The complex computations made by advanced software and prepared by econometricians and data scientists are not easily understood. Elucidating the steps taken in the process of the Responsible Business Simulator helps participants to grasp how you can get from scattered information and data to objectified facts and figures. Precisely the fact that the decision makers themselves can fine-tune the subjacent objectified data to a balance that fits the risk appetite of the company or organization means that the technical tooling is not just a black box but, on the contrary, it invites the participants to engage with the data. The two processes of strategic dialogue and data science are closely interlinked. These interdisciplinary qualitative and quantitative approaches are ideally also reflected in the team that advises and facilitates the decision-making process in companies and organizations. Purely data-driven advisors may overlook organizational matters and dialogue-focused advisors or facilitators may overlook the substantiation of facts and figures justifying ambitions, key outputs and choices to be made.

Notwithstanding the fact that we are grateful for the diversity of cases to test out the Responsible Business Simulator, we see that more research is needed on a larger scale. The more companies and organizations that use the Responsible Business Simulator and make themselves acquainted with the (free) software package included with this book, the more experience decision makers will gain with the integrated approach. IZZ is a good example of an organization that is convinced of the added value and has therefore developed a tailor-made version available for healthcare organizations.

Another direction for further research is to undertake more monitoring of the impact of the decisions taken over time for the prosperity of the company or organization and its stakeholders. Between the first runs of cases in 2012–2013 and the second runs in 2015–2017 we were able to get an early impression; however, we would also like to see results from more companies. At Rimetaal we could see that although the company had been taken over by Kliko, the strategic decisions towards sustainable production and employability of personnel continued. Above all, the decision to switch from a total cost of ownership revenue model to a lease model with a service contract had impact, and has now become the dominant business model. This revenue model was precisely the outcome of the Responsible Business Simulator and despite the turmoil the company had been in, the long-term vision was kept alive.

At the beginning of the book we wrote that we are living in the age of disruptive changes. Many innovations are now materializing that will have far-reaching impact on business models, the way we work, the way we source energy, the way supply chains may look like in the near future, and the way we make investments for the continuity of companies and organizations. We may think of the mass application in the coming decade of artificial intelligence, sensors, smart logistics, connected healthcare, smart homes, connected cars and smart grids for renewable energy sources. No matter in what kind of industry or service sector you are operating, decision makers will have to come with balanced decisions on investments to switch to new business models. With the Responsible Business Simulator we showed that uncertainty can be reduced by clarifying and quantifying the financial and non-financial benefits of investments in sustainable business models that are beneficial for people, the planet and profits.

Annemieke Roobeek
Jacques de Swart
Myrthe van der Plas, Amsterdam, April 2018

GLOSSARY

access-over-ownership model product strategy in which the customer does not buy a product, but only the access to it, so that the ownership stays with the producer.

action learning the exchange of knowledge in the course of several interactive sessions with stakeholders, while at the same time incremental decision making takes place about the principal key outputs that serve to achieve the enterprise's strategic objective.

action research a disciplined process in which, simultaneously, academic insight is acquired and change is realized in a real-life situation.

additional outputs additional outputs are outputs that do not directly influence the decision making but are used as complementary information next to key outputs. When it turns out that there is an additional output that should be taken into account in the decision making, then this additional output should be promoted to key output.

appreciation function appreciation functions translate what a particular score on a key output means to the decision maker. An appreciation function can take on multiple shapes.

binary variable a binary variable can take on only two possible states, in this book these are the values 0 and 1.

Responsible Business Simulator the Responsible Business Simulator is software designed to facilitate strategic decision making towards a circular economy. It elucidates hidden multi-dependencies and uses the power of visualization. It provides decision makers transparency in their strategic options.

circular economy an economy that is restorative and regenerative by intention and design, and which aims to keep products, components and materials at their highest utility and value at all times.

collective intelligence group intelligence that emerges from the collaboration and collective efforts of multiple different individuals on a wide variety of cognitive tasks.

corporate social responsibility company activities that combine economic growth with limited impact on natural and social resources.

decision maker the person whose point of view is used to design which inputs are internal and which inputs are external. It is assumed that the decision maker has the power to choose values for all internal inputs.

decision maker's option a decision maker's option is defined by assigning a single value to all internal variable inputs. It assumes that every option within the scope of the decision can be completely described by one value per internal variable input. Since there typically is more than one internal variable input, a decision maker's option can be thought of as a package of potential sub-decisions, where each potential sub-decision is represented by choosing a single value for the corresponding internal variable input.

dependencies dependencies are relationships between internal inputs, external inputs, intermediates and outputs within the model. Dependencies consist of linear dependencies and nonlinear dependencies.

external variable input external variable inputs are the inputs that are not in the hands of the decision maker and hence are also known as exogenous variables or out-of-control inputs. The values of these external inputs are adjusted during the decision-making process. Every external variable input can be thought of as a single aspect of external uncertainty affecting the outcome of the decision in scope.

fixed input fixed inputs are inputs of which the values are kept constant during the decision-making process. When it turns out that there is a fixed input for which it is useful to assess the effect of adjusting its value on the outcome of the decision, then this fixed input should be promoted to internal or external variable input, depending on the control the decision maker has on the input. In case of (partly) linear models, the constant first order derivatives are not considered as fixed input but as a separate input category named 'linear dependencies'.

input types of information for which data can be collected and fed into the simulation model in order to calculate outputs. Inputs may be variable and fixed inputs.

intermediate intermediates store the results of sub-steps in the calculations that convert inputs of the simulation model to outputs of the simulation model. Intermediates are used to make calculations easy and transparent. Intermediates are based on inputs and/or other intermediates.

internal variable input internal variable inputs are in the hands of the decision maker and hence also known as endogenous or in-control inputs. The values of these internal inputs are adjusted during the decision-making process. Every internal variable input can be thought of as a single aspect on which a sub-decision needs to be made.

internet of things the network of physical devices, vehicles, buildings and other items, embedded with electronics, sensors, software and network connectivity that enable these objects to collect and exchange data.

key output key outputs are outputs on which the decision will be based. These outputs can be thought of as the basis for the decision criteria. Key outputs are often referred to as Key Performance Indicators or KPIs.

linear dependencies linear dependencies are linear relations between variable inputs, fixed inputs, intermediates and outputs. Linear dependencies can be fed into the Responsible Business Simulator as matrix cells. The row of the cell represents the driver (ie the input or intermediate affecting an output or other intermediate), the column of the cell represents the destination (ie the output of intermediate that is affected by an input or other intermediate), and the value of the cell represents the constant first order derivative in the linear relation.

Monte Carlo simulation Monte Carlo simulation is a sampling method that can be used to simplify a complex reality. It involves the random sampling of a probability distribution such that a specified number of trials are produced that together form the shape of the new distribution.

non-linear dependencies non-linear dependencies are non-linear relations between internal inputs, external inputs, intermediates and outputs. These dependencies require programming in the Responsible Business Simulator.

outputs outputs are the final results of the calculations based on inputs. A distinction is made between key outputs and additional outputs.

performance-based contracting a product strategy where customers do not buy specific goods or services, but rather the performance of a system.

Poisson process a Poisson process is a random (stochastic) counting process. It is memoryless as there is a constant and continuous opportunity for an event to occur.

round table format a discussion format in which a topic is chosen beforehand and all participants are given an equal right to participate.

scenario a scenario is defined by assigning a single value to all external variable inputs. It assumes that every possible future outcome of all external uncertainty with respect to the scope of the decision can be completely described by one value per external variable input. Since there typically is more than one external variable input, a scenario can be thought of as a coherent combination of future developments, where every single aspect of external uncertainty is represented by choosing a single value for the corresponding external variable input.

shared value a meaningful benefit for society that is also valuable to the business.

simulation model the simulation model is part of the Responsible Business Simulatorand is a set of formulas modelling multi-dependencies. It converts the decision maker's options and scenarios into outputs.

stakeholder anyone who is or becomes directly or indirectly involved in or affected by the activities of a company or organization.

making strategic decisions to benefit people, the planet and profits an interactive process with stakeholders that addresses both financial and non-financial aspects. It comprises a seven-step process that leads to a clear strategic choice. The process is empowered by a unique modelling software named the Responsible Business Simulator.

sustainable development development that meets the needs of the present without compromising the ability of future generations to meet their own needs.

triple bottom line the TBL aims to measure the financial, social, and environmental performance of a company over time, rather than merely the traditional measure of corporate profit, and is based on three pillars people, planet and profit.

variable inputs inputs where the user wants to explicitly investigate the effect of variations in these inputs on outputs. Two types of variable inputs are distinguished internal variable inputs and external variable inputs.

ABBREVIATIONS

AIMMS	Advanced Integrated Multidimensional Modelling Software. This is the software package in which the Responsible Business Simulator is programmed.
CAPEX	Capital Expenses
CFP	Corporate Financial Performance
CHP	Combined Heat and Power
CO_2	Carbon Dioxide
CSI	Corporate Social Integration
CSP	Corporate Social Performance
CSR	Corporate Social Responsibility
DJSI	Dow Jones Sustainability Index
DSM	Dutch State Mines
DSO	Distribution System Operator
ESG	Environmental, Social and Governmental
GDP	Gross Domestic Product
GE	Grey Energy
GHG	Greenhouse Gas
GoO	Guarantee of Origin (or REC)
GPS	Global Positioning System
GRI	Global Reporting Initiative
GUI	Graphical User Interface
IRR	Internal Rate of Return
ISO	International Organization for Standardization
KNVB	Koninklijke Nederlandse Voetbal Bond (Dutch Football Association)
KPI	Key Performance Indicator
NGO	Non-Governmental Organization
NPV	Net Present Value
NRS	Non-Renewable Source
PCR	Polymerase Chain Reaction
RE	Renewable Energy
REC	Renewable Energy Certificate (or GoO)
RDT	Rapid Diagnostic Test
RS	Renewable Source
RVO	Rijksdienst voor Ondernemend Nederland, the governmental agency to stimulate entrepreneurship in the Netherlands
SDG	Sustainable Development Goals

STB	Smaller-the-Better, concerning the risk appetite of the decision maker
TBL	Triple Bottom Line
TCO	Total Cost of Ownership
UNDP	United Nations Development Programme
WHO	World Health Organization

INDEX